Power For: Feminism and Christ's Self-Giving

Power For: Feminism and Christ's Self-Giving

Anna Mercedes

t&t clark

Published by T&T Clark International
A Continuum Imprint
The Tower Building　　　　　80 Maiden Lane
11 York Road　　　　　　　　Suite 704
London SE1 7NX　　　　　　New York NY 10038

www.continuumbooks.com

All rights reserved. No part of this publication may be reproduced or transmitted in any form or by any means, electronic or mechanical, including photocopying, recording or any information storage or retrieval system, without permission in writing from the publishers.

Copyright © Anna Mercedes, 2011

Anna Mercedes has asserted her right under the Copyright, Designs and Patents Act, 1988, to be identified as the Author of this work.

British Library Cataloguing-in-Publication Data
A catalogue record for this book is available from the British Library

ISBN:　978-0-567-30345-5 (paperback)

Typeset by Newgen Imaging Systems Pvt Ltd, Chennai, India

In memory of my grandfather,
Ted William Broussard,
1920–1981,
from whom I inherited the spirit of *kenosis*.

Contents

Acknowledgments		viii
Introduction: Dangerous Doctrine		1
Chapter 1:	Christ's *Kenosis* and God's Power over Us	12
	Pauline Identity Politics	14
	Imperial Omnipotence	21
	Abstinence or Masquerade	24
	"Gentle Omnipotence"	30
	Toward Other Modes of Power	34
Chapter 2:	Beyond "Power Over": Relational Christology	39
	The Dissolution of God's Power over Us	40
	Theology of the Cross as Relational Christology	46
Chapter 3:	Power for Ourselves: Kenotic Erotics	63
	Divine *Kenosis* and Human Subjectivity	65
	Trinitarian Erotics	70
	Human *Kenosis* and Divine Subjectivity	77
	Kenosis and the Kinetics of Subjectivity	80
Chapter 4:	Beyond "Power-With": Martyrs and Masochists	85
	Feminism and Masochism	88
	Reading Masochism in Christian Asceticism	92
	The Suffering Self	99
Chapter 5:	Power for Resistance: Abuse and Self-Giving Care	110
	Self-Giving Care as a Resistance Strategy	114
	Theological Recognition of Power for Resistance	121
Chapter 6:	Power for Christ: Self-Giving and Incarnation	129
	A Yielding Power	132
	Chrism Conveyed	137
	Passionate Christ	148
Bibliography		154
Index		165

Acknowledgments

Many teachers have shaped me, but four have been major conversation partners in the course of this project, shaping the formation both of this manuscript and of the woman who wrote it: Catherine Keller and Gordon Lathrop, John Hoffmeyer, and Virginia Burrus. I extend my warmest thanks to them, and offer them this book in hopes of ongoing conversation.

There are several communities that have particularly shaped me as a theological writer: first, the congregation of First Lutheran Church in Greensboro, North Carolina, where I grew up. Next the campus community of the Lutheran Theological Seminary at Philadelphia from 1999–2003 most concretely set me on the path toward this book, including especially the dinner table of Marda Messick and Woods NeSmith, and conversations on a blanket on the quad. Bill Bixby, Katie Day, and Pamela Cooper-White have particularly continued their support through the years, as have the very wise Wendy Moen and Jessicah Krey Duckworth. Finally, my professors and friends at Drew Theological School, including Karmen MacKendrick as a visiting professor, both widened my theological vision and sharpened the precision of my own theological contributions. The Keller Collective particularly continues to sustain me.

Library communities have made a huge contribution, too: I thank Krauth Memorial Library at the Lutheran Theological Seminary at Philadelphia, the Drew University Library, and Alcuin and Clemens Libraries at my current schools, the College of Saint Benedict and Saint John's University.

I thank the Humanities Division here at CSB/SJU for a research course release in the fall of 2010, allowing me to finish this manuscript. I thank my students here for their enthusiastic encouragement and bright visions. And I thank my friends and colleagues in central Minnesota for fortifying me through the stages of writing.

I thank Violet Little and Paul Wenner for their support.

Portions of chapter 2 were published in *Stand Boldly: Lutheran Theology Faces the Postmodern World*, edited by Eric Trozzo, Berkeley, CA: Three Trees Press, 2008. I thank the Wittenberg Workshop for allowing this work to reappear here.

I also remain grateful to Dr. Timothy Wengert, particularly in his class on Melanchthon at the Lutheran Theological Seminary at Philadelphia in 2002, for helping me to understand the relationship between Luther and

Melanchthon's thought, and, most importantly, for teaching me the significance of the theology of the cross in my life.

I am grateful to Tom Kraft at Continuum for supporting me and this project with his confidence. I also thank Molly Morrison for her gracious and clear editorial work and Anna Turton her editorial assistance.

As the book neared completion, Deanna Thompson, Jennifer Jeanine Thweatt-Bates, and Martin Connell gave me the huge gift of reading all or part of the manuscript and offering strengthening suggestions. I thank each of them for such a gift of time.

My spouse, Richard R. Bohannon II, accompanied me through all the stages of writing, even when most of the words were off the page and hanging in the air between us as we bustled down Manhattan sidewalks in search of the next café.

And speaking of cafés, two special places have given me fertile writing space for this project: Infusion in Mt. Airy, Philadelphia, saw me through the very earliest stages, and The Local Blend in St. Joseph, Minnesota, nurtured its completion.

I became a mother in the midst of this book project, and I was able to keep writing because of Rick's co-parenting, my mom and her grandparenting, and the loving support of Sharon Ostendorf and her cozy daycare. Sharon enables me to offer my daughter the whole complex spectrum of who I am as her mother. I want Sharon to know that I could not have written this book without her.

It is with my local family that I am daily immersed in the thick yet pleasurable complexities of self-giving. My mother, Susan "Bruce" Nolan, has always believed in my theological voice: she started reading my writing to others at church when I was twelve. My maternal grandmother, Mercedes Nelson Broussard, now ninety, struggled unsuccessfully to find funding for college in the 1930s, and I am proud to be for her a granddaughter in the academy, writing books.

Along with the wide network of friends and family that inspire the person I am—too many to list here—my spouse and our child most intimately inform the pages of this book. Sylva's four-year-old delightfulness and affection redefine *kenosis* for me each day. I am mindful, too, of the child growing and kicking within as this book goes to press, and the ways this tender process of self-giving shapes my words.

Anna Mercedes
Epiphany 2011

Introduction: Dangerous Doctrine

Self-development is more important than self-sacrifice!
–Elizabeth Cady Stanton[1]

As part of an undergraduate course on feminist theology, I asked my students, "How can Christian theology exacerbate violence against women?" We were well into the course by then, and students gave numerous examples: scriptures about the silencing and subordination of women, masculine God imagery glorifying human males, the objectification of women as property in the Bible and in tradition, the equation of power and violence in some biblical accounts, and finally, the central theme of Jesus' redemptive suffering. Having read in our class the analysis of several contemporary feminist theologians, my students were able to articulate the ways in which theological teaching has too often translated into violence against subjugated peoples in the name of Christ. As Catherine Keller writes, "Christianity has been perennially tempted to glorify victimization in its glorification of its central victim."[2]

Yet despite their quick responses, my students remained skeptical, not so much for lack of understanding the tragic connections, but rather, I suspect, for fear of how such an admission of Christianity's guilt would erode their faith. My students stared at me, pensive and deciding: should I believe this difficult information, or should I consign it to academic theory and believe in God? It's hard to stretch faith to a place where tough interrogation and tough belief coexist: I watched my students try it on for size. They squirmed in their seats and wished I would dismiss class early. At those moments, when they hover between critical thought and faith, I seek to demonstrate that it is possible to exercise both, drawing on my work as both a feminist and a Christian.

I tell my students that I adamantly acknowledge the violence that Christian theology has supported. There are too many examples of lives shattered by the teaching of the churches in combination with unjust situations. Christian rhetoric can be dangerous, and has been particularly for subjugated persons.

---

[1] Quoted in Carol Gilligan, *In a Different Voice: Psychological Theory and Women's Development*. Cambridge, MA: Harvard University Press, 1982, 129.
[2] Catherine Keller, "Scoop Up the Water and the Moon Is in Your Hands: On Feminist Theology and Dynamic Self-Emptying," in *The Emptying God*, eds. John B. Cobb, Jr. and Christopher Ives. Maryknoll, NY: Orbis Books, 1990, 105–106.

Teaching us to be submissive does make it hard for us to distinguish strong acts of faith from sheer self-demolition.

And then my more adamant students insist: we are supposed to be humble before God; we are supposed to be obedient and trust God; we are supposed to "take up our crosses and follow." They tell me, as politely as they can: "Feminists aren't very faithful."

So I tell them that alongside and even *because of* my harsh appraisal of Christianity, I feel myself, as a Christian, called to humility, to generosity, to relationships that often involve suffering or pain. I ask them to imagine how feminist commitments might *coincide* with positions of vulnerability and submission. What if, having followed the feminist call to *come into ourselves*, we find ourselves *opening out*, wanting to be there for others and with others: in the erotic embrace, in social justice, in acts of courage where we might lose it all? I nudge them toward this possibility, stressing its feminist *and* Christian contours. And I can see in a few sets of diverted eyes and half smiles that they get it.

In this book I engage an element of the Christian tradition that has been particularly thorny for feminist appropriation: the self-giving of Christ, described by Paul in his letter to the Philippians as Jesus' "emptying" of himself. In formal theological language this self-emptying is termed *kenosis*, coming from transliteration of the Greek verb used in Philippians. Depending on who is using it, *kenosis* can refer to the "emptying," self-giving, or self-sacrifice involved in Jesus' social choices, in his death, or in Christ's incarnation in the first place.

The long legacy of female subjugation that has relied on women's sacrifice as a fundamental currency of patriarchal economies implicates self-emptying doctrine as a tool of hierarchical enforcement. Thus feminism's emphasis on women's self-development and self-assertion seeks to resist patriarchy by refusing the subordination and objectification of women and by calling women into their own agency. Because of this effort to resist patriarchy through self-development, contending with the self-sacrificial aspects of Christianity, as one group of feminist writers describes it, is like "swallowing a fishbone:" stuck in our throats, it is not clear how self-giving christology can nourish us![3] But as this book will seek to demonstrate, self-giving, or *kenosis*, can also function as a resistance strategy against patriarchy and other forms of oppression.

But Stanton's defiant claim, offered to a newspaper reporter covering the growing women's movement, highlights the apparent contrast of self-development and self-sacrifice. Self-giving and strength of self may easily seem opposed. This is partly because, under patriarchal systems, strength is often

---

[3] Daphne Hampson, ed., *Swallowing a Fishbone? Feminist Theologians Debate Christianity.* London: Society for Promoting Christian Knowledge, 1996.

unnecessarily equated with the ability to take, to claim, to rule, and not with the flexibility to give or to yield. In many real ways, the two are sometimes at odds. And yet, especially if strength is understood more widely than its meaning in a patriarchal system, they need not be polar opposites: it is possible for self-giving and self-development to coalesce. This admission is still a dangerous one for feminists, for the vulnerability of generosity and care has been abused so enduringly and so undeniably by those in power and particularly by Christian leaders. But there is other danger in ignoring the power of self-giving.

Christian theology can lead us into risky situations: this in itself is not a novel claim. Feminist theologians do not generally disapprove of all danger; rather, our criticism is of forces that disproportionately endanger women and other oppressed persons. And we see in aspects of Christian theology one such force. Christianity's complicity in violence against oppressed persons includes more than the already devastating history of inadequate and detrimental clergy response to abuse, and indeed the awful record of abuse perpetrated by clergy, still inadequately recognized as the crime it is. Theological motifs right at the center of Christian doctrine present some of the same messages about personhood that patriarchy has long imparted to women. These Christian teachings shape our understanding of ourselves and our reaction to abuse.

Melinda Contreras-Byrd, a practicing psychologist working with abused women, observes that "the life choices of many abused women epitomize what theologians have touted as true virtues, as spiritual strengths."[4] Thus, many feminist theologians challenge the overall rhetoric of humility, self-giving, or sacrifice in Christian theology. In 1960 Valerie Saiving wrote an article, "The Human Situation," that became pivotal to feminist theology's understanding of the ways gender norms and church doctrines intersect. In contrast to the long-standing tradition of understanding pride as the major form of sin—pride in terms of elevating oneself to godlike status, and depending on oneself instead of on God—Saiving clearly labels self-abnegating behavior, rather than pride, as the major form of female sin. Saiving posits that "the temptations of woman *as woman* are not the same as the temptations of man *as man*." Though "sin" has been understood as self-centeredness, she argues that this definition of sin does not adequately describe the fault of many women, for whom sin would be more accurately defined as a failure to come into their own, neglecting any degree of self-focus. Saiving describes "feminine forms of sin," which are "'feminine' not because they are confined to women or because women are incapable of sinning in other ways but because they are outgrowths of the basic feminine character structure," as including "triviality, dependence

---

[4] Melinda Contreras-Byrd, "A Living Sacrifice?," *The Other Side* 38.2 (2002): 20–23, this quotation 21–22.

on others for one's own self-definition; tolerance at the expense of standards of excellence; inability to respect the boundaries of privacy; sentimentality, gossipy sociability, and mistrust of reason—in short, underdevelopment or negation of the self."[5]

Saiving is not claiming that male humans are inherently egotistical or that female humans inherently are not. She is instead pointing toward the ways in which people are culturally conditioned to act in these ways according to gender. She criticizes the way Christian theology has overlooked the affects of female gendering. Saiving's analysis highlights the ways in which many women have been trained into a "character structure" that makes them overly self-giving.

By this analysis, Christian doctrines of self-giving can actually encourage a state of sin in that they support such a character structure. Similarly, Keller writes that "the call to agapic self-sacrifice may indeed provide the proper corrective to the hypertrophic masculine ego, which patriarchal society eggs on to inflated forms of ego development. But women sin in the opposite and complementary direction: that of the underdevelopment of the self."[6] Accordingly, while self-giving ethics may be appropriate for the stereotypical male, women may need a different doctrine, one that encourages self-fulfillment.[7]

Supporting this analysis, Carol Lakey Hess, in her study of women's development in communities of faith, finds that the self-effacing ethics of much Christian education leave women and girls in a state of "prophetic torpor." Self-giving ethics do not adequately exercise the prophetic muscles of individuals who are already prone to silencing their own thoughts. If these ethics are intended to induce righteous action and love for others, as they may do for the stereotypical male character, Hess finds that they fail to do so for women. "While it may seem as if a tradition's emphasizing self-abnegation cannot be said to diminish a person's capacity to care about others," Hess believes that "it can and does."[8] Thus a woman's ability to care for others is undermined by inability to care for herself: "when we anathematize resistance, self-love, and assertiveness, we ironically diminish the capacity of individuals and communities to care deeply about the world and others in it."[9] Thus Hess claims that "a theology that emphasizes self-sacrifice as the human *telos* functions to further enervate women's struggle for self-assertion."[10]

---

[5] Saiving, Valerie. "The Human Situation: A Feminine View," in *Womanspirit Rising: A Feminist Reader in Religion*, eds. Carol Christ and Judith Plaskow. San Francisco: Harper San Francisco, 1979, 37.
[6] Keller, "Scoop Up the Water," 105.
[7] For example, see my discussion of Lisa Dahill's treatment of Bonhoeffer in Chapter 5.
[8] Carol Lakey Hess, *Caretakers of Our Common House: Women's Development in Communities of Faith*. Nashville: Abingdon Press, 1997, 45.
[9] Ibid., 45.
[10] Ibid., 35.

But could self-sacrifice combine with self-assertion? While Hess is largely critical of theologies involving self-sacrifice, she does understand passion for justice as *connected to* sacrifice. She writes that in contrast to "imposed suffering or passive submission to an oppressive status quo, when one chooses to marginalize oneself and assertively suffer with the powerless, one is taking a firm stand against injustice." The distinction for Hess is in the "prophetic vigor" of chosen marginalization: "the purpose of this stance is to oppose, denounce, and vigorously resist suffering—not to passively accept suffering or, God forbid, glorify it as virtue-producing."[11] Hess realizes that theologies encouraging vigorous acts of justice need not discard all self-giving themes. As Hess beautifully observes, "the impulse of humility is often assertiveness. When God is understood to be the center of one's identity, the courage to assert oneself on behalf of justice is inspired."[12]

Already in the life of Jesus theologians can find an example of the way in which a pouring out of the self may also be experienced as an affirmation of identity. Yet such complexities of identity lie at the heart of feminist struggle with doctrines of self-giving. Keller emphasizes that feminist theology "will not be able to return . . . to embrace any ideals of self-sacrifice, self-denial, and selflessness" without first having "thoroughly struggled with the concrete contexts in which selfhood is engendered."[13]

In advocating a feminist embrace of self-giving here, I will draw upon Keller's early concepts of "separative" and "soluble" selfhood in order to indicate the limiting characterizations of selfhood promulgated under patriarchy. Building from second-wave feminist critiques, like that of Saiving, which emphasized the differing "sins" of masculine and feminine character, Keller writes of the separative self that "it is less precise to call this ego separate than separative, implying an activity or an intention rather than any fundamental state of being . . . Its sense of itself as separate, as over and against the world, the Other, and even its own body, endows it with its identity."[14] The soluble self in turn complements this separative ego, tending to dissolve into the other and lack a distinct sense of identity. Since "it is separation which prepares the way for selfhood,"[15] the soluble "individual" does not really establish selfhood at all. From a feminist perspective, the separative self is not problematic because of its isolation, for it is not truly isolated: it is in intense relation *over* and *against* and it is likely served by soluble others. Because its relations are structured by an aggression essential to its own sense of self, the separative posture remains problematic for feminism. The soluble will not therefore be helped by a conversion to separative personality, as though "women" need only

---

[11] Ibid., 49–50.
[12] Ibid., 44.
[13] Keller, "Scoop Up the Water," 106.
[14] Keller, *From a Broken Web: Separation, Sexism, and Self.* Boston: Beacon, 1986, 9.
[15] Ibid., 1.

become like "men" in order to establish themselves—an idea that feminism has long outgrown.[16] Rather, as Keller demonstrates, the self can be reconceived in a network of far wider relation, outside the polarized and underdeveloped characterizations of patriarchal subjectivity.

At a glance, the self-giving posture may offer an all-too-vivid parallel to the soluble posture of patriarchy's construction of femininity. However, Keller's work in shifting selfhood beyond the blinders of patriarchy already suggests that theological doctrine may also have different potential when separated from patriarchal metaphysics. Feminists may choose to reject not self-giving itself, but rather the patriarchal situation that inculcates the underdeveloped female self. For example, Keller is clear that she does not intend "to decry the gesture by which selves knowingly give themselves over as gift to the matrix of meaningful life that sustains them—the social ecology of love surely requires such circulation of energies."[17] Rather, she locates the problem not in this "gesture," but rather in the social context of the gesture, for "under conditions of systematic exploitation . . . the gift is snatched, generosity is abused, and selflessness as a religious ideal becomes a matter of convenience for the oppressors, who deploy the rhetoric of self-sacrifice to defuse resistance."[18]

The feminist claim that sacrifice and service wrongly consume many women's lives holds significant political impact in its sweeping accuracy (and that claim—issued strongly by the generation before me—quite concretely enabled my own theology to come to voice, making academic theological work more possible for the young woman I was and the mother I became). Yet the claim that it is unilaterally wrong for service to characterize people's lives overlooks the complexity of human experience, forgetting the people—women included—who choose service precisely as an expression of their own rich character, and also minimizing the extent to which all human lives, male and female, are embedded in layers of dependency and caregiving.[19] This last point has been particularly emphasized in womanist and Latina feminist work, where community and care have often been readily affirmed as good and life-giving, and indeed as necessary for survival.[20] In contrast, in

---

[16] Elsewhere, Keller finds none other than Simone de Beauvoir, a herald of feminism's second wave, to be subtly lauding the separative posture while decrying the limiting inseparability to which women have historically been conscribed. See Keller's "Feminism and the Ethic of Inseparability," in *Weaving the Visions: New Patterns in Feminist Spirituality*, eds. Judith Plaskow and Carol P. Christ. San Francisco: Harper San Francisco, 1989, 256–265.

[17] Catherine Keller, "More on Feminism, Self-Sacrifice, and Time: Or, Too Many Words for Emptiness," *Buddhist-Christian Studies* 13 (1993): 214–215.

[18] Ibid., 215.

[19] Eva Feder Kittay offers a philosophical and personal study of interdependency and care in her *Love's Labor: Essays on Women, Equality, and Dependency*. London: Routledge, 1999.

[20] See particularly Emilie Townes, *Breaking the Fine Rain of Death: African American Health Issues and a Womanist Ethic of Care*. Continuum: London, 2001, 168–186; Delores Williams, *Sisters in the Wilderness: The Challenge of Womanist God-Talk*. Maryknoll, NY: Orbis, 1993, 164–167; and Jeanette Rodríguez, "Latina Activists: Toward an Inclusive Spirituality of Being in the

much Euro-American feminist work, especially in feminism's second wave, community and care could seem the very oppressions from which liberation was desired. Overall, the necessities of care and community appear more readily when feminists consider the ways in which culture, including social class, impacts our definitions of what self-development and self-assertion look like.

But I have not simply called this book "Feminism and Christ's Self-Giving," because in writing about self-giving here I aim to emphasize a sort of power generated by it—a power that leans toward others and offers itself to them, a power that may be a power both for feminist aims and for the presence of Christ in the world. In that latter sense, this book offers a christology.

Lisa Isherwood observes that power is "an issue that feminists have had more ease denouncing than claiming."[21] If giving and care have seemed the essentialized female task, power has seemed the stereotypically male domain. Some feminist women have inarguably claimed "male" power for themselves, but feminists have also declared that they desire something different than the hierarchical dominance that has characterized patriarchal power. Most feminists, whether women or men, have understood their feminism to be a movement away from "power over"; they have wanted to be intentional about ensuring that their own empowerment not entail further oppression of others.

"Power over" is such a familiar form of power that for some such a model of power has become flatly equated with power itself, such that to be powerful means to be positioned over others, to dominate. But far from denouncing any and all power, many feminists have moved toward articulating and claiming other possibilities for power.[22] Feminists have asserted that power can still function outside patriarchal economies, and that power looks different when it is not dominating power—may look so different, in fact, that those inured to patriarchy may not even recognize it as power at all. Some feminists have demonstrated the power of nonviolent resistance. Others have intentionally mimicked "power over" in order to diffuse and transform it. Most popular in feminist theology has been the ideal of mutual power, what I will call here "power with." Though these strategies, which sometimes overlap, do not match patriarchy's power, still they are powerful, showing that there is power apart from sheer domination. And one of the most telling proofs of these powers is their *resistance* to hierarchical exploitation, to "power over."

Christians have long attested that Jesus of Nazareth exuded power, but the Gospel narratives do not describe his as an exploitive power over, though many

---

World," 114–130 in *A Reader in Latina Feminist Theology: Religion and Justice*, edited by María Pilar Aquino, Daisy L. Machado, and Jeanette Rodríguez (Austin: University of Texas Press, 2002).

[21] Lisa Isherwood, "The Embodiment of Feminist Liberation Theology: The Spiralling of Incarnation," *Feminist Theology* 12.2 (2004): 140–156, this quotation 143.

[22] Pamela Cooper-White offers a concise overview of this development in *The Cry of Tamar: Violence Against Women and the Church's Response*. Minneapolis: Fortress Press, 1995, 30–40 and 270.

later theologies would describe precisely an overpowering Christ. One way to understand Jesus' power is as a power with. Jesus stood in solidarity with suffering people; he did not lord himself over them. He empowered through his presence and company. His solidarity gives us an image of his power. Jesus' power with suffering people offers one illustration of his resistance to the imperial culture in which these people were immersed.

Jesus can also be read as wielding (or perhaps yielding) what I will call a "power for," as he lived committed to the benefit of others, passionate for God and God's people. Christians have revered this aspect of Jesus, for instance in Dietrich Bonhoeffer's description of Christ as the "person for others," and in other theologies that I will explore in this book. But this has been a tricky sort of christology for feminist Christians. For if our Christ is wholly committed to the benefit of others, how can such a Christ empower persons for whom care for others has functioned as oppression?

In order to develop a theology of kenotic power for ourselves, for resistance to exploitation, and for the ongoing life of Christ, I will explore throughout this book the ways in which doctrines of *kenosis* have related to power. In the first chapter I look particularly at four moments in the history of *kenosis*: the appearance of *kenosis* in Paul's letter to the Philippians, the transition of kenotic doctrines with the beginning of the Christian empire, the debates over *kenosis* by seventeenth- and nineteenth-century Lutherans, and the feminist *kenosis* recently proposed by Sarah Coakley. These four examples serve in Chapter 1 to demonstrate the ways in which doctrines of self-giving can support an idea of a God who is anything but. Instead of conveying a self-giving God, these theologies can serve to reify conceptions of God as one who does not share power, and who ultimately employs *kenosis* in order to exhibit power over us.

In Chapter 2 I push toward other theologies of self-giving and power by looking at the work of an odd quad: Rosemary Radford Ruether, Marta Frascati-Lochhead and her use of Gianni Vattimo, and the sixteenth-century reformers Martin Luther and Philip Melanchthon. The two feminist theologians in this chapter help me to demonstrate how doctrines of *kenosis* are able to move us away from theologies of God as an overbearing presence. Turning to the reformers, I seek to demonstrate that a theology of the cross—despite many critiques of its potential violence—can support a theology of a richly kenotic God, interested in passionate connection with those whom God loves, instead of a cold distance held in check by a dichotomy of power and powerlessness, with demands from the powerful for blood and suffering.

Chapter 3 explores a "kenotic erotics," demonstrating the twofold point that *kenosis* need not be an action born only of traditional *agape*, and that accordingly, there is something for us in *kenosis*—something self-supporting in self-giving. Just as many feminists have celebrated the revelations of self discovered in life's erotic dimensions, *kenosis* can offer a mode of action that empowers us by texturing our sense of self. In Chapter 3 I discuss Dietrich Bonhoeffer's christology and the way his Christ's self-giving serves human subjectivity, Hans Urs von Balthasar's kenotic trinitarian theology and the way his sense of divine *kenosis* ultimately generates both divine and human subjectivity through an energy much like *eros*, and Marcella Althaus-Reid's queer theology with her proposal that human erotic *kenosis* invites and transforms incarnations of divine subjectivity. Mindful, however, of feminist warnings about too much enthusiastic zeal for *eros* (critiques engaged in Chapter 6), Chapter 3 does not propose a strictly erotic sense of self-giving. Rather, many senses of love can infuse kenotic motion in the world, and *kenosis* need not be confined to that which we think of as "love."

If christic self-empting carries currents potentially agapeic and erotic, might it also sometimes carry dynamics in which desire and self-giving purposely collide with pain? Challenging feminist theology's model of mutual power, or "power with," Chapter 4 explores a controversial self-giving power in the strategy of masochism. Masochism has been a fraught topic for feminism, appearing—like *kenosis*—to be a topic that liberated women need avoid. To the contrary, Chapter 4 draws upon the historical and philosophical work of Virginia Burrus and Karmen MacKendrick, whose readings of ancient Christian hagiography convey a *productive* masochism. This chapter highlights the way in which self-giving might purposefully engage the dynamics it seeks to contort or resist, and thus again rediscover agency in abandon.

The fifth chapter looks to the powers of self-giving particularly for resistance. Following the recent psychoanalytic trend of emphasizing the resistance of abuse survivors rather than their victimization, the chapter describes studies of survivors' resistance that have demonstrated how resistance sometimes comes in the form of care. Greater theological recognition of kenotic forms of resistance would honor the strength of abuse survivors and in some cases even honor a particular sort of christic presence.

The concluding chapter draws on all the previous chapters in order to describe the power of self-giving to generate holy chrism, anointing the ever-shifting body of Christ in the world today. Several feminist theologies posit the ongoing incarnation of God by drawing on the theme of erotic power, but kenotic power offers a different way forward. Self-giving engages a force that differs from both the "power in mutual relation" common to feminist theology and the "power over" of patriarchal thought. Christic self-giving conveys a *power for*: for God's thriving in the world, and for our own.

This project began when my own experience taught me the vulnerability of the self-giving path. A seminary student at the time, I knew that my desire to be in the relationships in which I had been hurt was influenced by my fervor for Christian community and its privileging of self-giving character. Encountering feminism around this time as well, I learned that the self-giving message of Christianity had historically affected women differently than men and that it continues to support oppressive structures in which women are abused. Still, and perhaps because I was surrounded by such a strong community, I encountered in this same self-sacrificing community a force acting to deconstruct those very abusive structures.

I saw in the feminist theology I was reading several options for making sense of my own woundedness. The strongest and most predominant option seemed to be this: I could unlearn my self-giving tendencies and blame Christian theology for raising me to be a young woman too good at self-sacrifice. But this seemed like a subtle way for me to "blame the victim"—to blame myself. "If only I hadn't been so other-oriented" seemed the theological equivalent of "if only I hadn't worn such a low-cut blouse": "I was really asking for it."

In a brief article by Melinda Contreras-Byrd in *The Other Side* magazine I found my way toward another option. Even though she is a counselor, Contreras-Byrd emphasizes placing emphasis and blame for abusive situations *outside* of private, therapeutic context. She asks, "What if our true client is our society, and to focus anywhere else is to participate in subterfuge and untruth?"[23] Her article helped me toward the recognition that the kenotic tendencies in my own self are not directly causal of the violence I may encounter in the course of my days (nor are they totally unrelated to it, for good or for ill). Of course, self-giving *can* function as the inverse of self-aggrandizing, such that both roll together as the gears of a violent economy. And there are forms of psychosis that make some of us overly self-deprecating and even self-destructive. But a violent society can also crush the open heart because the *society*, not the heart, is ill (a possibility to which Christianity has born witness from the beginning). I realized that it was possible for feminist theology to say: instead of teaching our daughters and sons a delicate balance of self-preservation, let us work toward a world where our prodigally loving children will not be so easily crushed.

I want to say more to the young women and men with whom I work than "sometimes you have to look out for yourself too" or "strike a balance between yourself and other people." Part of my dissatisfaction with this advice stems from its dependence on the kind of individualistic metaphysics of selfhood from which feminism arose amidst the important human-rights emphases of the Enlightenment, but which would also come under criticism from feminism's own vision of relationality. This relationality speaks to a different concept of self in which "I" would not have a discrete self to balance against "others" with whom I relate. Our identities are more fluid, which is not to say that we are completely amorphous and indistinguishable from one another.

---

[23] Melinda Contreras-Byrd, "A Living Sacrifice?" *The Other Side* 38.2 (2002): 20–23, this quote 20–21. Also see Traci West, *Wounds of the Spirit: Black Women, Violence, and Resistance Ethics.* New York: New York University Press, 1999, 55 and 159.

There is a place for such "take care of others and also yourself" advice, of course, but it seems really unclear in actual practice and, perhaps worse, simply bland. Karmen MacKendrick writes disapprovingly of "an over sanitized and pastoral conception of love—as recognition, as 'I affirm you,' as a polite strengthening of discontinuity, as divorced as thoroughly as possible from pain or transgression." I want those I teach to know that Christian and also feminist loving can be more interesting than that. With MacKendrick, "I would work instead with an image of love as an impossible joyous abandon—a sense of being without recourse—which opens the self and thus undoes it."[24] And I might name that abandon *kenosis*.

---

[24] Karmen MacKendrick, *Counterpleasures*. Albany, NY: State University of New York Press, 1999, 156.

Chapter 1

Christ's *Kenosis* and God's Power over Us

In its second wave, feminism adopted the slogan "the personal is political." That which, under Victorian ideals, would have seemed private business—domestic abuse, reproductive cycles, the state of one's hymen, sexual satisfaction or lack of it—is all ultimately connected with social systems. These things—even the hymen—do not exist free of cultural context, but shape and are shaped by it.[1] And injustice in the home is a political issue, not a "private" problem.

The "christic" is also political. The messianic was political before Greek usage labeled this concept "Christ": messiahs were God's anointed serving political purposes, with the word even applying to foreign leaders who did right by the people of Israel.[2] Because the christic is political, theologies of Christ's self-emptying often serve to support particular politics, including gender politics. As we saw in the introduction, Christian self-giving is not a gender-neutral concept. Rather, Christian messages about care for others and sacrifice of self fall differently on ears that are patriarchically gendered as masculine or feminine. So long as females, racial minorities, and persons with less money are taught to be submissive while white, monied males are taught to be strong, Christian self-giving ethics will have different affects on different persons—especially when the spokespersons for these messages are at the top of the hierarchy. In such a patriarchal, racist, and classist context, no message about self-giving is politically neutral.

Theologies of self-giving are always about political power to some degree: who should have it, how to get it, what to do when you're crushed by it. This becomes even clearer when the broader topic of Christian self-giving is narrowed to the specific concept of *kenosis*. Because of its use in the New Testament and in the history of Christian doctrine, *kenosis* immediately invokes, not primarily Christian ethical behavior, as "self-giving" alone might, but our understandings of the nature and makeup of Christ: whether the metaphysics of the incarnation, the ramifications of the cross, or both and more.

---

[1] Joan Jacobs Brumberg, *The Body Project: An Intimate History of American Girls*. New York: Random House, 1997, 139–192.

[2] Cyrus II of Persia is referred to as God's "anointed" in Isaiah 45:1.

Self-giving may seem an obviously humble gesture, but the historical record of doctrines of *kenosis* tells a much more complicated story. Much of the time, though not always, theologies of Christ's *kenosis* have served to reify God's power over us. Christ's self-emptying itself has not necessarily functioned to reinstate God's power over us—indeed, it is the hope of this book that Christ's ongoing *kenosis* might be up to something else—but the theologies themselves have functioned this way.

When Christ was the name given to a Jesus who had lived among an oppressed minority group in the grip of the Roman Empire, his *kenosis*, particularly its collision with the cross, revealed in various theologies of the New Testament his ironic gaining of power. The kenotic life was a purposeful strategy, starting from a place under the heel of oppressive power. Later, when Christ was a name for the God of the empire, Christ's *kenosis* became itself a gesture of imperial power, of benevolent condescension that demonstrates its potency in being able to do so much while risking so little.

Feminism's resistance to and careful use of kenotic christology also reflects the political hopes and struggles of our day, and our visions of God's power and our own. Our theologies of Christ reflect our visions of good politics, our ideas about how power should flow in our day. The theology that I develop here does the same, proposing a way that Christianity's power might be graciously and healthfully operative in a pluralistic and postcolonial society, and for postmodern thinkers. Christ has always been more than our current understanding of Christ; Christ's eternal reality—whatever it might be—is not subject to our shifting christologies so much as to our human participation, or lack thereof, in this Christ. Different christologies direct us to different involvement in the work and power of God in the world. In that way, then, Christ's reality is very much at stake in our theologies, because our involvement as body of Christ in the world correlates in ways perhaps beyond our knowing with the vivacity of Christ.

Feminist theologian Sarah Coakley has undertaken a project with *kenosis* that resonates in many ways with the thesis of this book: for Coakley, *kenosis* is "not only compatible with feminism, but vital to a distinctively Christian manifestation of it."[3] While Coakley acknowledges the dangers of kenotic doctrine for women, she insists that "there is another, and longer-term, danger to Christian feminism in the *repression* of all forms of 'vulnerability,' and in a concomitant failure to confront issues of fragility, suffering, or 'self-emptying' except in terms of victimology. And that is ultimately the failure to embrace a feminist reconceptualizing of the power of the cross and resurrection."[4] Yet despite our common aims, and despite her feminism, Coakley's vision of kenotic empowerment is very much a "power over" model. While Coakley argues for a practice of kenosis in contemplative prayer beneath "gentle

---

[3] Coakley, *Powers and Submissions*, 3.
[4] Ibid., 33.

omnipotence," I will argue in this and following chapters for kenotic practice that, while potentially including prayer, carries one into the mess of interpersonal interactions, not as a product of kenotic practice, but as the practice itself: not so much receiving, as conveying, power.

This chapter presents four examples from the history of kenotic theology that especially demonstrate the use of kenotic doctrine to assert God's power over us. Paul's letter to the Philippians, which gives us the biblical home of kenotic theology, certainly asserts God's power over, but because it is a power into which persons are incorporated in Christ, the domination of divine power is at least tempered, if not transformed. Post-Constantinian patristic theologies, considered particularly here in Athanasius of Alexandria, struggle to interpret Christ's self-emptying as part of an omnipotent and unchanging God. Much later, the Lutheran "kenoticists" of the seventeenth and nineteenth centuries in turn struggle to express a historically imaginable *human* who nonetheless retained God's omnipotence and immutability. And finally, Coakley most recently offers a theology of "power in vulnerability" beneath nonexploitive, yet omnipotent, divinity.[5] This is by no means a comprehensive history of kenotic doctrine, and to the contrary we will encounter many other uses of the kenotic in later chapters. The work of this chapter is instead to specifically explore the ways that theologies of divine self-giving have, paradoxically, asserted a power-hoarding God.

Pauline Identity Politics

The Apostle Paul wrote his letter to the Philippians to address conflict in that congregation. He addresses that conflict by both the firm assertion of his own leadership power over the congregation and by the invocation of the sort of identity the congregants share in Christ. In the second chapter of this letter, Paul embeds a hymn about Christ in the middle of his instructions on concord, as follows:[6]

> Do nothing from selfish ambition or conceit, but in humility regard others as better than yourselves. Let each of you look not to your own interests, but to the interests of others. Let the same mind be in you that was in Christ Jesus,

---

[5] Ibid., 5.
[6] For the argument that the Philippians kenosis passage is a hymn, see Ralph P. Martin, "A Hymn of Christ: Philippians 2:5–11" in *Recent Interpretation and in the Setting of Early Christian Worship*. Downers Grove, Illinois: InterVarsity Press, 1997, xii. Against this interpretation, G. D. Fee has argued that the piece is Paul's own "exalted prose," in his "Philippians 2:5–11: Hymn or Exalted Pauline Prose," BBR 2 (1992): 29–46; cf. Ralph P. Martin, *A Hymn of Christ: Philippians 2:5–11 in Recent Interpretation and in the Setting of Early Christian Worship*, Downers Grove, Illinois: InterVarsity Press, 1997, xliv.

(verse 6) who, though he was in the form of God,[7]
did not regard equality with God
as something to be exploited,
(verse 7) but emptied himself,[8]
[taking the form of a slave],[9]
being born in human likeness.[10]
And being found in human form,
(verse 8) he humbled himself
and became obedient
to the point of death—
[even death on a cross].[11]
(verse 9) Therefore God also highly exalted him
and gave him the name
that is above every name,
(verse 10) so that at the name of Jesus
every knee should bend,
[in heaven and on earth and under the earth],
(verse 11) and every tongue should confess
that Jesus Christ is Lord,
[to the glory of God the Father].

The passage as a whole begins and ends with Paul's invocation of joy: he asks for the Philippians to make his joy complete through their harmony with one

---

[7] The Greek word here is *morphe*, often translated as "form," repeated again in verse 7 with Paul's redaction. Thus μορφη θεου is contrasted with μορφη δουλου. Fowl explains that though the most common use of *morphe* in Greek would refer to perceptible appearance, it seems unlikely that Paul would use *morphe* to mean that Jesus looked like God, since both Jesus and Paul stood in the tradition of the "unrepresentable God of Israel." Fowl suggests through comparison with other letters of Paul and with the Septuagint that "form" in verse 6 may denote "the glory, radiance, and splendor by which God's majesty is made visible to humans," and credits Marcus Bockmuehl, "The Form of God," with a similar interpretation of *morphe*. See Stephen E. Fowl, *Philippians*. Grand Rapids, MI: Wm. B. Eerdmans, 2005, 92.
[8] The Greek here is εαυτον εκκενωσεν, from κενοω, to make empty or void.
[9] The brackets represent possible redactions, discussed later. Also see the list of redactions in Martin, lix–lx.
[10] Within this hymn, paralleling Hebrew poetic form, Martin explains that "the second line completes and enriches the thought of the first" (*Hymn of Christ*, lviii).
[11] At this juncture there is a clear pivot in the hymn, contrasting the humiliation of the previous three verses with the exaltation of the later three. Martin explains that the "therefore . . . also" opening verse 9 serves "as a *peripeteia* in Greek drama, which reverses the hero-victim's fate and sets out the road to recovery and reinstatement of honor" (*Hymn of Christ*, lviii).

another, and concludes that he will rejoice even if he himself is "being poured out as a libation."[12] Paul's own flowing libation resonates with the emptying of Christ in the hymn.

In this letter to the Philippians, *kenosis* is about human activity as much as it is about Christ: self-emptying may appear in a metaphysical description of Christ, but it serves the rhetorical purpose of urging the congregation's own self-emptying. This is underscored by the possibility that the hymn may have been specifically baptismal.[13] This liturgical context directs analysis away from a more theoretical interpretation of Christ's "two natures," as would be common in the formulation of later Christian doctrine, and instead toward inquiry as to how the Philippians understood their own nature as baptized Christian people. Thus, though the hymn is overtly describing Christ, in the context of ritual initiation, it expresses what it means to live and have being in Christ as a baptized person.[14] The christic, anointed one—Christ—is the baptized person, or rather the community into which the baptized person is incorporated. In Isaiah, the people of Israel together become the messianic figure; here in Philippians, the Christian community becomes the Christ figure, taking on the christic "mind," as in verse 5. In Philippians, then, Christian identity is kenotic identity, making appropriation of Philippians difficult for contemporary feminists.

This difficulty is lessened, I would argue, if Philippians is read as a statement about being in Christ, about baptismal ontology, rather than as only an injunction to kenotic behavior. Both interpretations are possible because the introduction to the hymn (at verse 5) lacks a verb.[15] The Greek conveys that the Pauline audience should have "the same mind" in themselves, but the translator must determine how this "mind" connects to Christ. Is it exemplified by Christ? Is it given over by Christ to the Philippians? The NRSV translates verse 5 "Let the same mind be in you that *was in* Christ Jesus," while the RSV chose "Have this mind among yourselves, which *is yours* in Christ Jesus." Stephen Fowl's translation of Philippians 2:5 emphasizes exemplary ethics: "Let this be your pattern of thinking, acting, and feeling, which was also displayed in Christ Jesus."

But against the exegesis that Paul employs the hymn primarily in order to sway the Philippians toward an ethical imitation of Christ, Ralph Martin argues that Paul uses the hymn to offer pastoral comfort to the Philippians by reminding them of their ontological status in Christ: Paul comforts them

---

[12] See Philippians 2:2 and 2:17.
[13] Martin, 292–293.
[14] In this vein Martin writes that "in accepting the challenge of life in Christ [the Philippians] will 'become what they are' and they will work out in actual fact all that is potentially declared in baptism . . ." (Hymn of Christ, 293, also see xlviii).
[15] As Martin explains, "In leaving us with a verbless second part of the verse, literally 'which also . . . in Christ Jesus,' he has set the translator a conundrum . . ." (*Hymn of Christ*, xlviii). Or as Fowl has it, "The obscurity of the syntax in the Greek means that almost any translation into English is also going to be an amplification" (*Philippians*, 89).

with a liturgical allusion to their baptismal identity in one who, like them, has suffered, but then was also exalted. Martin suggests that instead of teaching the Philippians that they *should* be like the kenotic Christ, Paul tells the assembly that they already *are* of the kenotic Christ. Paul reminds the Philippians of their sacramental identity in Christ, demonstrating that their lives are already caught up in a kenotic economy by a sort of baptismal default. For Martin, "the Apostolic summons is not: Follow Jesus by doing as he did—an impossible feat in any case," but rather, "become in your conduct and church relationships the type of persons who, by that *kenosis*, death and exaltation of the Lord of glory, have a place in his body, the Church."[16] An ethics emerges secondarily from the primarily ontological import of the *kenosis* hymn.

If, indeed, the *kenosis* passage began as a corporate hymn, this communal character of the kenotic identity may further undergird the interpretation that the Philippians may have understood the transition from individualistic pursuit to group identity to be not one of ethical self-correction but rather a change effected at an ontological level already by and in Christ. But the stakes of such an ontology are raised by Paul through possible redactions made to the assembly's hymn. Several phrases that break from the poetic structure of the hymn may be Paul's own additions. These include in verse 7 "taking the form of a slave," in verse 8 "even death on a cross," in verse 10 "in heaven and on earth and under the earth," and finally in verse 11 "to the glory of God the Father." Paul's redaction of Philippians stresses a cosmically enthroned redeemer who has paradoxically suffered and died. Accordingly, Martin suggests that Paul may have redacted the community's hymn in order to emphasize the concept of "Christ crucified" that is so important to Pauline thought.[17]

Paul's possible redactions drastically alter the implications of the text for a contemporary feminist reader by glorifying the depth of the violence the Christ figure undergoes. The redactions emphasize both the gory depth of Christ's sufferings and the celestial height of Christ's exultation and juxtapose human execution with the glory of God. The kenotic trajectory of the text thus becomes all the more extreme. Before the redactions, the first half of the hymn sings of the incarnation and humanity of a Christ whose *kenosis* entailed birth and disclosure in human form, and thus obedience to death, to the mortal condition of all fleshy bodies. But after the redactions, the *kenosis* involves obedience to "death on a cross," a death more brutal than mortality alone would demand: an execution, a public shaming, an unjust death. Further, before the redactions the second half of the hymn sets Christ's humility in counterpoint with subsequent honor: Jesus' obedience to human life yields human obedience to Jesus, as knees bow and tongues confess. After Paul's

---

[16] Martin, 289–291. Here Martin cites R. Bultmann, *Theology*, I, 311: "'In Christ,' far from being a formula for mystic union, is primarily an *ecclesiological* formula."
[17] Martin, xvi.

redactions, the bowing "knees" are now far more than human: celestial knees join the entourage. Paul envisions a triumph in which *all* beings give obeisance to the executed one. And this executed one remains kenotic even at the end, giving all glory over "to the glory of God the Father."

Thus, before redaction, a contemporary feminist analysis might emphasize the embodied life that Christian self-emptying entails, drawing out a summons to obedience to our bodies, to our births and deaths, to the disclosure among ourselves that we experience in our skin, and to the limits of our material existence. This (pre-Pauline) *kenosis* into our own carnal state, to rootedness in the circumscriptions of our bodies, could be read to yield—not celestial transcendence—but a graced name and honor from the human community.

And yet, the pre-Pauline hymn is not the one handed down by the biblical canon to the later theological tradition. Instead, later doctrinal formulations of *kenosis* have as their source Paul's particular kenotic metaphysics. The immanent gore and shame of the flesh and the transcendent glory of the divine characterize the authoritative Pauline *kenosis*. Beaten and downtrodden persons throughout Christian history have therefore received this dynamic metaphysics as the "mind" that is theirs in Christ.

What difference does it make to feminists if *kenosis* is read as a way of being rather than a "should"? The reader's decision as to how Paul intends his audience to relate to the "mind" of the kenotic Christ—an intention left hazy by the missing verb in Philippians 2:5—can determine whether the text points toward the pursuit of redemptive suffering and shame or recognition of enduring life *despite* suffering and shame. Does Paul offer stern injunction or consoling hope? Is the message that in order to gain glorious honor, one should be like Christ, who was obedient to execution on the cross? Or is the message that one should rest in affiliation with the life of Christ, whose obedience met with suffering and shame, yet whose honor is great? While the first reading leads to the emphasis on redemptive violence that feminist theologians have rightly declared problematic, the second reading might offer—even within the economy of Paul's grandiose and gory *kenosis*—a recognition of the suffering and gore people regularly face and a promise that such travail, as Paul writes in his letter to the Romans, cannot separate them from the love of God that is in Christ Jesus.[18]

Feminist exegesis of this text has tended toward the first reading, finding the text to primarily direct its readers toward obedience and ethical imitation. Joseph Marchal's feminist rhetorical analysis of Philippians determines that "Paul's rhetorics inscribe certain power relations of authority and obedience, typically first to Paul's own benefit."[19] The structure of the letter favors an overall message of ethical imitation based on the orders of hierarchy: obedience

---

[18] See Romans chapter 8.
[19] Joseph A. Marchal, *Hierarchy, Unity, and Imitation: A Feminist Rhetorical Analysis of Power Dynamics in Paul's Letter to the Philippians*. Atlanta, GA: SBL, 2006, 193.

to Christ and, under Christ, to Paul himself. As Marchal explains, "the letter is Paul's attempt to establish a kyriarchal relationship between the Philippian community and himself . . . The rhetorics of the letter present the audience with a series of models, offered on hierarchical terms."[20]

Pheme Perkins's feminist interpretation of the text stresses the largely masculine audience of Paul's letter, evident through his militaristic and athletic imagery, and the listing of only male disciples as Christ-like examples. Though women were part of the congregation at Philippi, as indicated in Chapter 4, Perkins finds that Paul's overall message in the letter seems most directly to be addressed to the men. Perkins thus wonders to what degree "women might be considered 'brothers' called to imitate the example of the apostle."[21] Perhaps the instruction of humility does not wholly apply to Philippian women. Perkins also contends that Paul's intended audience is composed of people with power and social status to give up in imitation of Christ, because "the hymn starts not with the suffering Christ but with the Christ who is equal to God." Accordingly, "abused women whose ministers tell them to submit to husbands, are not in the position to copy the Christ of this hymn. Its challenge is addressed to persons of some status and power, just as Christ had the status of God."[22]

Yet Paul's letter may not be addressed only to those with power to lose. As Perkins herself explains, Paul writes this letter as an imprisoned leader, a context clear from Philippians 1:13. As he grants that he may be "poured out," Paul acknowledges the possibility that his own kenotic life will meet with death. The possibility that he will be executed presses upon Paul and on his congregation in Philippi, contributing to the rivalry and dissension among them as they anticipate the loss of Paul's leadership.[23] Caught in the concourse of a vast imperial system, they have found hope in an unlikely messiah who was crushed by that same empire. They have been persuaded by Paul's presentation of an alternate empire under Christ. Now, facing the execution of their own evangelist, they scramble for leadership and unity, mindful that the fate of Jesus and Paul could also be theirs. Paul writes to them that God "has graciously granted you the privilege not only of believing in Christ, but of suffering for him as well—since you are having the same struggle that you saw I had and now hear that I still have."[24] In Paul's presentation, which may be more than a patriarchal spin, suffering for Christ is a *privilege*. From this perspective, Paul may remind them of their christic identity, not to instruct them to suffer further, but precisely because they were already suffering.

---

[20] Ibid., 204.
[21] Pheme Perkins, "Philippians," in *The Womens Bible Commentary*, edited by Carol A. Newsom and Sharon H. Ringe. Louisville, KY: Westminster/John Knox Press, 1992, 343.
[22] Ibid., 344.
[23] Ibid.
[24] Philippians 1:29–30.

While the original context of the biblical text need not dictate the text's function today, in this case the original context relates directly to feminism's most common criticism of *kenosis*. If the *kenosis* passage was applied by Paul as a pastoral word to a troubled minority people under the heel of empire, then one cannot summarily push the kenotic strand of Christian doctrine under the umbrella of the Christian correction to a masculine bias. The letter may have brought the strength of renewed identity to a vulnerable people: a kenotic identity politics. The "Enlightenment male" of later theologies, seeking to make of himself a God, may hear resonance of his sin in Paul's critique of individualistic pursuits, but Paul's letter is addressed to different men and women who needed strength in the face of a threatened future.

Reading the hymn as a pastoral reminder of identity in Christ rather than as injunction to imitative practice need not imply an already powerful audience or a message not intended for more disenfranchised persons. Although the more ethical interpretation allows for the question of for whom this ethic is appropriate (perhaps those with power to lose), the conclusion that Paul sets up an identity structure "in Christ" assumes that variously empowered people would be located within that communal identity. Indeed, from this more ontological exegesis, it seems exclusive to deny women or subjugated people access to a kenotic identity, as though one were claiming that they should not be "in Christ" because they are too poor. The more ontological perspective suggests the power of identity "in Christ," in the form of the kenotic exalted one, rather than the prescription of the imitation of that Christ as an antidote to the overprivileged. This Pauline kenotic ontology emphasizes the dignity of generous and humble postures under and against oppressive regimes. While such a scriptural message can be used as a tool of patriarchal reinforcement, it can also, precisely because it offers a self-giving ontology, be read as fortification against exploitation.

Differing interpretations lead to different implications for imagining God's power over us. If, with his invocation of *kenosis*, Paul is reasserting the Philippians' Christian identity as their subtle power over oppressive regimes, then the letter's sense of God's power over us still leaves room for human power, even placing God's power at the service of their power for resistance. But if Paul's use of the *kenosis* hymn and his reference to his own outpouring function to assert Paul's own power over the Philippians, then the Bible's one explicit reference to *kenosis* already serves the purposes of hierarchal ecclesiastical power. It seems possible, also, that Paul could have done both of these things: asserting his dominance in order to induce submission to his concept of ontology in Christ.

The Philippians' example of kenotic theology remains ambiguous in its assertion of God's power over us. The result of Christ's *kenosis* is ultimately that all knees shall bow to Christ. But if Christian people are to have the "mind" of Christ in them, then one implication is that they, too, will gain power over:

over all the other worldly powers that dominated the Philippians' experience. From a feminist perspective, this seems both good for human empowerment and dangerous, as this hierarchical power is gained only at the expense of others, expressed in an ability to dominate and demand the submission of the bent knee.

Imperial Omnipotence

The patristic age saw a radical shift in Christian politics as the regime of the Roman Empire itself became Christian. The theme of the suffering of Christ shifted along with the changing politics of the day. During this time, unlike in the periods of sporadic martyrdom, the *kenosis* of Christ became inconsistent with the increasingly imperial model of Christ. How can a Christ as mighty as the emperor, calling the people to obedience, also empty out, becoming like a servant? How can such a Christ in any way lose control or even suffer in the throes of an incarnate life? The christological debates about the "two natures" of Christ—divine and human—struggle to work out these seeming contradictions (while also working out all manner of political rivalries).

Perhaps the most major shift comes alongside the transition of Christianity from a loosely defined entity, subject to suffering at the hands of power-holders, to an increasingly ratified entity able to subject others to suffering. The Christ who could unify an empire would need to be, rather than a Christ understood differently in different places, one kind of Christ, and a mighty one at that. And a kenotic Christ is an inconvenient model for an emperor seeking to consolidate his empire and fortify his ability to coerce.

In contrast, for Irenaeus, living before the Christian empire in a time of Christian persecution, Christ's suffering was far from problematic. To the contrary, as I will again discuss in Chapter 4, Irenaeus hypothesizes that if there were two natures of Christ, the suffering one must be superior.[25] The suffering of Christ offered Christ's most glorious aspect, for in it Christ recapitulated and made new the whole creation of the world. Irenaeus's fixation on martyrdom was wrapped together with his understanding of Christ's suffering: In Christ's pouring out on the cross, the whole world is poured out and begun anew; in the martyr's pouring out, Christ's own death is again recapitulated. Thus, in Irenaeus's thinking, Christ's *kenosis* was something in which humans participated, albeit in a manner gory to many modern ears. There was an ongoing flow of creation and re-creation with each martyr's death. Over time attention would shift from what the kenotic Christ would mean for human life—more clearly the aim in a pastoral letter like Philippians or in a baptismal rite as with the pre-Pauline hymn—to what such a Christ means for our image of God.

---

[25] Irenaeus, *Against Heresies* 3.18.5.

Peter Brown connects the discourse of power and poverty with the christological debates of the time, noting that from a political context of the "permanent and overwhelming presence" of a "godlike autocrat" arose "vehement Christological debates . . . on the precise manner in which and, above all, on the precise extent to which God had condescended to join himself to human beings in the person of Christ."[26] By this analysis, the self-emptying of Christ was debated not only to demarcate the orthodoxy of the newly legal church, but also for the purpose of theorizing the right use of omnipotence. Brown stresses that "the emperor was to show . . . condescension to his subjects, as the rich stooped to hear the cry of the poor and as God himself had once stooped to join himself, through his incarnation, to the impoverished flesh of the human race."[27]

Athanasius's christology provides a strong example. In the context of the emperor and his masses, christological doctrine could serve to ratify an idea of divinity as the powerful control governing over the flux and misery of the poor and suffering. Athanasius has difficulty explaining Christ's sufferings, for Christ is not the poor; Christ is as an emperor! Aloys Grillmeier explains that for Athanasius the Logos cannot suffer, and therefore his theology required another subject of suffering.[28] Athanasius asserts that it is the humanity in Christ that suffers, while the Logos "accomplishes his sacrifice 'not by offering his body but by making himself visible in the body.'"[29]

Athanasius's fourth-century christology provides a striking contrast to second-century Irenaeus, for whom the suffering part of Christ was clearly the better part. As Irenaeus wrote in *Against Heresies*, "an impassible Christ did not come down into Jesus, but Jesus, since he was Christ, suffered for us . . ."[30] But in Athanasius the divine Christ is not a suffering self.[31] Rather, the divine is the unsuffering strength that infuses the suffering masses with stability. In Athanasius, as Virginia Burrus explains, "The Logos' gift of stability is posited as alien to a materiality defined by its self-dissolving tendencies."[32] It is as though Christ's ability to stabilize matter parallels the church's stabilizing social structure. If the Christian is the suffering self, the church shall be her savior. Ecclesial power, not the suffering persons themselves, embodies christology. The body of Christ, ironically, should not be broken.

---

[26] Brown, *Power and Persuasion in Late Antiquity: Towards a Christian Empire*. Madison, WI: University of Wisconsin Press, 1992, 155.
[27] Ibid.
[28] Aloys Grillmeier, *Christ in Christian Tradition*, vol.1: *From the Apostolic Age to Chalcedon*, trans. Bowden. London: A. R. Mowbray and Co., 1965, 201.
[29] Ibid., quoting Athanasius, *De Incarnation* 16:4.
[30] Irenaeus, *Against Heresies* 3.18.3.
[31] I discuss Judith Perkin's work on the trope of "the suffering self" in late antiquity in Chapter 4.
[32] Virginia Burrus, *"Begotten, Not Made": Conceiving Manhood in Late Antiquity*. Stanford, CA: Stanford University Press, 2000, 46.

Rebecca Lyman writes that "Athanasius' theological concerns were . . . embedded in an ongoing religious and philosophical shift toward the transcendence and reduced access to the divine during the fourth century."[33] Likewise, resonating with Brown's observation about later christology and imperial power, Richard Horsley and Neil Asher Silberman conclude that "the image of Christ was slowly transformed from that of an alternative king to that of a *model* emperor—presiding over a shadow government in heaven and showing by example how things should be done on earth."[34]

Shifts in early Christianity involved both this reduced access to divinity and also, in the analysis of Horsley and Silberman, an abstraction of the source of Christian opposition. Horsley and Silberman emphasize this shift particularly between Pauline and later pseudo-Pauline texts. For example, quoting the pseudo-Pauline letter to the Ephesians, they write that "in contrast to Paul's own career of struggle against a succession of earthly opponents, the Letter to the Ephesians concluded that 'we are not contending against flesh and blood, but against the principalities, against the powers, against the world rulers of this present darkness, against the spiritual hosts of wickedness in the heavenly places'."[35] Judith Perkins also points out that "martyrs' struggles were described as being not with persecutors, but with the devil over whom they triumph through pain and suffering."[36] Meanwhile, imperial power itself becomes less demonized.

Kenotic doctrine comes not to challenge imperial domination but to detail the proper compensatory use of imperial power. Abuses of power garnished by "condescension" and "generosity" become sanctified, and from feminist perspective seem merely token gestures, providing strong ground for critiques like that of Daphne Hampson (discussed later). Rather than any common baptismal incorporation into Christ, *kenosis* now explains the mind-set appropriate to godlike persons, whether emperor or bishop (or man). As Lyman explains of Athanasius, he "repeatedly stated that the Logos took on the weaknesses of human nature; yet his actual exegesis tended to separate the Logos from the experiences of the flesh in order to defend his divinity."[37] Doctrines of Christ's self-emptying became a way to reify divine omnipotence over human travail.

---

[33] Rebecca Lyman, *Christology and Cosmology: Models of Divine Activity in Origen, Eusebius, and Athanasius.* New York: Oxford University Press, 1993, 131.

[34] Richard Horsley and Neil Asher Silberman, *The Message and the Kingdom.* Minneapolis: Fortress, 1997, 225. Also resonating with Brown and Perkins, Horsley and Silberman write that "a new generation of Christian leaders accepted and creatively adapted the main elements of the dominant imperial milieu to their own spiritual ends" (225).

[35] Horsley and Silberman, 225. For Horsley and Silberman, the pseudo-Pauline letters bear witness that "for many churches, the Roman Empire was no longer the main enemy but rather the earthly environment in which Christianity would have to exist peacefully until the second coming of Christ" (225).

[36] Judith Perkins, *The Suffering Self: Pain and Narrative Representation in the Early Christian Era.* London: Routledge, 1995, 32.

[37] Lyman, 153–154.

Rather than human suffering participating in and even recapitulating the power of God, during the time that Christian leaders gained political power, power was theologically repackaged into God and not in the masses of the body of Christ. Coakley, discussing the eighth-century Eastern context, notes the total control exercised by the divine in John of Damacus's theology, wherein "the divine fully permeates" the human.[38] As Coakley rightly indicates, while patristic anxieties about the preservation of a classical notion of God were put to rest by these sorts of "kenotic" christologies, feminist anxiety is instead augmented: for here is "a divine force that takes on humanity by controlling and partly *obliterating* it (and all, seductively, in the name of *kenosis*)."[39]

Abstinence or Masquerade

Though the incarnation and suffering of Christ were always discussed by Christian theologians, *kenosis* itself does not come specifically under debate until the seventeenth century among groups of Lutheran reformers. As Graham Ward explains, "the doctrine of *kenosis* was not a point of intense theological debate until the seventeenth century" and was "a particularly Protestant debate."[40] In two periods, first in the seventeenth century and then again in the nineteenth, Lutheran "kenoticists" vigorously debated what Christ's self-emptying could mean.[41]

The fervent debates over *kenosis* in the modern period can be explained in multiple ways. The formation of new churches after the Reformation called for new doctrinal formulations, mirroring the consolidating pressures of the Constantinian age. Also, however, Lutheran kenoticism peaks just as the modern age dawns, shedding newly critical light on historical study of the human person of Jesus, alongside the Enlightenment focus on the autonomy and agency of the human person.[42] As a converse to the concerns of the patristic

---

[38] Coakley, *Powers and Submissions*, 15.
[39] Ibid.
[40] Ward, "Kenosis: Death, Discourse and Resurrection," 15–66 in *Balthasar at the End of Modernity*, by Lucy Gardner, David Moss, Ben Quash, and Graham Ward. Edinburgh: T&T Clark, 1999, 25.
[41] The Formula of Concord had not provided a decided view on the matter of Christ's *kenosis*. The formula explains: "And this majesty, by reason of the personal union, Christ always possessed, but in the state of his humiliation he humbled himself, and, for this reason, truly grew in age, wisdom, and favor with God and men. Wherefore, he exercised this majesty not always, but as often as seemed good to Him, until, after his resurrection, he fully and entirely laid aside the form of a servant, but not human nature . . ." See *Epitome*, article 8, paragraph 16, in *The Book of Concord*, eds. Kolb and Wengert. Minneapolis: Fortress, 2000, 511, cf. Schmid, 389.
[42] See John Macquarrie, "The Pre-existence of Jesus Christ," in *The Expository Times* 77.7 (1966): 199–202, particularly page 199, and Wolfhart Pannenburg, *Jesus: God and Man*,

christological councils, kenoticism in the seventeenth century and onward serves to underscore the *humanity* truly present in Christ.[43] Pannenburg explains that as historical-critical scholarship became increasingly important, this physical emphasis was meant to "harmonize the old Christological dogma with the modern, historical picture of the life of Jesus in his mere humanity."[44] Ward has also suggested that the renewed focus on *kenosis* in this period corresponds to modernity's fixation on death (though I challenge this interpretation in Chapter 2).[45]

The first wave of kenoticism in the seventeenth century alternated between two schools of thought, represented by the Giessen and Tübingen theologians. The controversy concerned the nature of the *communicatio idiomatum*, or communication of properties, between the two natures of Christ, that is, the divine and the human. The Giessen theologians advocated *kenosis* as a renunciation of divine powers while in human form, while the Tübingen theologians understood *kenosis* as a concealment or *krepsis* of divine powers in Jesus' human life.[46] It was the difference between an abstinence and a masquerade.

For the Tübingen school, the debate began over the problem of the omnipresence of Jesus' human flesh. They understood his flesh to be present everywhere from the moment of conception, entailing an "absolute presence," or what nineteenth-century historian Schmid later describes as "uninterrupted nearness" to all creatures. With this nearness omnipresence was exercised by Christ even during the humiliation of the incarnation (indeed, immediately and simultaneously accompanying the incarnation), and thus the human Christ did not actually renounce any power but simply concealed it. The Tübingen theologians determined that Christ "in the state of humiliation . . . had been as to his person ignominious and obscure."[47]

John Gerhard of Jena explains why the Tübingen christology was unacceptable to him and to other Lutherans at Giessen: "If by *kripsis*, or hiding, there be understood a simulation, we deny that the self-renunciation should be thus described." Instead, Gerhard insists that rather than simulation "there was a true and real self-renunciation, embracing both . . . abstaining from the use . . . which the apostle calls *kenosis* and . . . the assumption of a servile form, and extreme humiliation, which the apostle joins to the *kenosis*."[48] For Giessen, *kenosis* involves abstaining from the use of divine power. Those of the Giessen school denied that Christ governed all things in secret while in the state of humiliation. They

---

translated by Lewis L. Wilkins and Duane A. Priebe. Philadelphia: Westminster Press, 1968, 310.
[43] See Pannenburg, 310 and Ward, "Kenosis," 27, 29.
[44] Pannenburg, 310.
[45] Ward, "Kenosis," 26–28.
[46] The Tübingen theologians of this period particularly include Johann Brenz, Osiander, Nikolai, and Thummius, while Giessen is represented by Martin Chemnitz and others.
[47] Tübingen's position as summarized in Schmid, 391.
[48] Gerhard of Jena, 1582–1637, as quoted in Schmid, 382.

claimed that Christ truly renounced the use of such power. In so doing, explains Schmid, "they rejected absolute omnipresence" as put forth by Tübingen, claiming instead that "the divine nature of Christ was intimately present to creatures at all times, but not so the human nature."[49] Schmid summarizes the difference sharply: those at Tübingen "characterized it as only exceptional, when Christ, during his life upon earth, in certain cases renounced the exercise of the dominion belonging to his human nature," whereas those at Giessen "considered it exceptional, when Christ, during his life upon earth, made use, on the part of his human nature, of the right of divine majesty that belonged to him."[50]

The 1624 *decisio Saxonica* mostly favored the Giessen school.[51] John Quenstedt, nephew of Gerhard, demonstrates the view that was affirmed by the Saxon Union: "Christ Jesus, when he had taken upon himself the form of a slave, neither laid aside the divine nature itself, nor in any way resigned the form of God, but that he did not entirely and fully exercise it, and did not make an ostentatious display of it . . ."[52] Despite the 1624 decision, the different schools continued to promulgate their own teaching on christology, but as the conversation was largely interrupted by the Thirty Years' War, Lutheranism eventually shifted to an overall favoring of the Giessen christology.[53]

Seventeenth-century kenoticism helped make it possible to speak of Christ living an actual human life without being completely overridden by the divine nature. Still, Pannenburg stresses the limitation of this kenoticism: "the Godman of this Christology who merely declined to use his glory remained a sort of fabulous being, more like a mythical redeemer than the historical reality of Jesus of Nazareth." In seventeenth-century kenoticism, no power is given away and none is really shared. *Kenosis* either hides away the massiveness of God's power over us or demonstrates God's overpowering capacity even to refrain from the use of such power. In either case *kenosis* protects God's ability to overpower us, while any gestures of power with or power for only serve to reinforce how little such gestures actually affect God.

At this point, as Jürgen Moltmann emphasizes, "neither group was prepared to talk about a *kenosis* of the *divinity* of the eternal Logos. They merely wished to make room for the true and real humanity of Christ's life on earth."[54] Or as Pannenburg explains, in contrast to later kenoticism, "this conflict

---

[49] Schmid, 391–392.
[50] Ibid., 393.
[51] For overviews of the controversy see Pannenburg, 307–323; Schmid, 389–393; or Gottfried Thomasius, "Christ's Person and Work" (1857), in *God and Incarnation: In Mid-Nineteenth Century German Theology*, ed. and trans. Claude Welsh. New York: Oxford University Press, 1965, 429.
[52] Quenstedt of Wittenberg, 1617–1685, as quoted in Schmid, 384.
[53] Schmid, 384.
[54] Moltmann, "God's *Kenosis* in the Creation and Consummation of the World," in *The Work of Love: Creation as Kenosis*, ed. John Polkinghorne. Grand Rapids, MI: Wm. B. Eerdmans, 2001, 139.

involved . . . only the exaltation and humiliation of Christ *according to his human nature*, not a humiliation and self-emptying of the Son of God himself."[55] That was the work of kenoticism's next wave, which would introduce the emphasis on the divine self-limitation with which Coakley contends. Nineteenth-century kenoticists, Moltmann explains, "took as subject of Philippians 2 not the Christ-who-has-become-human, but the Christ-in-his-becoming-human."[56] As Bonhoeffer summarizes this development, now "the Logos, humbling itself, becomes a human being," rather than the Logos, incarnate as human, subsequently being humiliated. The effect is that "the historical picture of Jesus Christ is thus freed from the inner violence of needing to repress" its divine character.[57]

Nineteenth-century kenoticism began again with Lutherans in Germany, but would this time become a more far-reaching conversation.[58] The most influential kenoticist of this period is Gottfried Thomasius, who stressed explicitly the "self-limitation of the divine."[59] Thomasius envisioned an actual limit experienced by "the eternal Son of God" who "gave himself over into the form of human limitation, and thereby to the limits of a spatio-temporal existence, under the conditions of a human development, in the bounds of an historical concrete being, in order to live in and through our nature the life of our race in the fullest sense of the word, without on that account ceasing to be God."[60] Thus, for Thomasius, the *kenosis* of Philippians 2 applies to the incarnation, the simultaneous exchanging of the form of God for the form of a servant. Thomasius writes that "the assumption of human nature, in the determinateness in which the Son of God willed it and made it his own for the purpose of redemption, *i.e.* the assumption of the flesh, took place by means of the *kenosis* of himself, and could be carried out only in this way."[61] The incarnation is the self-limitation of "disincarnate logos" choosing to enter flesh and its conditions.[62] Then, however, "the earthly life of the redeemer," "as the divine-human continuation of the incarnation," "is at once revelation and divesting," continuing the *kenosis* and revealing God in the process.[63] Over

---

[55] Pannenburg, 309, cf. Schmid, 376–377.
[56] Moltmann, "God's *Kenosis*," 139.
[57] Bonhoeffer, Dietrich Bonhoeffer, "Lectures on Christology," *Dietrich Bonhoeffer's Works*, vol. 12. Minneapolis: Fortress Press, 2009, 348, cf. Pannenburg, 310.
[58] The conversation grew particularly in Britain, in the work of Gore, Weston, Mackintosh, and Taylor. See Stephen W. Sykes, "The Strange Persistence of Kenotic Christology," 349–375 in *Being and Truth: Essays in Honor of John Macquarrie*, ed. Alistair Kee and Eugene Thomas Long. London: SCM Press, 1986.
[59] Thomasius as quoted in Pannenburg, 310; cf. Thomasius, "Christ's Person and Work," 72.
[60] Thomasius, "Christ's Person and Work," 48.
[61] Ibid., 56.
[62] Ibid., 47. Thomasius elaborates here that "this divine-human person can only have originated through God's determining himself to actual participation in the human mode of being . . ."
[63] Ibid., 67.

the lifetime of the historical Jesus, the incarnate Logos partakes by "ethical necessity" or a "necessity of freedom" in "the divine-human continuation of that self-limitation by the way of humbleness and suffering, by the way of the cross throughout" and "thus goes ever farther on the course once taken."[64] Jesus' life follows a kenotic trajectory.

The most cumbersome aspect of Thomasius's kenoticism is found in his distinction between the "immanent" and "relative" attributes of God: "Immanent attributes are absolute power (freedom) and eternity, absolute holiness, truth, love; the relative attributes . . . are omnipotence, omnipresence, omniscience."[65] The relative attributes describe how God *relates* to the world; they are "activated" by the essential immanent attributes. Thomasius imagines that in the *kenosis* of the incarnation, God renounces God's way of relating to the world in an emptying of the relative attributes. This *kenosis* of relative attributes—in other words, this shift in God's relation to the world—enables God "to experience in truth a humanly natural life, a life in the flesh, and to redeem us." Thomasius employs his distinction between immanent and relative characteristics to explain the limitations he sees in seventeenth-century kenoticism. As to the Giessen idea that Christ would voluntarily refrain from use of divine power while in the flesh, he writes that "omnipotence is nothing but the employment, *i.e.* the activation, of absolute power in the whole of the world; a non-employment of omnipresence or omniscience beside or with the possession thereof is an internal contradiction . . ."[66] Because omnipotence (admittedly a noun) is for Thomasius something like an active verb, in deciding not to use it (to do it), then one does not have it. "Renunciation of the use is thus here *eo ipso* divesting of the possession . . . Thus we say simply: During his earthly state of life the redeemer was neither omnipotent nor omniscient nor omnipresent."[67] In the flesh "the mediator neither used nor possessed the divine omnipotence that is the form of appearance and activation of absolute power in the world."[68]

But at the same time, God does not renounce being God in "holiness, truth, love," and God's "essence thereby suffers no diminution." Thomasius explains

---

[64] Ibid. On this ethical point Thomasius elaborates that Christ "used the absolute power which dwelt in him only for his mediatorial vocation. And he could not use it otherwise than for this purpose, because he *ought* not" ("Christ's Person and Work," 70).

[65] Ibid., 94. For Jürgen Moltmann's discussion of this see "God's *Kenosis* in the Creation and Consummation of the World," 137–151 in *The Work of Love: Creation as Kenosis*, ed. John Polkinghorne. Grand Rapids, MI: Wm. B. Eerdmans, 2001, 139.

[66] Thomasius, 71.

[67] Ibid.

[68] Ibid., 70. Problematically in Thomasius's theology, Christ's incarnation becomes the center of history, where "the entire pre-Christian influence of god, not simply on Israel but also on the pagan world, is a propadeutic to Christ" ("Christ's Person and Work," 86). Though for Thomasius Christ's incarnate life becomes the centerpoint of all history, one could also use Luther and Melanchthon's criticism of scholastic theology to claim that the shift effected is in human understanding of God, finding God outside the expected "relative attributes," rather than in the nature of Godself.

"the immanent attributes God cannot give up because he would thereby give himself up." Thus, Thomasius can claim that the "incarnate one," though "no *all*-mighty, *all*-present, *all*-knowing man," actually "is and remains the absolute power, truth, holiness, love, *i.e.* essentially God."[69]

Curiously, then, God's *kenosis* into the human condition is possible for Thomasius precisely because God does not need or depend upon creation. "The relative attributes he can renounce because the world, and thus also the relation to it, is not necessary for him."[70] In other words, because God is essentially free (an immanent attribute), God can afford to let go of God's manner of relating to the world, emptying out omniscience and omnipotence. As Hans Urs von Balthasar affirmatively describes Thomasius's thought, "since this self-limitation of the Godhead takes place in absolute freedom, being the work of love, it does not suppress God's divinity."[71] More critically, I would point out that God is able to become enmeshed in the world here precisely because God is not dependent on the world. Thus, oddly, in positing a deeply incarnate and limited God, Thomasius manages to reiterate God's freedom from flesh and creation. Thomasius hovers between power over and power with.

In his day Thomasius's christology met with fervent criticism. But responding to criticism of his christology, Thomasius writes: "As I proceed to a self-limitation of the eternal Logos in the incarnation, I find myself quite in the middle of the ecclesiastical stream, wholly in the course of the Christological ideas and tendencies of our Lutheran doctrine."[72] He comes to "understand the *kenosis* as more profound than has hitherto been customary,"[73] presumably speaking about the seventeenth-century kenoticists, since he sees himself in harmony with Luther. To his objectors, Thomasius argues:

> God *can* go just as far in his self-divesting as he *wills* in his love. The objections raised against this from some sort of *a priori* concept of immutability cause me as little concern as the name 'theopaschitism' by which one intends to cast suspicion on this whole mode of thinking. In any event, the depth of the condescending, self-sacrificing love of God will be deeper than the highest peak of our speculation.[74]

---

[69] Thomasius, 94, cf. Moltmann, "God's Kenosis," 139.
[70] Ibid.
[71] Hans Urs von Balthasar, *Mysterium Paschale*. Edinburgh, Scotland: T&T Clark, Ltd., 1990, 31.
[72] Thomasius, 90, cf. 89, where he writes: "I am unable to hold both things firmly together, namely the full reality of the divine and human being of Christ (especially the full truth of his naturally human development of life) on the one hand, and on the other hand the full unity of his divine-human person, without the supposition of a self-limitation of the divine Logos coincident with the incarnation."
[73] Ibid., 100–101.
[74] Ibid., 100.

Though Thomasius's christological system proved cumbersome with his distinctions between immanent and relative attributes, his work subtly reasserts the message of the *theologia crucis* as he presents a God willing to descend deeply into human existence. Thomasius seeks to determine the meaning of *kenosis* in relationship to us. Coakley sees Thomasius's work as a "real *novum*" in kenoticism, introducing the suggestion of a "self-limitation of the *divine* realm."[75] But I read Thomasius as a faithful, if quirky, expositor of his Reformation heritage, a heritage discussed in Chapter 2.

"Gentle Omnipotence"

Many contemporary theologians have explored *kenosis*, and their work will be discussed throughout this book. I turn to Sarah Coakley's theology of *kenosis* now, however, both because she is one of the few feminists to focus on this theme specifically, and because her work offers this chapter yet another example of the way in which doctrines of *kenosis* can be used to reify concepts of God's power over us.[76]

Coakley pushes theologians, especially feminist ones, to "rethink the standard binary of 'power' and 'submission'."[77] Instead of supporting the opposition of this binary, Coakley seeks power in submission, asking: "How . . . is divine power to be seen as alluring and sustaining human (dependent) responsibility?"[78] Coakley's assertion about power in submission nonetheless attains that power through a lending of power from above.

Coakley defends *kenosis* partly in response to post-Christian feminist theologian Daphne Hampson, who finds *kenosis* to be in simple contradiction to any doctrine of salvation for women.[79] For Hampson *kenosis* may inform male ethics, supplying a check to the overinflated ego, but "for women, the

---

[75] Coakley, *Powers and Submissions*, 19, cf. 20–21, 23, and 38. Coakley traces the twentieth-century theologies of God's own *kenosis*—theologies she determines are masculinist—back to Thomasius. I find Thomasius to be less novel than she suggests, and while it seems that some of the theologians she critiques, like Moltmann, were influenced by Thomasius, I find the kernel of the divine *kenosis* idea to far predate him, at least to the Lutheran Reformation, but perhaps even in the *logos* christologies circulating in early Christianities. Pannenburg sees in Thomasius a return to patristic interests with *kenosis*. The new element in Pannenburg's analysis is not the self-limitation of the divine, but rather the physicality of that limitation, "no longer understood in the merely moral sense of a humble bending down to humanity, imparting to it unification with God" (*Jesus: God and Man*, 310).

[76] For an appreciative discussion of Coakley's contributions on *kenosis*, see the symposium on her work published as *Svensk Teologisk Kvartalskrift* 85.2 (2009).

[77] Coakley, *Powers and Submissions*, x.

[78] Ibid., xiv.

[79] Coakley's earlier dialogue with Hampson is in *Swallowing a Fishbone? Feminist Theologians Debate Christianity*, ed. Daphne Hampson. London: Society for Promoting Christian Knowledge, 1996.

theme of self-emptying and self-abnegation is far from helpful as a paradigm." Hampson concludes that "*kenosis* is a counter-theme within male thought. It does not build what might be said to be specifically feminist values into our understanding of God."[80]

Coakley analyzes Hampson's criticism of *kenosis*, showing the ways in which Hampson's analysis ignores the many different textures of kenotic theology and adequately critiques only certain types. Hampson's bone to pick, Coakley suggests, is rightly with the "speculative 'kenoticism' devised by early twentieth-century British theologians exercising their (perhaps guilty) social consciences."[81] Here Coakley lists Frank Weston, Charles Gore, and P. T. Forsyth.[82]

The transparent patriarchal colonialism of these particular theologians illustrates yet again how political frameworks shape christological constructions. These christologies are as inflected by the colonialism of their age as much as earlier christologies had been by Roman imperialism.

Still, Coakley's largest disagreement is not with Hampson but with those she dubs "new kenoticists."[83] Coakley herself scorns this kenoticism, which understands Christ's *kenosis* to be paradigmatic not of perfected human nature but of the *divine* nature. As Coakley puts it, "submission has become paradoxically *identified* with divine power." She finds deeply problematic those theologies of *kenosis* that hazard any submission or vulnerability on the part of the divine: that is, any divine *kenosis*. By emptying the powers of divinity, Coakley determines that these theologians negate the strength that humans could draw upon in kenotic vulnerability before (the nonkenotic) God. For Coakley this sort of theology "appears to make 'God' both limited and weak (by a process of direct transference from Jesus' human life to the divine), and so endanger the very capacity for divine transformative 'power'."[84] She relegates such christology to

---

[80] Daphne Hampson, *Theology and Feminism*. Oxford: Blackwell, 1990, 155. Hampson offers that an example of such a feminist value would be "the mutual empowerment of persons." But for Hampson, the kenotic theology of the incarnation, which in Hampson's interpretation endorses "a giving up of power in favor of powerlessness," ultimately supports hierarchy rather than mutuality in the divine/human relationship and thus lacks adequate emphasis on the sharing of power (154).

[81] Coakley, *Powers and Submissions*, 11.

[82] Ibid., 19–22.

[83] "New kenoticism" was first John Macquarrie's term, but he uses it somewhat differently than Coakley (cf. Coakley 24). Macquarrie distinguished between "new" and "old-style kenotic theories" in a short article from 1966 and then continued the comparison in a 1974 publication. In his 1966 article Macquarrie counts himself among the new kenoticists, though later he is less clear, becoming critical of its reactivity "against what it regards as the speculative or even mythological character of the old-style kenoticism," resulting in a sort of "adoptionist christology" that is an "impoverishment" of the concept of *kenosis*. See "The Preexistence of Jesus Christ," *The Expository Times*, April 1966, and "Kenoticism Reconsidered," *Theology: A Monthly Review* 77 (March 1974): this quote p. 123. For a reading of Macquarrie's kenoticism, also see S. W. Sykes, "The Strange Persistence," 358.

[84] Coakley, *Powers and Submissions*, 30.

a "popular male theological strategy."[85] Here she cites a wide variety of figures, from Moule and Robinson to Barth and Balthasar and Moltmann.[86]

Coakley wants instead to advocate, drawing upon 2 Corinthians 12:9, "the possibility of a 'strength made perfect *in* (human) weakness' . . . of the normative concurrence in Christ of non-bullying divine 'power' *with* 'self-effaced' humanity."[87] By a telling redaction to 2 Corinthians, Coakley emphasizes that *human* strength is made perfect in its ceding to divine omnipotence. For Coakley, the perfect human situation is crafted by the pairing of nonkenotic divinity with kenotic humanity.

Coakley's emendation of 2 Corinthians is telling: could not strength in weakness be characteristic of *divine* strength, not just human strength? In 2 Corinthians 12, Paul is recounting a revelatory conversation with the divine, who says to Paul, "My grace is sufficient for you, for power is made perfect in weakness." The NRSV includes the note that "other ancient authorities read *my power.*" Surely the passage itself does not rule out the possibility that weakness may perfect divine, and not only human, power.

The problem for Coakley in a concept of divine *kenosis* is a human "seepage" into the divine.[88] But any "seepage" presumes a different notion of the divine to begin with: an originally nonkenotic God who could be contaminated by the change wrought through Christ. If God's nature was always kenotic, no seepage has taken place—only an eroding of a classical theology of God's nature. But Coakley assumes that the human is contaminating the divine rather than that God was always so "contaminated" by God's love for creatures, such that the life and death of Jesus were in accord with the ways of the God of Israel.

In opposing theologies of divine *kenosis*, Coakley resists dismantling her "power over" model of God, though she is mindful of those feminist theologians who have endorsed submission and vulnerability in situations of shared power, or "power with."[89] In order to secure power in God, Coakley insists on a traditional model of God's power: an intensely patriarchal model of power. For her, other models necessarily spell weakness for God.

With a strategy different from what she sees operative in "new kenoticism," Coakley turns attention not to any *kenosis* of the divine, but rather to strictly human *kenosis*. Focusing on gospel descriptions of Jesus, Coakley asks: "If Jesus' 'vulnerability' is a primary narrative given, rather than a philosophical embarrassment to explain away, then precisely the question is raised whether 'vulnerability' *need* be seen as a 'female' weakness rather than a (special sort of) 'human' strength."[90] The kenotic Christ reveals the perfected human

---

[85] Ibid., xv.
[86] Coakley, xiv, xx, and 10.
[87] Ibid., 31.
[88] Ibid., 23, cf. 31.
[89] Ibid., 33.
[90] Ibid.

state as willfully vulnerable. In advocating "willed ceding to the divine" in contemplative prayer, Coakley accounts for feminist concerns by stressing that (a) the divine is not abusive; (b) the contemplative *kenosis* itself is a sort of "power in vulnerability," not a final negation of all power; and (c) submission to God is revealed in Christ as the proper *human*—not only female—posture. For Coakley the perfected humanity revealed by Christ undoes traditional gender stereotypes by endorsing only one ideal type: the kenotic human before God.

Coakley articulates "a vision of Christological *kenosis* uniting human 'vulnerability' with"—her version of—"authentic divine power (as opposed to worldly or 'patriarchal' visions of power)," such that the human is "wholly translucent to the divine."[91] This "authentic divine power" comes from a "gentle omnipotence."[92]

Thus, Coakley argues for contemplation as "a graced means of human empowerment in the divine which the feminist movement ignores or derides at its peril."[93] Prayer is enfleshed, and thus this contemplative *kenosis* is incarnational.[94] She describes kenotic contemplative prayer as "an ascetical commitment of some subtlety, a regular and willed *practice* of ceding and responding to the divine."[95] She insists on *kenosis* beyond theory; she advocates contemplative *practice*, a "practiced dependency on God," befitting the liturgical context of the *kenosis* hymn recorded in Philippians.[96]

To her credit, Coakley has practiced her sort of "spiritual *kenosis*" with prison inmates, teaching this practice to them and practicing it with them.[97] She has seen firsthand and in shared company across gendered, racial, and socioeconomic differences the work of kenotic power. She repeatedly met with a group of inmates who chose to commit to the contemplative practice, and the men participating demonstrably experienced communal and personal strength through the practice of silent group prayer. This empowerment proved true for them despite the risk that these men who have been silenced by imprisonment would feel further silenced under God in such prayer. Coakley reports:

> Many of the men new to the practice found it hard to relax or to bear the inner turmoil that the silence engendered. At such times I felt strongly the influence of my inner group of more experienced practitioners, whose gentleness and poise were the best advertisement for the long-term efficacy

---

[91] Ibid., 18.
[92] Ibid., 37.
[93] Ibid., xvii.
[94] Ibid., 68.
[95] Ibid., 34.
[96] Ibid., xx and 34.
[97] Spiritual kenosis is Coakley's term; see *Powers and Submissions* 33 and 37.

of the undertaking. Gentleness, poise, peace and solidarity were indeed manifest ways of "bucking the system," if only for a short and blessed interval in the prison day.[98]

This contemplative *kenosis* provided the men with a form of empowering resistance to their literal confinement, what Coakley names a "jail break."

Toward Other Modes of Power

While Coakley argues that "wordless prayer can enable one, paradoxically, to hold vulnerability and personal empowerment together, precisely by creating the 'space' in which non-coercive divine power manifests itself,"[99] I want for feminism the ability to keep this paradoxical combination through a wider sense of *kenosis* than contemplative prayer alone. A "non-coercive divine power" is certainly better from a feminist perspective than a coercive one, but I imagine a wider *kenosis* in which, rather than waiting for the divine to come, to "manifest itself," it is one's own arrival that simultaneously manifests personal empowerment and divine power, as these coalesce in a moment of incarnation. Coakley also imagines incarnation: "for it is a feature of the *special* 'self-effacement' of this gentle space making—this yielding to divine power which is no worldly power—that it marks one's willed engagement in the pattern of the cross and resurrection, one's deeper rooting and grafting into the 'body of Christ'."[100]

For her feminist construction of *kenosis*, Coakley sees in the Giessen theologians and their insistence on a kenotic human nature a christology that "might have some life in it as far as a feminist reconstruction is concerned."[101] Giessen offers her a theological model in which the human Christ chooses to renounce God's overwhelming powers, thus demonstrating for Coakley that perfected human nature is found in dependent submission to God's power. She sees in Giessen "a vision of christological *kenosis* uniting human 'vulnerability' with authentic divine power (as opposed to worldly or 'patriarchal' visions of power), and uniting them such that the human was wholly translucent to the

---

[98] Sarah Coakley, "Jail Break: Meditation as a Subversive Activity," *Christian Century* 121.13 (2004): 19.
[99] Coakley, *Powers and Submissions*, 5.
[100] Coakley, *Powers and Submissions*, 35. Coakley admits some danger that makes her "vulnerability" truly vulnerable, but it is hardly the sort of vulnerability one might face in kenotic activity beyond the specific space of contemplative prayer, or "the defenseless prayer of silent waiting on God" (34). While this prayer maybe defenseless in its approach to God, it nonetheless could carry a number of other defenses: privacy of thoughts and experiences, and assumedly the safety of one's body while praying. Coakley mentions the danger of a sudden breakthrough from the psyche (36).
[101] Ibid., 17.

divine."¹⁰² She favors a reading of *kenosis* as an operation of Christ's human, but not divine, nature. For her this strategy safeguards the immutability and omnipotence of God. Thus, though many feminists have found the doctrine of God's omnipotence problematic, this is precisely the doctrine that Coakley maintains in her kenotic christology. She claims that this all-powerful God is a source of empowerment for all humans, women included, as they imitate the human nature of Christ and place themselves in contemplative humility before God.

Clearly, Coakley is not critical of classical understandings of God. She is, however, critical of the way in which Enlightenment understandings of the human person yield a correspondingly powerful idea of humanity: "a sovereign self-possession and autonomy that is capable of rising above the weaknesses and distractions of human desires and human tragedy."¹⁰³ For the Christ figure, in whom the divine and human are said to coexist, Coakley finds Enlightenment assumptions about humanity to be particularly problematic. If God is potently self-possessed and so is the perfect human person, then in the person of Christ, the "two natures" are each consummately self-contained and unyielding. Coakley asks, "How can the natures of *two* such 'individuals' concur christologically?"¹⁰⁴ She solves this conundrum by softening the human figure: "What, we may ask, if the frailty, vulnerability and 'self-effacement' of [the gospel] narratives *is* what shows us 'perfect humanity'?"¹⁰⁵

Practicing such self-effacement in contemplative prayer, she suggests, is an exercise of "'power-in-vulnerability,' the willed effacement to an omnipotence which, far from 'complementing' masculinism, acts as its undoing."¹⁰⁶ Her argument is that Christ's humility pulls the rug out from under patriarchal posturing, showing it to be an improper way to live. However, while she succeeds in undoing gender hierarchy on an intrahuman level, she only reinstates this hierarchy between humans and God. Rather than undoing gender stereotypes through her christology, she instead lumps all of humanity, in Christ, into a feminized state of submission beneath a traditionally masculinized diety, thus reinstating the dichotomy of a masculine power and female submission, and between masculine divinity and feminine materiality. She insists on an omnipotent God positioned in prayer over a kenotic humanity: a humanity that, in *kenosis*, can "cease to set the agenda" and "'make space' for God to be God."¹⁰⁷ Yet what precisely is God *being* here, and why must God require so much space and free reign in order to be Godlike? Coakley's formulation

---

¹⁰² Ibid., 18.
¹⁰³ Ibid., 25.
¹⁰⁴ Ibid.
¹⁰⁵ Ibid., 26.
¹⁰⁶ Ibid., 37.
¹⁰⁷ Ibid., 34.

implies that God's virility thrives when hovering over the disarmed, submissive human: a violent tableau all too familiar to women.[108]

Coakley stresses that she is not advocating a submission to violence: "By choosing to 'make space' in this way, one 'practices' the 'presence of God'—the subtle but enabling presence of a God who neither shouts nor forces, let alone 'obliterates'."[109] Yet, even if the possibility of abuse is removed, her portrayal of contemplative space-making still calls to mind an old-fashioned heterosexual coupling between a male (God) and a female (humanity): the submissive one makes space to willingly receive the potency of her divine lover. Consensual and nonviolent, yes—but not a transformation of gender norms. We will not undo the gender stereotypes Coakley hopes to dismantle unless we take apart heteronormativity too. In what other, wider ways might we practice the presence of God through *kenosis*?

Coakley's tenacity for a traditional mode of divine power is a subtle point in her work, because she seeks to articulate a transformed notion of divine power, wanting to "*redefine* divine 'power' creatively."[110] For example, Coakley sees in Giessen "the possibility raised here of a vision of christological *kenosis* uniting human 'vulnerability' with authentic divine power (as opposed to worldly or 'patriarchal' visions of power), and uniting them such that the human was wholly translucent to the divine . . ."[111] She describes her vision of God as "non-bullying."[112] Perhaps it is in this gentle "authenticity" that she sees a "*reformulation* of the very notion of divine 'power' and its relation to the human."[113] And yet the subtraction of violence, while significant, does not transform traditional dynamics of power and submission, or of a patriarchal God. In Coakley's formulation, human power can be perfected in weakness, while for the divine, the patriarchal rules still apply, with the important caveat that the divine is gentle and nonabusive. But to put it bluntly, a nice man in power is still a man in power—power over everyone else—and this is not a transformation of patriarchy. Coakley wants human subjectivity to be found in dependence on God, but where is human subjectivity when the person

---

[108] Elsewhere, Coakley presents another version of this same binary through midrash on the narrative of Isaac's binding in which Isaac becomes symbolic of Coakley's ideal feminist self: a stereotypically masculine divine exercises his power over a consistently and voluntarily passive human, cleansing her of her own desires and filling her with his. See Coakley, "In Defense of Sacrifice: Gender, Selfhood and the Binding of Isaac," in *Feminism, Sexuality and the Return of Religion*, ed. Jack Caputo, forthcoming.

[109] Coakley, *Powers and Submissions*, 35.

[110] She writes that "it is one thing, of course, to *redefine* divine 'power' creatively, another to shear God down to human size, to make God intrinsically power*less*, incapable of sustaining the creation in being" (*Powers and Submissions*, 24).

[111] Coakley, *Powers and Submissions*, 18.

[112] Ibid., 31.

[113] Ibid., 22.

is "wholly translucent"?[114] As theories of sadomasochism demonstrate, power and submission may be transformed not by the absence of pain but by the presence of agency (a topic discussed at more length in Chapter 4).

Coakley wants "absolute dependence" for humans, a "right dependence," a "right *kenosis*."[115] Coakley argues that "the apparently forced choice between dependent 'vulnerability' and liberative 'power' is a false one," and while I would agree that vulnerability and power comprise a false dichotomy, her insistence on strictly human dependence indicates her resistance to imagining divine power apart from "power over." She will not allow dependence to characterize the divine realm. In this way God is still held over humanity, maintaining a cosmic contrast between power and vulnerability. Coakley's answer to her own question, "How . . . is divine power to be seen as alluring and sustaining human (dependent) responsibility?" would, by my reading, be: through invited power over us. She writes that Christ "instantiates" "the unique intersection of vulnerable 'non-grasping' humanity and authentic divine power, itself 'made perfect in weakness'."[116] But since she has denied divine weakness, it seems she must mean: made perfect in *our* weakness. Patriarch indeed.

It seems that for Coakley, divine power is proved as such by its capability to sustain creation and human responsibility.[117] If that is the goal, must "power over" be maintained? Arguing against theologies of divine self-emptying, Coakley writes, "It is being urged that the 'limitations' of Jesus' human life are in some sense directly *equatable* with what it is to be 'God'," entailing "the *identification* of 'God' as permanently 'limited.'"[118] Her reading is correct; these theologies do largely affirm a kenotic limit in God, as I will explore more fully in the following chapters. But for Coakley these theologies further suggest that God "becomes intrinsically devoid of omniscience and omnipotence (at least in anything like the traditional definitions)."[119] Here I would suggest that we may be able to move away from the traditional understanding of omnipotence without yet suggesting that God is devoid of it.

The holy bearing of a limit only need render God im(omni)potent if one understands all-power to mean power to remove limits. Such an understanding

---

[114] Coakley writes that "this special 'self-emptying' is not a negation of self, but the place of the self's transformation and expansion into God" (*Powers and Submissions*, 36). When discussing subjectivity in her introduction, Coakley cites Hegel's master/slave dialectic but without exploring how such a dialectic would entail a converse dependency of God on us. She acknowledges in her mention of Hegel that the slave would "have the edge" on the master, but she does not carry this over to a theology in which God would in some way be transformed by creation. See Coakley, *Powers and Submissions*, xiii and xx.

[115] Coakley, *Powers and Submissions*, 68 and 5. For Coakley this dependency on God serves as the "fulcrum" for our other interpersonal dependencies.

[116] Ibid., 38.

[117] Ibid., xiv and 24.

[118] Ibid., 23.

[119] Ibid., 24.

of power is indeed patriarchal. It assumes that the one in power can do whatever he wants and has control over everything: omni-power as total control. But power need not function only in that way. The current of divine presence, a current that fosters life, heals, makes new (and is, thereby, powerful) works through the setting and keeping of limits, as in: "I will be your God, and you shall be my people,"[120] the fettering of the divine heart by *hesed,* by covenant loyalty, itself a fecund limit.

Unlike Coakley, many feminists have criticized theologies of God's omnipotence because omnipotence is so classically characteristic of patriarchal theologies. While it should be clear by now that I find Coakley's use of omnipotence to be patriarchal, with a stereotypically masculine divine firmly over us, I do wonder about other possibilities for the idea of God's all-power. Can the idea of omnipotence function outside a patriarchal economy? Surely God's power finds other modes of expression, but can *omni*potence also find expression apart from domination without collapsing into contradiction? Is it impossible to let power play and flow and go and yet maintain omnipotence? What if God's power is kinetic, generated in motion?

It is possible that the feminist critique of omnipotence is focused on the patriarchal idea of what power is, as power over, while divine, all-encompassing power might manifest itself in different ways such that God's omnipotence is almost unrecognizable to us, arbitrary to our relationship with God. Rather than asserting that the theological idea of God's omnipotence is flatly wrong, I would say instead that asking after omnipotence is the wrong question to be asking—wrong as in unfruitful and even counterproductive. As the next chapter will show, my own Lutheran heritage helps me to articulate the possibility that, whether or not God is omnipotent, God may be uninterested in revealing that side of God to us, that perhaps God even finds omnipotence irrelevant (even irreverent?) in relation to us.

---

[120] Jeremiah 7:23, cf. Jeremiah 11:4 and 30:22, Exodus 6:7, and Ezekiel 36:28.

Chapter 2

Beyond "Power Over": Relational Christology

As demonstrated in the previous chapter, doctrines of self-emptying have again and again been used to bolster the idea of God's overbearing power. Considering this record, how might we think of Christ's self-giving apart from the metaphysics of "power over"? We might, as Rosemary Radford Ruether has done, imagine Christ marking the end of God's power over. Her approach is somewhat similar to the kenotic philosophy of Gianni Vattimo, taken up by Marta Frascati-Lochhead in her project on *kenosis* and feminist theology. As I will explore in the first part of this chapter, a major problem with both of these approaches is the characterization of God's relationship with ancient Israel, and thus with contemporary Jews, as problematically *prior* to this self-revelation of God. This danger is partly dismantled if we instead imagine the kenotic revelation to be one in Christian *thinking* about God (as is possible with Frascati-Lochhead's framework) rather than some fundamental shift in God's way of being.

Whatever way we move away from power over, it will need to be in such a way that any divine self-giving is congruent with the scope of God's character in the Hebrew Bible. Even though doctrines of *kenosis* are christological, in order to remain fecundly kenotic rather than lording Christian power over others, especially Jews, theologies of *kenosis* will need to be generous and yielding in relation to Jews and other religious people.[1] (Would that this were obvious of all Christian doctrine!) If *kenosis* supports a theology that is violent or supersessionist, then we are back at power over.

After describing Ruether and Frascati-Lochhead's uses of *kenosis* and the ways in which they critique a metaphysics of overwhelming power, I will then turn to what may seem an unlikely source for constructing a kenotic theology

---

[1] While *kenosis* is at its root in Philippians christological, themes like *kenosis* emerge in other spiritual traditions. Jewish tradition carries the concept of *zimzum*; see Jürgen Moltmann's discussion of this in "God's *Kenosis* in the Creation and Consummation of the World," 137–151 in *The Work of Love: Creation as Kenosis*, ed. John Polkinghorne. Grand Rapids, MI: Wm. B. Eerdmans, 2001. Buddhists have *sunyata*, discussed in *The Emptying God*, eds. John B. Cobb, Jr. and Christopher Ives. Maryknoll, NY: Orbis Books, 1990.

apart from power over: the sixteenth century's Martin Luther and Philip Melanchthon. They may seem unlikely for at least two reasons. First, Luther's theology was hardly good in relation to the Jews of his time. Especially in the later portion of his career, Luther instructed the burning of synagogues—a teaching that would be appropriated tragically by the Third Reich centuries later. Second, Luther's "theology of the cross" has been the object of much feminist contention.[2] This is because it seems to condone the very thing I will use it to critique: God's power over us, particularly seen in the cross as a sadistic power.

Too many women and other historically oppressed persons have been told to patiently endure their suffering in the name of Christian discipleship. They have been told to bear their crosses—whether their cross is a slave master or an abusive spouse. Feminists have rightly protested these abusive theologies.[3] Luther's theology of the cross, which claims that God is rightly understood only through "suffering and the cross," may seem an obvious example of such a theology. But I will argue here for a reading of Luther's theology of the cross as a theology of God's power given *for* God's beloved people. Luther's theology of the cross, particularly when read beside Melanchthon's "benefits of Christ," can be read as a kenotic theology expressing God's identity as a God for us.

The Dissolution of God's Power over Us

In her *Sexism and God-talk*, Ruether writes *kenosis* as the intentional self-humiliation of the divine patriarch. She engages *kenosis* through a feminist midrash on the Philippians text. In her midrashic scene, God the Father sits anxiously on his throne in heaven, while on earth all is chaotic. Even in his celestial realm the whispers of the long-suppressed Queen of Heaven nag him relentlessly. He wonders: Could my suppressive and oppressive politics be the source of earthly problems? "I and the kings of earth have come to resemble each other too closely. By calling me Father, Lord, and Ruler, they claim the power to rule the earth as I rule the heavens . . . Men teach women their place on earth, following My example."[4] These thoughts catalyze the patriarchal God's *kenosis* in the form of incarnation into the virgin's womb. The heavens are torn apart, Mary is pregnant, and Joseph feels moved to protect her illegitimate child. Outpoured light, like a comet, sears the sky, and its sound leaves a trace

---

[2] Diana Thompson responds to this contention in her *Crossing the Divide: Luther, Feminism, and the Cross*. Minneapolis: Fortress Press, 2004.

[3] See Joanne Carlson Brown and Carole R. Bohn, eds, *Christianity, Patriarchy, and Abuse: A Feminist Critique*. Cleveland, OH: Pilgrim Press, 1989, and Rita N. Brock and Rebecca Ann Parker, *Proverbs of Ashes: Violence, Redemptive Suffering, and the Search for What Saves Us*. Boston: Beacon Press, 2001.

[4] Ruether, *Sexism and God-talk: Toward a Feminist Theology*. Boston: Beacon, 1993, 2.

of Philippians: "Being in the form of God, he did not count equality with God as a thing to be prized, but emptied himself and became a servant."[5] Thus, God the Father becomes a servant in the incarnation of Jesus; God's *kenosis* in Jesus is the *kenosis* of divine patriarchy. God's power over drains away at Bethlehem.

In this way the theological motif of *kenosis* offers Ruether a way in which to rework the Christian tradition she has inherited by using another part of that tradition. Through midrash she creates friction between the Philippians hymn and the legendary image of God as a giant old man enthroned above, finally re-presenting God as a servant. In Ruether's midrash it seems as though the Philippians hymn is in a sense *God's* baptismal hymn, the melody by which God is washed into kenotic life, beckoned to the font perhaps by the lingering, luring voice of the Queen of Heaven: a still, small voice within, renewing the integrity of the divine self. The divine refusal of dominance opens the door toward Ruether's feminist theology.

Ruether also reads a kenotic message in the synoptic narratives of Jesus. This Jesus "calls for a renunciation, a dissolution, of the web of status relationships by which societies have defined privilege and deprivation." Jesus "manifests the kenosis of patriarchy, the announcement of the new humanity through a lifestyle that discards hierarchical caste privilege and speaks on behalf of the lowly."[6]

The problem with this vivid deconstruction of God's power over us is its implication that the God of Israel, prior to the life of Jesus of Nazareth, was an overbearing patriarch. In her work on feminist theology and anti-Judaism, Katharina von Kellenbach has demonstrated that feminist theologians perpetuate anti-Judaism when they posit the life of Jesus as a more egalitarian turn in God.[7]

In her later work, Ruether's use of self-emptying shifts. In her *Gaia and God*, Ruether advocates an ecofeminist ethic that involves self-limitation. Here Ruether writes: "Many spiritual traditions have emphasized the need to 'let go of the ego,' but in ways that diminished the value of the person, undercutting particularly those, like women, who scarcely have been allowed individuated personhood at all." She argues that "we need to 'let go of the ego' in a different sense" as "we are called to affirm the integrity of our personal center of being, in mutuality with the personal centers of all other beings across species and, at the same time, accept the transience of these personal selves."[8] Ruether's kenotic ethic here affirms the transience and diversity of life. Her ethic involves

---

[5] Ibid.
[6] Ibid., 137.
[7] Katharina von Kellenbach, *Anti-Judaism in Feminist Religious Writings*. Atlanta, GA: Scholars Press, 1994.
[8] Ruether, *Gaia and God: An Ecofeminist Theology of Earth Healing*. New York: HarperOne, 1994, 251.

a confluence of self-fullness and selflessness in that the affirmation of one's "personal center" is simultaneously the affirmation of a vast connection.

Ruether's sense of kenoticism in *Gaia and God* inspires Marta Frascati-Lochhead's own appropriation of *kenosis*.[9] As Marta Frascati-Lochhead summarizes, "Ruether advocates an ethic of self-limitation: self-limitation of the species through birth control and family planning for the sake of nature, and self-limitation of the consumption of the affluent for the sake of the poor as well as for the sake of the earth."[10] Ruether's feminist theological method offers Frascati-Lochhead her best example of the *kenosis* of feminist theology itself: feminism's own letting go of ego.

Frascati-Lochhead brings to contemporary feminist theology the Italian philosopher Gianni Vattimo's use of *kenosis* as the dissolution of metaphysics. Vattimo, deeply influenced by Heidegger and Nietzsche, sees in the *kenosis* of the Christian incarnation a hermeneutical event emptying divine truth into the secular realm, shifting the separation of transcendence. In this way Christian meaning disaffiliates from overarching metaphysics of being and ceases to be received as an overbearing truth claim: a relentless power over. This is for Vattimo the nihilistic vocation of Christ's incarnation, Christ's self-emptying. Thus, "rather than the destruction of the Christian tradition, nihilism is, Vattimo argues, the product and fulfillment of the Christian tradition, of Christian *caritas*."[11] As Frascati-Lochhead explains, "the point Vattimo wants to make is that in God's self-emptying love, the destiny of Christianity becomes *kenosis* as this event of transmission, self-emptying, secularizing in which we are immersed and of which we cannot give any 'objective' appraisal."[12]

For Vattimo the hermeneutical effect that the kenotic incarnation has on metaphysics can be understood as a type of mending or healing rather than as a pure, triumphant erasure. Vattimo's use of the term *kenosis* is informed by Heidegger's use of *Überwindung* and *Verwindung*. Vattimo's kenotic secularization is not *Überwindung*: it is not an overcoming or a superseding, not a reestablishment of metaphysical foundations, of another power over. Rather, following instead the barely translatable concept of *Verwindung*,[13] *kenosis* involves

---

[9] Marta Frascati-Lochhead, Kenosis *and Feminist Theology: The Challenge of Gianni Vattimo.* Albany, NY: State University of New York Press, 1998. Frascati-Lochhead claims that in Ruether "feminism is not involved in the retrieval of a golden age of prophetic faith. There is no pure Christianity, there is no message from the past that has been invulnerable to appropriation by dominant powers" (202). But Frascati-Lochhead finds her inspiration in Ruether's recent work; in *Sexism and God-talk*, a "pure past" does seem to remain operative, perhaps accounting for Elisabeth Schussler Fiorenza's claim that Ruether still holds allegiance to an ancient primordial purity.

[10] Frascati-Lochhead, 207.

[11] Ibid., 35.

[12] Ibid., 155.

[13] For another discussion of *Verwindung* see Barbara Muraca, "Getting over 'Nature': Modern Bifurcations, Postmodern Possibilities," in *Ecospirit: Religion and Philosophies for the Earth*, eds. Laurel Kearns and Catherine Keller. New York: Fordham, 2007, 156–177.

"acceptance, resignation, deepening, healing, distorting." As Frascati-Lochhead explains these aspects of *kenosis*, "taken together they define an attitude, a way forward, distinct from the way of progress, of *Uberwindung*."[14] *Verwindung* is not a new beginning, but a way forward that unfolds from within "the contaminated, polluted soil of metaphysics."[15] It is not a triumphalist end of metaphysics so much as a healing of it. Overbearing power is not replaced, as though stamped out and overpowered, but is instead purposely contorted to serve a different future.

Frascati-Lochhead brings into conversation with Vattimo "the crisis of feminist theology"[16] at the end of feminism's second wave as feminist women from multiple backgrounds made it clear that "feminist theory has often resulted, unintentionally, in the exclusion of women."[17] For Frascati-Lochhead this "crisis" draws into question "the metaphysical status of feminist claims,"[18] as there cannot be said to be one metaphysical good for all women if that good has in fact functioned to oppress some women. If "feminism" had come to function as a white, heterosexual power over others, then feminism itself was in need of *Verwindung*.

So for Frascati-Lochhead, it is to this metaphysical crisis in feminism that Vattimo's concept of *kenosis* can speak: "Vattimo's philosophy can offer itself as a resource to feminist theology, helping it to interpret its own relationship to patriarchal metaphysics and to understand nihilism in a way that does not degenerate into a relativism which serves only the powerful."[19] Feminism criticizes patriarchy, "unmasking the deep patriarchal structures that pervade traditional theological thought." The problem, summarizes Frascati-Lochhead, remains that "if feminism succeeds in replacing the metaphysics of patriarchy with a metaphysics more congenial to the interests of women, will not the 'errors' of patriarchy only be reproduced, albeit in a different form?"[20] Feminist scholars have sought to address this problem in various ways,[21] but Frascati-Lochhead introduces the work of Vattimo in order to explore another possible way of relating to the patriarchal tradition inherited by feminist theology: "What is ultimately emptied in the process of secularization, as Vattimo describes it, is the violence of strong metaphysical structures, and the ability of these structures to impose silence."[22] The proliferation of hermeneutics brought on by secularizing *kenosis* involves a multiplicity of voices, as in the multiple voices of third-wave feminism. While there is not metaphysical truth

---

[14] Frascati-Lochhead, 74–75.
[15] Ibid., 150.
[16] Ibid., 3.
[17] Ibid.
[18] Ibid.
[19] Ibid., 35.
[20] Ibid., 33–34.
[21] Specifically, Frascati-Lochhead discusses Nancy Fraser and Linda J. Nicholson, Susan Brooks Thistlethwaite, Sheila Davaney, Rebecca Chopp, and Morny Joy.
[22] Frascati-Lochhead, 161.

to undergird all feminism, there is, as in Vattimo's work, the guiding principle of *caritas* to provoke feminist claims.

Frascati-Lochhead asks "Can feminist theology be viewed as a secularization of patriarchal theology? Can feminist theology be viewed as kenotic?"[23] She offers that one feminist theoretical example of a kenotic *Verwindung* can be found in Donna Haraway's work. "In the way in which the cyborg both belongs to and yet distorts Haraway's 'informatics of domination' it exhibits both the acceptance and the distortion that belong together in *Verwindung*." The cyborg organism thus lives in the ambiguous space of the third wave. Frascati-Lochhead explains that "with Haraway's help, we are able to sketch how 'weak thought' understood as nonfoundationalism, dissolution of metaphysical structures, *Verwindung*, might find development even in the area of sexual difference where Vattimo himself is silent."[24]

Though Frascati-Lochhead also looks to Rebecca Chopp and Sallie McFague for a recoding of feminism's metaphysical heritage, it is in the work of Ruether that Frascati-Lochhead sees the most exemplary kenotic *Verwindung* of patriarchal inheritance.[25] For Frascati-Lochhead, "Ruether effectively challenges the hypothesis of a grand narrative leading to an unambiguous overcoming of patriarchy and ecological violence. One appropriates what one can and never assumes that what one is able to reconstruct . . . provides the key to fixing once and for all the patriarchal and hierarchical dominations that characterize contemporary experience."[26] I notice that this is a marked shift

---

[23] Ibid., 158.
[24] Ibid., 147.
[25] Rebecca Chopp's concept of "emancipatory transformation" involves, in Frascati-Lochhead's words, "not corrections of, or supplements to, the social-symbolic order, but rather a reordering, a 'rending and renewing' of the order itself" (Kenosis *and Feminist Theology*, 168). Though this reordering demonstrates a sort of *kenosis* of patriarchal metaphysics, Frascati-Lochhead determines that because Chopp locates feminist theology on the margins of the social-symbolic "monotheistic ordering," "the center/margin metaphor continues to dominate Chopp's discourse throughout her work." Thus, Chopp ultimately presents a new metaphysics, such that "multiplicity appears as the way things really are, a reality which can only be adequately seen from marginal positions" (177–178). Frascati-Lochhead concludes that "in the last analysis, Chopp does not avoid a dualism that inevitably signals the continuing dominance of metaphysics. The world is divided into center and margin" (179). In contrast, following the metaphysical *kenosis* that Vattimo describes, Frascati-Lochhead argues that "the multiform feminist discourses and visions that differ from one another and from the social-symbolic order attest to the impossibility to found Christianity on a transcendent metaphysical basis" (178). Frascati-Lochhead also finds McFague's work indicative of a *kenosis* in feminist theology, especially in the "secularizing thrust that McFague discerns in the relation between 'postmodern science' and Christian faith" (184). McFague's kenotic method works by using both theology and science to move beyond a human-centered cosmology: "The destabilization of anthropocentrism leads to the subversion of the hegemony of reason and of a dualistic metaphysics" (186). However, Frascati-Lochhead determines that overall McFague maintains too much "residual metaphysical realism" in her use of "postmodern science" to be exemplary of Vattimo's *kenosis* applied to feminist thought.
[26] Frascati-Lochhead, 205.

from the unambiguous overcoming offered in Ruether's earlier midrash. But in Ruether's recent work, Frascati-Lochhead finds that "feminism, in its transmission of the messages of the past, accepts, heals, distorts the tradition, even forcing it to say things that it has not said before."[27]

For Frascati-Lochhead, the process of rummaging through the theoretical baggage of the past and reusing that which is helpful for a new construction is itself a practice of *kenosis*. Citing both Ruether and Keller, Frascati-Lochhead highlights the idea of "feminism of a recycling of culture" that "provides us with a metaphor that, in many ways, evokes Vattimo's understanding of secularization or *kenosis*."[28] The feminist movement is both a product of secularizing *kenosis* and an object of it: "Kenotic feminism assigns itself to the very process that has produced it."[29] Thus, "feminism belongs to *kenosis* and it consigns itself to recycling. Feminist theology as the *kenosis* of patriarchy finds its destiny in its own dissolution, in the *Verwindung* of the structures feminism itself creates."[30]

I find that Frascati-Lochhead avoids in a way that Vattimo does not the reinstatement of a "power over" metaphysics. Frascati-Lochhead uses a Vattimo-inflected *kenosis* to curb feminist theology's own tendencies toward power over, tendencies toward adopting its own totalizing truth claims in a way that ultimately oppresses and does not empower. While Vattimo posits the incarnation as a pivotal moment in the history of Being, such that Christian incarnation marks the dissolution of totalizing meaning (though, indeed, theologies of the incarnation have functioned to the contrary!), in his work Vattimo favors not the Philippians passage, but rather a passage from Hebrews: "In many and various ways God spoke to the people of old through the prophets, but now in these last days he has spoken to us through his son."[31] For him this text points to the way in which meaning is allowed, through the incarnation of God's word, to proliferate, to distort one conclusive meaning into multiple and perpetually reconstructed meanings. But his use of that text also highlights his supersession of Jewish tradition: the way that God was received in the past through the prophets is revealed in the incarnation to be premature and ultimately violent (due to the challenge of thinking Being apart from metaphysical violence). The nihilistic work of Christian *kenosis*, as Vattimo presents it, relies on a contrast with Jewish monotheism in order to function,

---

[27] Ibid., 202.
[28] Ibid., 205. Here Frascati-Lochhead is referencing both Ruether's "Ecofeminism and Healing Ourselves, Healing the Earth" (Paper and lecture presented at the Vancouver School of Theology, July 1995), 3, and Keller's "Talk About the Weather: The Greening of Eschatology," in *Ecofeminism and the Sacred*, ed. Carol J. Adams. New York: Continuum, 1993, 43.
[29] Ibid., 208–209.
[30] Ibid.
[31] See Vattimo's use of Hebrews 1:1 in his *Belief*, trans. Luca D'Isanto and David Webb. Stanford, CA: Stanford University Press, 1999, 79.

and that contrast is its own sort of overcoming, its own sort of supersession.[32] In this way Vattimo's *kenosis* slips back into a gesture of *Uberwindung* in regard to Judaism.

It is in an attempt to use *kenosis* as *Verwindung* that I turn next to my own Lutheran tradition. Vattimo's technique with *kenosis* can, I suspect, work differently if we read *kenosis* as a Christian practice, a hermeneutics that we apply to our own way of thinking God (here I am not so far from Frascati-Lochhead's use of *kenosis* as a way of doing feminist theology). Rather than a point in God's history (for here it seems Vattimo overly conflates divine history with our history of trying to think Being), self-emptying can be a Christian interpretive practice, providing a hermeneutics of "weak" Christian identity, a deconstruction of any firm hold on truth. Our attempts to know God themselves empty out: we can be sure of little of God except (to invoke Vattimo affirmatively here) by the guiding thread of *caritas*.

God's friendship with us, God's kenotic leaning toward us, gives us a little daily bread of truth rather than a revelation of mighty omnipotence. And this *caritas*, if the reader will allow a skip backward through the centuries, is not so different from the *caritas* that can be derived from the *pro nobis* Christ of early Lutheran theology (though, of course, Heideggerian philosophy would have been alien to Luther's own agenda).

Theology of the Cross as Relational Christology

When Luther and Melanchthon discuss Christ's self-giving, they emphasize that Christ did not only "empty" out, but rather *effluit nobis*: Christ poured out *for us*. They insist that knowledge of the crucified Christ provides no benefit unless a person understands Christ to be addressing him or her directly. Though Lutheran theology of the cross has been criticized for its supposed fixation on death or its implication of redemptive suffering, this intimate intentionality of the *kenosis* of Christ demonstrates that the importance of this christology lies less in morbidity and brutality and more in the vector of second-person address.

A shift away from a power over model of God already begins in the grammar of second-person address. The import of this grammatical detail for christology would be the difference between "Christ does this for all people" and "Christ does this, specifically, for you now." Such address was articulated by Luther in the language of "suffering and the cross," but was stated differently by Melanchthon as the "benefits of Christ." Luther claimed that a theologian

---

[32] See my further analysis of Vattimo in my "A Christian Politics of Vulnerability," 41–54 in *The Sleeping Giant Has Awoken: The New Politics of Religion in the United States*, eds. Jeffrey W. Robbins and Neal Magee. New York: Continuum, 2008.

of the cross understands God by looking at the cross; Melanchthon taught that to know Christ was "to know his benefits." Read together, understanding comes in the benefits of the cross for oneself. Perhaps if Melanchthon's "beneficial" language had always been paired with Luther's *theologia crucis*, much of the contemporary criticism of Luther's fixation on suffering may have been thwarted, for the dangers of the theology of the cross would have been partly curtailed.

The second-person address of Lutheran christology reveals something of the character of the God making the address: a desire to communicate with and be in a particular relationship with "you." This desire of God's is not primarily for the sake of self-contemplation, like some Aristotle's unmoved mover; in such a situation, as Catherine Keller has critically observed, "God loves god in us if we are graced."[33] It is not God's narcissistic desire, but neither is it a general or diffuse desire "for others." Rather, this is a specific desire to be in relationship *particularly with you*. Thus, intimate, pointed, relational desire fleshes out the character of God.

Luther's theses for the 1518 Heidelberg Disputation provide the most straightforward presentation of his theology of the cross, though one can trace this doctrine at work through much of his thought. Theses 19 through 21 read:

> That person is not worthily called "theologian" who looks at the invisible things of God through understanding created things, but who understands the visible and hindward things of God through looking at suffering and the cross. The theologian of glory calls the evil thing good and the good thing evil. The theologian of the cross calls the thing what it is.[34]

Rather than an explanation of the cross among other topics of Christian significance, this theology is for Luther the key to all theological inquiry. It offers a conversion of hermeneutics, articulating the speculation through which faithful understanding is given.

In these "crucial" theses, Luther alternates between two different Latin verbs, *conspicio* and *intellego*, to describe the theologian of glory and the theologian of the cross. A person may understand (*intellego*) all of creation and in so doing look at (*conspicio*) the aspects of God revealed in creation, as with the medieval method of analogical theology. But, claims Luther, a person may actually reach understanding (*intellego*) of the hidden things of God by looking

---

[33] Keller, *Broken Web*, 36.
[34] Luther, Heidelberg Disputation, 1518 (Weimar Addition 1:354). Similarly Melanchthon writes: "Philosophy reckons the most despicable evils in place of the best virtues... Divine law commands that we love our enemies; reason that we hate them ... There are certain impulses of the soul with which reason flatters itself, such as those by which it is born to 'glory'." (*Didymi Faventini* oration, *Melanchthon Werke* 1.80.35–1.81.29. Also see Schneider, *Philip Melanchthon's Rhetorical Construal of Biblical Authority*. Lewiston, NY: Edwin Mellen Press, 1990, 198–199.

at (*conspicio*) suffering and the cross.³⁵ The hermeneutical eye shifts away from abstract contemplation on the way the world works to suffering and the cross, yielding understanding, rather than speculation, of part of God. Because "the theologian" for Luther would here include anyone seeking God, not just those engaged in formal professional work, the *theologia crucis* articulates the location of conversion and the locus of continuing catechesis, as though Luther is trying to mark the meeting ground for human and divine, the alchemy of the burning bush. "Suffering and the cross" mark the places where God makes Godself known: the sites of revelation.

In his own work on *kenosis*, Graham Ward reads Luther's theology of the cross as a fixation on death, and thus as a telltale sign of a Lutheran complicity with the projects of modernity.³⁶ Ward determines that "what marks distinctively Luther's understanding of *kenosis* is a preoccupation with finitude and death" such that "the glorification of death . . . is played out in Luther's *theologia crucis*."³⁷ Indeed Luther's theology vehemently implements morbid language. Luther declares, for instance, that "living, or rather dying and being damned, make a theologian, not understanding, reading or speculating."³⁸ But to mark his theology as either preoccupied with death or enamored with death's glory misses Luther's theological agenda. Ward conflates the theology of the cross directly with death, while what is at stake with the cross for both Luther and Melanchthon is a "hermeneutics of the cross," a defining of theological method.

Ward misses this method when he reads Luther to be infatuated with death rather than revelation, with morbid closure rather than life-giving disclosure. Accordingly, Ward determines that for Luther "the crucifixion becomes *the* defining theological moment, separated from time and creation, fixed eternally," in contrast to Ward's reading of patristic understandings, wherein the incarnation "was not an event to be isolated for forensic theological analysis, ripped atomistically from the fabric of history."³⁹ For Ward this pinning of the crucifixion as the metaphysical event par excellence proves that "Luther's teaching on *kenosis* is therefore concomitant with a culture obsessed with, and fearing, death."⁴⁰ Indeed Luther's culture did obsess over death, but his *theologia crucis* can be read as an attempt at remedy rather than an unknowing symptom. Lutheran christology

---

[35] I thank John Hoffmeyer of the Lutheran Theological Seminary at Philadelphia for pointing out to me this alternation of verbs.
[36] Ward presents taxidermy as one such project.
[37] Graham Ward, "Kenosis: Death, Discourse and Resurrection," in *Balthasar at the End of Modernity*, by Lucy Gardner, David Moss, Ben Quash, and Graham Ward. Edinburgh: T&T Clark, 1999, 26–27.
[38] Martin Luther, *Luthers Werke* (Weimar edition), vol. 5.163.28–5.163.29.
[39] Ward, "Kenosis," 27.
[40] Ibid., 27–28.

need not be read as a theology participating in the fetishization of death. Rather, here is a theology struggling to address its context in the vernacular, applying the gospel directly to the stumbling block of its time and seeking to dismantle it. The functional piece of this theology is not the cross itself or death itself but the *pro nobis* nature of the participation of God in the cross and in death, speaking a word directly to the people of the time.

While Luther's trope of "suffering and the cross" certainly cannot be separated from the event of Jesus' own passion, and indeed would make little sense without that narrative root, the cross extends into a wider concept. In Luther's commentary on Philippians 2, for example, Christ's incarnation itself enables the connection that brings humans into a life-giving focus on God.[41] This implies that "suffering and the cross" entails for Luther not just the moment of Jesus' passion, but the reality of the incarnation itself. But even more so, "suffering and the cross" extends to encompass the suffering in the life of the particular human being brought to Christ. As Alister McGrath explains, Luther's *theologia crucis* insists that "God is particularly known through suffering" such that "the 'theologian of the cross' regards . . . suffering as his most precious treasure, for revealed and yet hidden in precisely such sufferings is none other than the living God, working out the salvation of those whom he loves."[42] Thus, in response to Ward, the historical event in question is not only the crucifixion of Jesus, but each event of conversion to Christ in people's lives. McGrath further explains that "the significance of suffering . . . is that it represents the *opus alienum*," the alien work of damnation, "through which God works out his *opus proprium*," the proper work of justification.[43] The theologian of the cross looking at "suffering and the cross" beholds her own humiliation.[44] While this explanation may sound dreadful to the feminist ear (a matter addressed later), it does demonstrate that when Luther claims that "the CROSS is our theology," he does not speak of a cross, as Ward claims, "separated from time and creation, fixed eternally," but rather the cross in the life of each Christian.[45] In this sense it is quite the opposite of what Ward detects: Luther describes a cross eternally *contextualized*, a cross

---

[41] See my analysis of Luther's Philippians commentary in "Who Are You? Christ and the Imperative of Subjectivity," in *Transformative Lutheran Theologies: Feminist, Womanist, and Mujerista Perspectives*, ed. Mary Streufert. Minneapolis: Fortress Press, September 2010.

[42] Alister E. McGrath, *Luther's Theology of the Cross: Martin Luther's Theological Breakthrough*. New York: Basil Blackwell, 1985, 150–151.

[43] Ibid.

[44] McGrath summarizes the operation of the *theologia crucis* thusly: "Before man can be justified, he must be utterly humiliated" (151).

[45] Luther (Weimar edition), 5.176.32–5.176.33; the capital letters are Luther's.

pro nobis.⁴⁶ As Deanna Thompson explains, Luther expressed "an intensely experiential understanding of religion."⁴⁷

Feminist theologians do have good reason to worry about a theology that always begins in suffering and humiliation. Luther's theology can undoubtedly be misused to argue that suffering is necessary in order to encounter God. But those familiar with Luther's thought will quickly realize that Luther could not have argued that any human act was necessary for a relationship with God without undermining his whole argument for salvation by grace alone.⁴⁸ By prescribing "suffering and the cross" as the locus of God's revelation, Luther is not prescribing further human suffering; rather, he is arguing that God meets us *where we already are*.

Though Melanchthon does not himself develop a *theologia crucis*, comparison of his thought with that of Luther's demonstrates that his understanding of "the benefits of Christ" fulfills the same role in his theological system as "suffering and the cross" do for Luther. Melanchthon has been criticized for his humanizing of Luther's work, but Luther himself praised Melanchthon, leaving little room for doubt that Melanchthon's work shares with Luther's a common theological agenda.⁴⁹

In explaining how the benefits of Christ introduce themselves to people, Melanchthon, like Luther, posits a location of revelation, firmly establishing that the benefits of the cross are not something people can parse out on their own. In his 1519 commentary on Romans, Melanchthon writes that "among the theological *loci* . . . there are some in particular which are of the very greatest importance to us: SIN, LAW, GRACE, so that the rest contain disputations

---

⁴⁶ Instead of a preoccupation with death, Luther's historical context at the beginning of modernity is perhaps most evident in his focus on the personal experience of God's grace (here Ward offers a helpful analysis; see his pages 28 and following). In this way Lutheran theology seems in line with its "evangelical" name. Qualifying this claim, however, Luther's theology of the encounter with God was rooted in the sacraments and the liturgy of the church, and thus a corporate personhood. The encounter of "suffering and the cross" of which Luther speaks would have been rooted for him in the encounter of the Word of God preached in communal assembly (the hermeneutical function of "law and gospel" preaching) and extended in the sacraments. The individual life of piety where a contemporary mind might suspect a "personal" encounter with God may to Luther reek of a spirituality of righteous works!

⁴⁷ Thompson, *Crossing the Divide*. Minneapolis: Fortress, 2004, 4.

⁴⁸ Thompson explains that "'being humiliated' is a work God does to us rather than a work we do to ourselves. This act of God is none other than an attack on the sin residing within the sinful self" (*Crossing the Divide*, 19).

⁴⁹ In addition to his Heidelberg Theses on what it takes to be a theologian, Luther claims that "he who desires to become a theologian has the Bible, and after that he can read the *loci* of Philip. When he understands both, he is a theologian, and to him all theology will stand open" (Weimar edition, *Tischreden* 5.5511, as in Schneider, 205). Luther is referring here to Melanchthon's 1543 loci. An example of criticism of Melanchthon's humanism, however, comes from Moltmann: "Although in his polemic against Erasmus in 1525 [Luther] once again put forward his theology of the cross against the rising humanism of the modern age, the humanism of Erasmus, with the aid of Melanchthon, found its way into Protestantism and encouraged the Protestant ethic of achievement" (*Crucified God*, 72).

more inquisitive than useful. For in these three the *summa* of our justification is comprehended."[50] Accordingly, John Schneider aptly writes that "this was perhaps Philip's schoolmastery way of stating Luther's 'theology of the cross'," in that Melanchthon would always view "the essential core of Christianity as consisting of this little theology in triplicate—law, sin, and grace—rather than in the sacred mysteries of the triune and incarnate Son of God."[51] These three are the loci that "had the most to do with *us* as broken human beings in search of truth and virtue."[52] Melanchthon writes that faith alone lifts the burden of law and sin, comforting suffering consciences. Faith is the "immense benefit" for the "blessed ones, to whom it is granted so to know Christ."[53] In the triplicate of "sin, law, grace" people know the good intentions of God for them, and thereby have faith.

Melanchthon writes that God took on flesh out of a desire to be known: "God desired indeed to be known, but in order to be known he came down in the flesh, nay rather, he was made flesh." Thus, Melanchthon presents the incarnation itself as a result of God's desire to be known by us; in Christ God takes a form that the human mind can recognize. God's "immense majesty" remains incomprehensible to us, so God therefore accommodates the human mind and presents us with a "scopus." Melanchthon writes that "Christ has been proposed to us as a *scopus* upon whom the human mind could successfully fix its eyes." The temptation of theologians has been to ignore this focal point, such that "each imagines for God a new form," but this is a dangerous exercise, for "when we despise this *scopus*, about to fly upward to heaven, it is inevitable that reason be imperiled, that it wander like a vagabond."[54]

Melanchthon's *scopus* plays the role of Luther's "suffering and the cross." Schneider draws attention to this juncture: "Here we behold Melanchthon giving his own expression to Luther's theology of the cross and its epistemic value system." Yet Schneider also notes the distinction in Melanchthon's articulation of the *theologia crucis*: "A change of one's scope does not always mean that other objects are in themselves beyond description, nor that one ought never to talk about them, but only that one has shifted the focus to first-order objects of knowledge, to the *loci causae* that are at the heart of the matter."[55] Schneider's observation, however, does not signal a strong deviation from

---

[50] Melanchthon in Schneider, 138. Original text in Ernst Bizer, *Texte aus der Anfangszeit Melanchthons*. Neukirchen: 1966, 90.

[51] John R. Schneider, *Philip Melanchthon's Rhetorical Construal*, 138.

[52] Ibid.

[53] Melanchthon as translated in Schneider, 140; text in E. Bizer, *Texte*, 91.

[54] Melanchthon as in Schneider, 193; text in *Melanchthon Werke* 1.75.29–1.75.31 and 1.76.1. Here Melanchthon also elaborates the necessity of a "*scopus*," in that "the common opinion of the fathers was that those who had seen God would not survive."

[55] Schneider, 193. Schneider further explains here that "to have said that in Christ God gave us a *scopus* . . . now seems a somewhat different thing from saying that in Christ God gave us a logical paradox, or that this event implied that human concepts in no wise apply to the nature of God."

Luther's theology of the cross; Luther does not claim that people should never look anywhere other than the cross, and he does not deny natural knowledge of God, but claims instead that there is danger in such speculation without first being made a fool in Christ. Similarly, Melanchthon grants "that it is a pious thing to investigate those incomprehensible mysteries" but that "it is certainly impious and perilous to attempt such a thing by human cleverness rather than by the divine scriptures."[56] Both Luther and Melanchthon, then, stress the peril in looking into the mysteries of God by means of academic pursuit. They insist that only God can reveal God's self, and that such revelation cannot be achieved through smart thinking. Where Luther trains the eye to look at the "suffering and the cross," Melanchthon trains the eye to look at "law, sin, and grace," or the *scopus* of Christ.

Concretely, Melanchthon directs persons to scripture as the site of revelation. As the *theologia crucis* points to the possibility of understanding the invisible things of God in seeing Christ crucified, looking away from the *scopus* of the Gospels only looks to a realm of obscured vision. Melanchthon's *scopus* holds the same hermeneutical role as Luther's cross: the *scopus* summarizes God's "alien" and "proper" works, the *opus alienum* and *opus proprium*, "taking away everything" and then teaching belief. The stress is on a conversion exacted by the grace of God, a conversion away from the obscured vision available through the lens of one's own efforts. Accordingly, Jaroslav Pelikan likens Luther's theology of the cross to Melanchthon's benefits of Christ, explaining that "the polemical target of both these propositions was a theological method that the authors attributed to scholasticism, which treated the truth of the Christian faith as objects of intellectual curiosity without reference to the cross and benefits of Christ."[57]

In an oration defending Luther, Melanchthon criticizes the "metaphysicians" who write about "those things which are attributed to God by men . . . unity, intellect, will, simplicity."[58] Luther likewise condemns scholastic theology, declaring that because people put to "wrong use" the knowledge of God they infer from created things, "God determined on the contrary to be known from sufferings" so that "in this way those who did not worship God as made known in his works might worship him hidden behind sufferings."[59] Luther explains the danger he sees in "high-flying ideas of seeking God" somewhere other than in "Christ crucified."[60] In hating the cross and sufferings, people "certainly love

---

[56] Melanchthon as quoted in Schneider, 194. Text in *Melanchthon Werke* 1.76.8.
[57] Jaroslav Pelikan, *Reformation of Church and Dogma*. Chicago, University of Chicago Press, 1984, 156.
[58] Melanchthon as quoted in Schneider, 192; text in *Melanchthon Werke* 1.75.8, 1.75.13.
[59] Luther, *Early Theological Works*, *Luther: Early Theological Works*, ed. James Atkinson. Louisville, KY: Westminster/John Knox Press, 2006, 291.
[60] Ibid., cf. Melanchthon, *Annotations on First Corinthians*, ed. and trans. John Patrick Donnelly. Milwaukee: Marquette University Press, 1995, 43: "There is a rich knowledge of God through nature, just as fleshy justice is in appearance a most upright life, but because it flows from a perverse judgment about God, it is nothing except vanity and sin."

works and the glory that goes with them."[61] The theology of the cross is thus directly related to Lutheran emphasis on justification by grace alone. It is also predictably related to politics, for to deny the insights of medieval scholasticism was also to deny insights of the Roman church.

Heidelberg thesis 24 clarifies Luther's position that wisdom itself is not evil, but that the person "who has not learnt the theology of the cross puts the finest things to their worst possible use."[62] Thesis 29 claims that those who would apply themselves to "the Aristotelian philosophy" cannot do so without danger unless they are first made foolish in Christ."[63] McGrath explains that "Luther readily concedes that man has a natural knowledge of God," but if "a theology were constructed on the basis of this natural knowledge of God, Luther insists that the inevitable consequence would be nothing less than idolatry and heresy."[64] Thus, it is not that a Christian is incapable of thinking about God without the benefits of the cross, but rather that she will inevitably misconstrue who God is, as a God in no particular relationship to her. And thus, God may then seem—naturally—a God above it all, over us.

But such a notion of God is ineffectual precisely because it has no benefit for you, or in my words, no relation to you. In his 1519 introduction to Luther's work on the psalms, Melanchthon writes: "[W]hat will it profit to have known that God is merciful and wise, unless you take it into your own soul that to *you* he is merciful, to *you* he is wise? And that is truly to know God."[65] For Melanchthon, one is made a Christian in the revelation of God as a God who does salvific things for you yourself. Melanchthon writes that those who value philosophical abstraction for knowledge of God have "placed beatitude in perfect virtue and perpetual tranquility of the soul" while not seeing "the mystery hidden for so many ages—the benefit of Christ."[66]

Read beside Luther's thought, the benefit of Christ parallels the hiddenness of God revealed in the cross. Likewise, the "cross" is important as a theological

---

[61] Luther, *Early Theological Works*, 292.
[62] Ibid., 278.
[63] Ibid., 280, cf. Melanchthon "How corrupt are all the theological hallucinations of those who have offered us the subtleties of Aristotle instead of the teaching of Christ!" (*Loci Communes* 1521, 19).
[64] McGrath, 161–162.
[65] Melanchthon as quoted in Schneider, 102, text in Weimar edition of Luther's Works, vol 5:25.
[66] Melanchthon (1520) as in Schneider, 167, text in *Melanchthon Werke* 1, 32.7–32.11. For Melanchthon, philosophy and the gospel conflict so greatly that "when philosophy is allowed in, the gospel is at once clouded over and Christ is clouded over." He condemns the attempt at righteousness in philosophy: "Philosophy attributes everything to our own powers and works, the gospel takes away everything and teaches that there is no other justification except by believing in Christ" (Melanchthon, *First Corinthians*, 39). Elsewhere Melanchthon writes that the "stupidity" of the scholastics in their discussions on the mysteries of God "could be left unnoticed if those stupid discussions had not in the meantime covered up for us the gospel and benefits of Christ" (1521 *Loci Communes*, 21). He uses the same verb here for "covered up" as for "clouded over," earlier.

topic not for its glamorization of death but for its hermeneutical function: the cross remains important so far as it is *beneficial* for you, effecting for you God's own self-disclosure. This need not be read as a glorification of death; rather, human suffering offers a unique and powerful lens, sharply bringing something of God's nature into focus.[67]

Looking elsewhere, we see only God's power. In abstract investigation, Melanchthon writes, "Nothing is discovered except size and power. Goodness is not taken into account. Thus it happens that our minds are not lifted up by such knowledge to trust in God, to love God, etc."[68] Our thinking may also cause us to fixate upon divine potency rather than divine beneficence, for "where we seem to know God most precisely, there we wander further from him because we contemplate only his power. We do not discern his goodness."[69] Thus, though Melanchthon far predates the feminist critiques of omnipotence, and would have likely been completely unaware of the gender-based reasons for such a critique, he offers his own criticism of imaging God's power over us: it shows us nothing of God's goodness, God's benefit for us. As we have seen, Melanchthon's thought here connects with the divisions Gottfried Thomasius later made between the relative and immanent characteristics of God, with the relative characteristics like omnipotence being those that the divine Logos renounces in *kenosis*.

Overall, the problem Melanchthon detects in a philosophical pursuit of God is that we cannot thereby discern God's love for us. We would miss the nearness of God's relatedness to us. "While we seek after the wise God, his wisdom alienates us from him because it is not understood."[70] The "wondrous administration of this world" (as with Luther's *facta*, or "created things," in the Heidelberg Disputation) is not the proper place to set one's eyes.[71] Rather, "the Lord God Almighty clothed his Son with flesh that he might draw us from contemplating his own majesty to a consideration of the flesh, and especially of our weakness."[72]

Contemporary feminists are rightfully celebratory of our bodies and their power, and so this sixteenth-century rhetoric about the weakness of our flesh may sound abhorrent, but feminists can also recognize that our bodies are good and beautiful precisely because they are mortal and changing and in need of the care of others. An affirmation of embodiment need not entail delusions about the very real pains we all feel and share in our bodies. And it is there, in that honest embodied place, that Luther and Melanchthon might

---

[67] Mary Solberg explores this theme in her epistemology of the cross, *Compelling Knowledge: A Feminist Proposal for an Epistemology of the Cross*. Albany, NY: State University of New York Press, 1997.
[68] Melanchthon, *First Corinthians*, 43.
[69] Ibid.
[70] Ibid.
[71] Ibid.
[72] Melanchthon, *Loci Communes* 1521, 21.

argue that the incarnate one is already sitting in companionship with us, such that a groundedness about embodied suffering is in fact beneficial to us.

In Luther's Philippians commentary, he writes of the way in which the *kenosis* of Christ pulls our eyes down from the heavens and places them on the proper scope: the weakness of our own bodies. For Luther, the weakness of our human embodiment (and not our physical death) is our Golgotha: "Through the regime of his humanity and his flesh, in which we live by faith, he makes us of the same form as himself and crucifies us by making us true humans instead of happy and proud gods: humans, that is, in their misery and their sin."[73] As I have argued elsewhere, it is the case that Luther's understanding of sin here is guilty of the masculine bias Valerie Saiving finds in traditional doctrines of sin.[74] More helpfully, however, the new life effected by Christ's humanity is a resurrection to true humanity: to the flesh once thought unimportant or beneath God, to our weakness. The suffering of the theology of the cross is the suffering that inheres in the process of becoming truly human subjects. This is a theme picked up by Bonhoeffer's christology, discussed in the next chapter.

In their own way, in the benefits of the cross, Luther and Melanchthon offer a way to move beyond power over. Or rather, they testify to God's power—an intimate, local power—to turn us away from the gravitational pull of overpowering theologies. In this way, God draws us into our own power. Luther and Melanchthon would not recognize the reasons for our contemporary feminist struggles for empowerment, but they did see increased capacity and ability in the conversion to the Christian life, for here people became, almost spontaneously, ebulliently self-giving.

Again emphasizing the vector of Christ's *kenosis* as a *kenosis* for us, Luther writes that Christ "lived, labored, worked, suffered, and died," and further, "did all this for our sake, that he might serve us and that all things which he accomplished in this form of a servant might become ours."[75] In this way Christ parallels the situation of all Christians as Luther understands it. They are rich in God and need "no work and no suffering" to be righteous, but having "the mind of Christ in them" (as Philippians exhorts) they work and suffer anyhow, for the sake of others. Melanchthon, who like Luther draws deeply on Paul for his understanding of the Christian life, also expresses the spontaneity of good works. The Pauline *scopus* presents the "three supreme *loci morales* in Christian doctrine," and "everything that can be said about vices, virtues" flows from law, sin, and grace "as from a fountain."[76] So, despite Lutheran criticism of

---

[73] Luther's commentary on Philippians 2, as translated in Moltmann 212–213, gender language amended. German text in Weimar edition of Luther's Works, 5.128.36.
[74] See note 41 in this chapter.
[75] Luther, *A Treatise on Christian Liberty*, trans. W. A. Lambert. Philadelphia: Fortress, 1957, 29.
[76] Melanchthon as translated in Schneider, 194, text in *Melanchthon Werke* 1.79.5. On the development of Melanchthon's *scopus* in his commentary on Romans, see Timothy Wengert, "Phillip Melanchthon's 1522 Annotations on Romans and the Lutheran Origins

meritorious works, the doctrine of salvation by grace alone certainly maintains "good works" as allowable, even expected as an obvious lifestyle, but shifts them out of the realm of obligation and into the category of acts of "Christian liberty." Rather than a person who was required to do good things, the Christian was continually remolded by the spirit of God into a person who *wants* to do them, spontaneously—not as an imposed imperative but as a self-propelled desire.

But far from a kenotic wellspring, a richness of subjectivity, Ward writes that in Luther's theology "*kenosis* as self-emptying is here a putting to death of the self. *Kenosis* is servitude and bondage (in Luther's theological understanding of bondage as freedom)."[77] Ward himself develops a kenoticism with a focus on resurrection. Yet Luther's *kenosis* does involve new creation, indeed resurrection, under his "understanding of bondage as freedom." In his "Christian Liberty" Luther writes that "although the Christian is thus free from all works, he ought in this liberty to empty himself, take upon himself the form of a servant, be made in the likeness of men, be found in human form, and to serve, help and in every way deal with his neighbor as he sees that God through Christ has dealt and still deals with him."[78] The Christian engages in self-emptying voluntarily; *kenosis* is an act of freedom. The Christian thinks to herself, "My God has given me in Christ all the riches of righteousness and salvation without any merit on my part . . . I will therefore give myself as a Christ to my neighbor, just as Christ offered himself to me; I will do nothing in this life except what I see is necessary, profitable, and salutary to my neighbor, since through faith I have an abundance of all good things in Christ."[79] Luther understands this ethic to be the message of Philippians, for "the Apostle has prescribed this rule for the life of Christians, namely, that we should devote all our works to the welfare of others, since each has such abundant riches in his faith that all his other works and his whole life are a surplus . . ."[80] With this excess, the person can then "by voluntary benevolence serve and do good"[81] to the neighbor.

This is desire for the sake of others, which is driven by plentitude, not neediness or lack. Neither is it a self-giving demanded of us, or of Jesus, by God. Accordingly, Deanna Thompson reframes atonement in terms of *friendship*: "God's atoning work for us on the cross is done through Jesus' befriending humanity . . . Friends freely choose to be in relation to one another. Is that not an appropriate image of Jesus's willingness to give of himself? Jesus was not paying a debt to God. Jesus the Friend acted freely, giving his very life on behalf of his friends."[82]

---

of Rhetorical Criticism," in *Biblical Interpretation in the Era of the Reformation*, eds. Muller and Thompson. Grand Rapids, MI: Eerdmans, 1996, 118–140.
[77] Ward, "Kenosis," 27.
[78] Luther, *Christian Liberty*, 29.
[79] Ibid., 30.
[80] Ibid., 28–29.
[81] Ibid.
[82] Deanna Thompson, *Crossing the Divide*, 136–137.

As noted earlier, Ward claims that "what marks distinctively Luther's understanding of *kenosis* is a preoccupation with finitude and death."[83] But in Luther *kenosis* can be read, to the contrary, both as the birth cry of new subjectivity and as the fecund trajectory of a life of Christian freedom; while death is integrated into this life, it is not stagnated in finitude. Thus, Luther writes that "a Christian lives not in himself, but in Christ and in his neighbor. Otherwise he is not a Christian. He lives in Christ through faith, in his neighbor through love. By faith he is caught up beyond himself into God. By love he descends beneath himself into his neighbor."[84]

While Lutheran theology certainly expresses finitude in terms of the limits of a human ability to know God on one's own, this same theology expresses that "by faith" she is drawn beyond herself, with God, to her neighbor, empowered for myriad relationships in the limitlessness of God. *Kenosis* becomes the form of life of each Christian, her own practice of incarnation, the reason for bearing "Christ" in her name. Just as the Christian is not bound to do good works to earn righteousness, so none of the work a Christian does for her neighbor obligates that neighbor to more work: "For a man does not serve that he may put men under obligations."[85] Christian *kenosis* is power *for* the other, not power over the other.

When Melanchthon presents his "benefits of Christ," this involves, as does Luther's Heidelberg Disputation, a determination of who can be called a Christian at all. For a person who is ignorant of the loci of sin, law, and grace, Melanchthon declares: "I do not see how I can call him a Christian." Melanchthon cannot imagine how else the person could come into relationship with Christ, "for from these things Christ is known, since to know Christ means to know his benefits, and not as *they* teach, to reflect upon his natures and the modes of his incarnation." Melanchthon asks, "For unless you know why Christ put on flesh and was nailed to the cross, what good will it do you to know merely the history about him?[86]

So for Melanchthon, a person cannot be called Christian unless she knows that the *kenosis* of Christ is *for her benefit*. Similarly, Luther preaches about the two natures of Christ in his 1522 Christmas sermon, asking, "What difference does that make to me? That he is man and God by nature, that he has for his own self; but that he has exercised his office and poured out his love, becoming my Savior and Redeemer—that happens for my consolation and benefit."[87] For

---

[83] Ward, "Kenosis," 26.
[84] Luther, *Christian Liberty*, 34.
[85] *Christian Liberty*, 30.
[86] Melanchthon, *Loci Communes* 1521, 21–22.
[87] Luther, as in Jaroslav Pelikan, *Reformation of Church and Dogma*. Chicago: University of Chicago Press, 1984, 156, text in Luther's Works, Weimar edition, 10 (I) 1.147. Also see Timothy Wengert, *Philip Melanchthon's Annotations in Johannem in Relation to Its Predecessors and Contemporaries*. Geneva: Librairie Droz, 1987.

Luther, rather than giving evidence of two discernable natures, the *kenosis* of Christ provides evidence that, though free to avoid work and suffering, Christ took these up anyway for us, in order to serve us.[88] Christ freely becomes, as Bonhoeffer would later have it, "the person for others." The outpouring *kenosis* of Christ matters not because it makes some glorious show of death or because it helps elucidate a metaphysics protecting a classical notion of God through a "two natures" doctrine, but because it catalyzes faith in us. This is a *kenosis* for our benefit.

Melanchthon and Luther are not discussing what makes a *stronger* Christian or stronger theologian. Rather, they are making a sharp delineation: some are clearly not called "theologian" or "Christian."[89] Melanchthon and Luther are discussing what it actually means to *be in faith*: to know God's good intentions for you. Luther explains that "it can happen that someone's face may be familiar to me but I do not really know him, because I do not know what he has in his mind. Now what good does it do you to know that God exists if you do not know what God's will is toward you?"[90] The "face" of God in the "created things" may be familiar to a person who nonetheless does not know the intentions of God for him, the good benefits hidden in God's "mind" for him. For both reformers, the Christian theological *scopus* involves the surprising encounter with what God has done *for you*. Luther points to the cross, Melanchthon to the scriptural presentation of sin, law, and grace. More specifically, Luther announces abruptly that the cross alone is our theology, and the rhetorician Melanchthon helpfully explains that sin, law, and grace are the cross rhetorically construed. To know Christ is to look at the cross. To

---

[88] See Ward's discussion of this in "Kenosis," 26. Here, while seeking to prove that Luther's *kenosis* finally concerns servitude, Ward raises what is in my analysis Luther's main point: the kenotic work of Christ is in service to God's people, *effluit nobis*.

[89] Luther makes a similar distinction when discussing the way in which a true theologian—again a Christian, not an academic—can distinguish between the functions of law and gospel. Being a theologian does not mean being especially smart or academically educated; rather, a person's being a theologian indicates that law and gospel have done their work, and thus the person has come to know the law and the gospel's benefits for her. In his 1535 Galatians commentary, Luther writes that "whoever knows well how to distinguish the Gospel from the Law should give thanks to God and know that he is a real theologian," and also that the "distinction between the Law and the Gospel, is necessary to the highest degree; for it contains a summary of all Christian doctrine" (LW 26.115–117). For further discussion of the necessity of this distinction for Luther see Ebeling, *Luther*, 110–140, and Oswald Bayer, *Martin Luther's Theology: A Contemporary Interpretation*, trans. Thomas H. Trapp. Grand Rapids, MI: Eerdmans, 2008, 58–67.

[90] Luther in his 1535 Galatians commentary, Luther's Works, American edition 26: 399–401, gender language emended. Preceding this, Luther writes, "There is a twofold knowledge of God: the general and the particular. All men have the general knowledge, namely, that God is, that he has created heaven and earth, that he is just, that he punishes the wicked, etc. But what God thinks of us, what he wants to give and to do to deliver us from sin and death and to save us—which is the particular and the true knowledge of God—this men do not know." In other words, people do not on their own know God as a God for them.

know Christ's benefits is to be worthy of the name "theologian." To be met by a Christ for you is to be a Christian.

Luther also writes about the reason that "Christ" bears this name, writing in a 1525 sermon that "Christ is not called Christ because he has the nature of humanity and of God, but by his office and work which he took on, not because he took on flesh and blood, but because he poured out those things for us [*sed quod ista effluit nobis*]. This makes us Christians."[91] Christ's *kenosis* is a *kenosis* "for us," a *kenosis effluit nobis*. Christ is known as Christ not through abstract metaphysics of the incarnation, but through self-giving action for us. It is as though Christ *becomes* the "anointed one" in the streaming chrism of Christ's own kenotic outpouring.

While Melanchthon and Luther both stress salvation apart from scholastic comprehension, they each do so with their own unique emphasis: plainly, Luther's *passiones et crux* point more strongly to suffering, whereas Melanchthon's *beneficia* point more fully to benefits. Luther points to the God who is intimately familiar with suffering. He stresses that only our own suffering—especially that suffering which puts works to naught, that passionate encounter with our own impossibility—will allow us to look intently on the hindward things of God. Suffering and the cross are hindward things in the same way that for Melanchthon Christ's cursed flesh is the foolish thing: these are the unlikely things of God. Though Melanchthon stresses suffering much less, he makes the "crucial" point perhaps more clearly than Luther: the foolish, hindward things are benefits *for us*.

The benefits of Christ—or, read together with Luther, the benefits of the cross—offer to contemporary christology an emphasis on the intimate intentionality of God's work in Christ. One can read in this christological tradition the vector of *God's* incarnate "emptying," a *kenosis* of eagerness and purposeful direction in the service of God's people. Instead of a problematical atonement exacted between Son and Father through an economy of suffering and death, the *kenosis* of Christ can convey God's desire to connect with God's people and to share life with them. The hermeneutic of the cross directs christological meaning into second-person address between God and those beloved by God. The "address" where God's beloved reside is one laced with the humiliations and pains of incarnate life; in Christ, God meets them there.[92]

Discussing Philippians 2 in "Christian Liberty" Luther writes: "Paul means this: Although Christ was filled with the form of God and rich in all good things, so that he needed no work and no suffering to make him righteous

---

[91] Luther in a sermon from 1525, Weimar edition 16, 217–218.
[92] Discussing the connection between humiliation and Christ as God for us, Dietrich Bonhoeffer writes that "because Jesus wants to be our freedom, he must first become a stumbling block for us before he can be our salvation. Only by being humiliated can Christ become *pro nobis*. See "Lectures on Christology," *Dietrich Bonhoeffer's Works*, vol. 12. Minneapolis: Fortress Press, 2009, 358.

and saved (for he had all this eternally), yet he was not puffed up by them and did not exalt himself above us and assume power over us."[93] Though God holds a richness beyond our understanding, God does not choose power over us.

From the perspective of a theology of the cross, perhaps the question of God's omnipotence remains the wrong place to point our attention. Other modes of God's power are both unknown to us and arbitrary to our relationship with God. God has chosen to relate to us more intimately rather than through overwhelming power. Just as "good works" come spontaneously to the person addressed and renewed by God, perhaps intimate connecting comes spontaneously to God, the stirring and giving of incarnate power flowing as God's own delight, God's proper work. Following this line of thought, omnipotence might be a rather boring and lonely mode for God to live in—before we even begin to imagine its implications for us. God may still be all powerful, but that power may be quite other than a power over us, especially if "all" power can be a shared experience.

It would be inaccurate to presume that Luther and Melanchthon shared in contemporary feminist concerns about omnipotence. They were not protofeminists. Anything like contemporary gender theory is absent from their thought. Their arguments did have implications for gender, both positive and negative—for example, in the emphasis on clergy marriage or in the closing of female monastic communities—but women's needs and interests were far from their thought.

And yet, as we have seen, these reformers did offer a critique, if not of omnipotence itself, of relating to God in this way. It is as though they describe omnipotence as an impossible, or at least unfruitful, relation (not necessarily an impossibility in itself). They would not have claimed that omnipotence was impossible for God, but they claimed in their way that it is impossible for us to know God in this way. (And Thomasius, in his time, would claim that omnipotence, as one way God relates, could be shed without changing God's essential nature). For Luther and Melanchthon, God is the sort of God who chose not to lord power over us, and instead chooses to serve God's beloved, to relate to us kenotically.

And, while Luther and Melanchthon were certainly not striving for women's liberation, they did have their own political reasons for critiquing ideologies of God's power over us. They were not attuned to women's exploitation, but they would have been familiar with exploitation by the Roman church of their day, which was claiming too much power in God's overpowering name. Roman church structure at the time supported the idea that God's power is far over us, beyond common comprehension. If, however, as Luther, Melanchthon, and other reformers taught, God wishes to be known more intimately, more

---

[93] Luther, *A Treatise on Christian Liberty*, trans. W. A. Lambert. Philadelphia: Fortress, 1957, 29.

directly, then the political powers over are subverted by such a theology. Justification by grace alone is a richly political strategy even as it is a strong theological claim. This is particularly clear in the way that Luther's own arguments softened once political power was more firmly on his side: as Moltmann points out, during the peasants' war, Luther teaches submission to the powers that be, not a radical revelation of God's empowering presence for common people. Of course, the developing doctrine of the "two kingdoms" can explain Luther's attitude here, but that only offers further proof that doctrine and politics are not far apart.

Luther's emphasis on God known for you was not yet modern individualism, because in his thought the God known in suffering and the cross was consistently present in a communal context: in baptism and eucharist. This was not a modern "me and Jesus" moment, because the "me" was still communally experienced. But neither was it totally free of a sense of individual empowerment, for it fueled rather bold social protest. It tapped a movement that was building long before Luther—seen, for instance, in Wycliffe or Huss—that refused to concede God to the political powers as a God of power over, claiming instead a God committed to relationship with all God's people—the ones who couldn't understand Latin or afford penance, or even the many who couldn't quite pull off holiness. To put it into language more familiar to contemporary feminism than to the Reformation period, theirs was a God of relational passion.

Thus, though early Lutheran theology may on the surface seem fixated on death or suffering, it can function for life-giving purposes, and as best we can tell, its writers intended it that way. Contemporary scholars have demonstrated that we must be vigilant about the ways that cross theologies have functioned as weapons and continue to perpetuate abuse.[94] We can heed these cautions and yet at the same time look for and honor ways that this dangerous theology can also empower those who are survivors of abuse and those who know the oppression of unyielding power over them. Deanna Thompson, Cynthia Crysdale, Wonhee Anne Joh, and Mary Solberg have all retrieved aspects of the theology of the cross in their feminist theological work.[95]

---

[94] See Delores Williams, *Sisters in the Wilderness*. Maryknoll, NY: Orbis, 1993, especially 164 and following, and the anthology on contemporary interpretations of the cross ed. Marit Trelstad, *Cross Examinations: Readings on the Meaning of the Cross Today*. Minneapolis: Fortress, 2006.

[95] Thompson's thorough exploration of "Luther, Feminism, and the Cross" (*Crossing the Divide*, 2004) finds particular promise in the commitment of a theology of the cross to call a thing what it is, especially in regard to victims and oppressors, while also emphasizing the hope of the resurrection and the friendship embodied in God's acts in Christ. Crysdale (*Embracing Travail: Retrieving the Cross Today*. London: Continuum, 1999) stresses a twofold experience of the cross. The first involves "one's own wounds" or the "experience of being crucified," and the second one's own experience of "crucifying," "sabotaging," and destruction (154). Through this twofold experience the Christian comes to *identify* with the story of the cross and then to *participate* in this story. This choice involves "embracing

Coakley reads Lutheran christology to be an obliteration of the human because of the full presence of God in the human.[96] This full presence, however, need not be bulky and dominative, crushing us with its presence. The full presence of God, for instance in the Eucharist, is fully a presence *for*: the body of Christ, given for you.

As in Ruether's midrash on *kenosis*, Luther and Melanchthon would have seen in Christ's incarnation a defining moment in history; they would have seen Jesus the Christ as the fundamental proof of God's intentions for us. "Apart from this man," Luther wrote, "there is no God."[97] But this is not to say, either, that Luther saw in Christ a change of heart in God. Rather, Luther reads Christ present throughout the Hebrew Scriptures. While this is not quite the anti-Judaism of which Kellenbach warns feminist theologians, neither is it at all helpful for contemporary Jewish and Christian relationships. It seems to me that we Christians can say that what we see God doing in Christ is consistent with the way God relates to God's covenanted people—that is, being there for them—without saying, in the manner of some Christians before us, that the Hebrew Scriptures stand as a typology of Christ or anything like herald and preparation for Christ. God has been God, and God has been loving God's people.

Perhaps the second-person intimacy of the "benefits of the cross" can offer Christians a *Verwindung* that healthfully distorts power over theologies. In the benefits of the cross one encounters a divinity choosing not to be with us as an overbearing transcendence, trying instead to thwart our attempts to think Being in that way. We encounter and generate a truth that is revealed in moments of sacrament and gritty life, as interpretive communities receive the *caritas* of God, and move forward on that momentum, not overpowered but empowered by the "touch" of a different transcendence.[98]

---

pain, choosing to love, to forgive others, letting go of justice as revenge. So one becomes an agent of God's communication, an architect of salvation, through resistance and surrender . . . Imitation of Jesus is not sweetness and light. Nor is it masochism. It involves choosing to be a Self oriented to God and abiding in God's love in a way that courageously confronts evil as woundedness and evil as sin" (154). Solberg (*Compelling Knowledge*, 1997) expounds an "epistemology of the cross" based on her experiences in El Salvador.

[96] Coakley, *Powers and Submissions*, 29.

[97] Luther, "Confession Concerning Christ's Supper, 1528," in *Martin Luther's Basic Theological Writings*, 2nd edn, ed. Timothy Lull. Minneapolis: Fortress, 2005, 266.

[98] See Mayra Rivera, *The Touch of Transcendence: A Postcolonial Theology of God*. Louisville, KY: Westminster/John Knox Press, 2007.

Chapter 3

Power for Ourselves: Kenotic Erotics

What happens to the lovers in theology? Where are the amorous impatient relations in theology? We need to reflect on this, because God's kenosis is a kenosis of love which does not need to be subjected to delays.

–Marcella Althaus-Reid[1]

From its second wave onward, feminism has recognized "the power of the erotic" in women's lives.[2] Audre Lorde famously wrote in 1978, "When we begin to live from within outward, in touch with the power of the erotic within ourselves . . . we begin to be responsible to ourselves in the deepest sense." Lorde connects this erotic living directly to increased self-awareness, "for as we begin to recognize our deepest feelings, we begin to give up, of necessity, being satisfied with suffering and self-negation, and with the numbness which so often seems like the only alternative in our society . . ."[3]

If *eros* has signaled strength of self to feminists, *kenosis* has most often signaled precisely the opposite, a *lack* of self-awareness. Doctrines of self-sacrifice or self-giving have seemed to require the sacrifice precisely of a woman's desires. Little attention has been given to whether *kenosis* could be the expression of her desires.

---

[1] Marcella Althaus-Reid, *The Queer God*. London: Routledge, 2003, 48.
[2] Examples of feminist theologies of *eros* include Mary Daly, *Pure Lust*. Boston: Beacon, 1984; Rita Nakashima Brock, *Journeys by Heart: A Christology of Erotic Power*. New York: Crossroad, 1988; and Carter Heyward, *Touching Our Strength: The Erotic as Power and the Love of God*. San Francisco: Harper & Row, 1989. These theologies have been criticized by other feminists, and I address these critiques in chapter 6. See Kathleen Sands, "A Response to Marcella Althaus-Reid's *Indecent Theology: Theological Perversions in Sex, Gender, and Politics*," *Feminist Theology* 11.2 (2003): 175–181 and "Uses of the Thea(o)logian: Sex and Theodicy in Religious Feminism," *Journal of Feminist Studies in Religion* 8.1 (1992): 7–33; Alyda Faber, "Eros and Violence," *Feminist Theology* 12.3 (2004): 319–342; and K. Roberts Skerrett, "When No Means Yes: The Passion of Carter Heyward," *Journal of Feminist Studies in Religion*: 71–92. In addition, Barbara J. Blodgett queries the usefulness of feminist theologies of *eros* for adolescents in her *Constructing the Erotic: Sexual Ethics and Adolescent Girls*. Cleveland, OH: Pilgrim Press, 2002.
[3] Audre Lorde, "Uses of the Erotic: The Erotic as Power," in *Sister Outsider: Essays and Speeches*. Berkeley, CA: Crossing Press, 1984, 58.

So while feminists have often been eager to say "yes" to erotic power, perhaps "kenotic power" has sounded too much like a contradiction, with self-giving too like the agapeic love of which feminists have reason to be weary. *Agape*, that selfless love, has seemed only a nice name for the regulations of traditional women's roles. Self-giving can seem, if we follow Saiving's reasoning, more a sin for the self-diffused than any loving mark of character, any strong expression of self. Based on this critique, it would seem, *contra* Althaus-Reid, that any "amorous impatient relations" in feminist theology must be ones of *eros* and not *kenosis*, since so many persons need more fullness of self, not less.

And yet Althaus-Reid is not the only one to imagine *kenosis*—with erotic contours—as a vehicle toward fullness of self. *Kenosis* need not be seen as uniformly agapeic. For example, would one describe the self-giving of God described by Luther and Melanchthon as purely agapeic? For there is certainly something in it for God, and in that sense the *kenosis* is not beyond self-interest. God gets relationship out of *kenosis*. As Melanchthon writes, "God desired to be known." In a sense, God comes into Godself as a God we know and love, as a God for us, through *kenosis*. God gets the pleasure of Godself through it.

However, there remains quite a bit of theological baggage around the suggestion that desire could prompt God's actions. As Catherine Keller aptly summarizes, "The metaphor of the divine Eros . . . remained until the twentieth century virtually unspeakable in theology . . . The Aristotelinized deity could not by definition desire; desire had come to signify lack—and isn't 'He' already perfect and self-sufficient?"[4]

Divine *eros* was most systematically disputed in the last century by Anders Nygren, whose *Agape and Eros* designated *agape* as clearly divine and *eros*, or "desire," as resolutely human. Human love, that is *eros*, was acquisitive and greedy, not self-giving like *agape*.[5] Yet many theologians have disagreed with Nygren, and have begun to articulate something like a divine *eros*, or a confluence of *eros* and *agape*.[6]

---

[4] Catherine Keller, "Afterword: A Theology of Eros, After Transfiguring Passion," in *Toward a Theology of Eros: Transfiguring Passion at the Limits of Discipline*, eds. Virginia Burrus and Catherine Keller. New York: Fordham University Press, 2006, 369.

[5] Anders Nygren, *Agape and Eros*, revised ed., trans. Philip S. Watson. Philadelphia: Westminster Press, 1953.

[6] The new ability to speak the "metaphor of divine Eros" in the twentieth century is largely thanks to process theology. See particularly chapter 5, "Risk the Adventure: Passion in Process," in Keller's *On the Mystery: Discerning God in Process*. Minneapolis: Fortress, 2008. Also, many interdisciplinary voices working on the topic of theological *eros* are gathered together in *Toward a Theology of Eros: Transfiguring Passion at the Limits of Discipline*, eds. Virginia Burrus and Catherine Keller. New York: Fordham University Press, 2006. On the contested distinctions between *eros* and *agape*, see particularly the introduction by Burrus, where she discusses Nygren, the theological afterword by Keller, and Mario Costa's chapter entitled "For the Love of God: The Death of Desire and the Gift of Life."

This chapter will argue that one confluence of *eros* and *agape* may be found in *kenosis*. For though good Christians have been taught to deny self-interest, and thus *eros*, in themselves and in their God, in the flow of a kenosis that generates power for the sake of others, self-interest may function quite differently. For self-interest, now tethered by agapeic energies, expresses not destructive greed but rather the wealth of the self's own want. *Eros* in *kenosis* offers a revelation of subjectivity: self-giving that brings self-satisfaction. In contrast, a flat conflation of *kenosis* with *agape* misses the self-interested contours that can adhere in *kenosis*—the ways that *kenosis* may generate power for ourselves.

This chapter has two foci: the power of *kenosis* to generate subjectivity and, relatedly, the ways in which *kenosis* expresses *eros*. In Dietrich Bonhoeffer's christology, Christ's *kenosis* enables human subjectivity. In Hans Urs von Balthasar, the Father's primal *kenosis* triggers triune subjectivity, and triune *kenosis* makes room for the subjectivity of all created beings. A similar dynamic is affirmed by Jürgen Moltmann and Michael Welker. Then, in Marcella Althaus-Reid, in a converse of Bonhoeffer, human *kenosis* enables the transformation of divine subjectivity. In both Balthasar and Althaus-Reid, the *kenosis* that triggers and transforms subjectivity is a self-emptying born of desire. Self-giving may be born, not of a lack of self-interest, but of an intensity of it.

Divine *Kenosis* and Human Subjectivity

In the previous chapter, I presented the ways in which both Luther and Melanchthon offer theologies of a God who is resolutely positioned *for us*. By turning to a later reader of Luther, Dietrich Bonhoeffer, I explore here how such a theology might be truly "for us" in terms of our subjectivity. In Bonhoeffer's christology, God in Christ beckons us to subjectivity.

Though Bonhoeffer does not develop an explicit theory of kenosis, his christology is deeply based in the incarnate, self-giving Christ. Accordingly Ronald Carson wrote in 1975, "I am now persuaded that J. A. T. Robinson pointed us in the right direction when he suggested in *Honest to God* that it was something like a kenotic christology toward which Bonhoeffer was tentatively working in the *Letters*."[7] And Bonhoeffer's portrayal of Christ's *kenosis* is one that enables, heals, and regenerates human subjectivity. In being radically for us, Christ makes *us* possible.

Bonhoeffer criticizes both the seventeenth- and nineteenth-century kenoticists, finding them to ultimately leave both the divinity and humanity of Christ incomprehensible. This is most problematic for Bonhoeffer because "everything depends on the whole of God, the Omnipotent and Glorious

---

[7] Ronald A. Carson, "Motifs of Kenosis and Imitation in the work of Dietrich Bonhoeffer, with an excursus on the Communicatio Idiomatum," *Journal of the American Academy of Religion* 43 (1975): 542.

One, being the one who becomes human and who comes to meet us in Jesus."[8] As with the *theologia crucis*, everything depends on the recognition of God's very self come to meet us, fulfilling God's desire to be known by us.

Bonhoeffer demonstrates an even stronger return to the *theologia crucis* than does Thomasius. Luther's insistence on the fullness of God existing to us only in the person of Jesus is echoed in Bonhoeffer's claim that "Jesus the human being is God . . . he is so as *the* human being, not in spite of his humanity or beyond his humanity."[9] God's being human—one way to read the *kenosis* of the Philippians hymn—presents God's subjectivity to us, not as some window to a further divine nature, but as the full revelation of God for us.

For Bonhoeffer, this means that the earlier Lutheran kenoticists went astray in seeking to diagnose the divine nature, thinking that "they could define *in abstracto* the divine and human natures in such a way that they had to fit into each other."[10] In contrast, for Bonhoeffer, "there is no 'divine nature' as all-powerful and ever-present." Rather, "if we are to describe Jesus as God, we would not speak of his being all-powerful or all-knowing; we would speak of his birth in a manger and of his cross." In other words, if we speak of Christ as God, we speak of Christ's "weakness."[11]

Consistently Bonhoeffer contends that hypothetical natures of God and humanity cannot be the beginning of a christology. Abstract natures of Christ drive a person to ask *how* two natures are possible in the incarnate one. Rather, the beginning question for Bonhoeffer must be *who*, as in "who is this person here with me?"[12]

Like Luther and Melanchthon before him, Bonhoeffer is critical of christology that, instead of being expressed "for us," speaks of God and humanity in abstract ways. As Clifford Green explains, "Christ is present as person not in isolation but *only in relation to persons*."[13] Christology must be relational—and the relation is specific, directed toward us. Bonhoeffer writes that "the being of Christ's person is essentially relatedness to me. His being-Christ is his being-for-me . . . The very core of his person is *pro-me*."[14] Christ carries a passionately kenotic leaning at the core.

---

[8] Bonhoeffer, "Lectures on Christology," 349. Bonhoeffer also finds that these kenoticists "do not make the humanity of Christ understandable," but rather turn the human into a kind of "demigod living on earth" (349).

[9] Ibid., 354, cf. 311. Bonhoeffer continues, again with resonance to Luther's theology of the cross: "It is Jesus Christ the human being who ignites faith" (354).

[10] Ibid., 349.

[11] Ibid., 354. Here students' notes from the christology lectures refer to Bonhoeffer quoting Luther's Christmas hymn, "All Praise to You, Eternal Lord."

[12] See Bonhoeffer's discussion of the "who" versus the "how" question in "Lectures on Christology," 302–303, 307, and 311.

[13] Clifford J. Green, *Bonhoeffer: A Theology of Sociality*. Grand Rapids, MI: Wm. B. Eerdmans, 1999, 209.

[14] Bonhoeffer, "Lectures on Christology," 314. Also see the discussion of this point in Green, 209.

Here it may become clear how the topic of the last chapter, the "for you" nature of God's desire and God's *kenosis*, might be essential for the subjectivity of God. For Bonhoeffer, the "pro-me" of Christ is essential to Christ's own subjectivity. The *pro nobis* is an ontological statement about Christ: "I can never think of Jesus Christ in his being-in-himself, but only in his relatedness to me."[15]

The essence of God is kenotic. God's subjectivity is kenotic. Further, this *kenosis* is no diffuse spill of the self, but is particularly geared toward the beloved of God. In the revelation of the beloved, God is God.

Thus for Bonhoeffer, "it is not only useless to meditate on a Christ-in-himself but godless, precisely because Christ is not there in-himself, but rather is there for you."[16] This means that one cannot accurately form an idea of God and then apply it to Christ; rather, "we say of this human being, Jesus Christ, that he is God."[17] The human is no less than God. "This person's being God is not something added onto the being human of Jesus Christ,"[18] and neither does being God subtract from Christ's humanity; instead, the human Christ plainly is God. In resonance with Luther's theology of the cross, if a theologian wants a description of the divine qualities, all that theologian can do is look at Christ, that is, encounter Christ as for her, and thus recognize the vitally "for-you" texture of the divine.[19]

To be placed before God involves a new focus on oneself, upon which the *kenosis* of God was always focused. Christ's *kenosis* necessitates awareness of the self. As Bonhoeffer writes, "Now our question has been turned around. The question we have put to the person of Christ, 'Who are you?' comes back at us: who are you, that you ask this question?"[20] Thus, the kenotic encounter involves a moment of double revelation: encounter with God and oneself. The *kenosis* of Christ presses the question of one's own subjectivity.

Resonating with Luther and Melanchthon's criticism of scholastic knowledge of God, Bonhoeffer criticizes attempts to decipher the nature of Christ apart from any encounter with Christ-for-you. In Bonhoeffer's work, as Green explains, "the point is not to reject reason but to transform and re-establish it so that it is not an instrument of domination."[21] Again, the self-giving of Christ-for-you serves to move beyond power over.

---

[15] Ibid., 314.
[16] Ibid.
[17] Ibid., 353. One must avoid "the attempt to unite two isolated existing realities" (354).
[18] Ibid., 353.
[19] This radically relationally located christology has an impact on Bonhoeffer's concept of "truth." For Bonhoeffer, "truth here is something that takes place between two persons, not something eternally at rest within itself. Truth happens only in community between two persons" ("Lectures on Christology," 316–317; also see the discussion in Green, 213). Here Bonhoeffer bears some resemblance to postmodern understandings of truth. For example, Gianni Vattimo writes of truth in interpretive communities (see the discussion of Vattimo in chapter 2).
[20] Bonhoeffer, "Lectures on Christology," 305, cf. 307 and Green, 226–227.
[21] Green, 226 footnote 130, citing Bonhoeffer's *Gesammelte Schriften* III, cf. Green 214.

For Bonhoeffer, the transcendence present between persons is not one of dominating power over each other. Bonhoeffer claims that the "who" question is the only question that goes beyond our own selves, that presses into the transcendent.[22] Thus, christology makes its statement of transcendence not by stressing the divine nature of Christ, but in the human person of Christ. Green explains that "transcendence does not refer to an inaccessible otherness or beyondness of God; it refers to the present Christ. But the present Christ is 'other,' 'outside' the self, in such a way that he cannot be drawn into the dominating power of the self-sufficient ego."[23] Thus, as Green summarizes, Christ "is *pro nobis* as *extra nos*," and Christ's transcendence "is not an attribute of Christ-in-himself but a relationship of Christ whose Personstruktur is a *pro-me*-Sein."[24]

It is precisely through a self-emptying that is a strong assertion of the non-solubility of the self that our own subjectivity is served by Christ. Christ's action is most unfocused on Christ's self precisely in being, strongly, the christic self. *Kenosis* offers a double power for ourselves: in the selves we are and the selves we serve.

In Bonhoeffer's analysis it is part of Christ's transcendent power to remain apart from another person and to avoid simply merging with him or her as the final outworking of the *pro-me* trajectory.[25] Bonhoeffer sees the dominating ego as the major human problem.[26] In other words, he considers only the separative self in Keller's terms. And Bonhoeffer determines that for her own salvation, the egotistical person needs Christ to resist being drawn into her egotistical orbit.

For Bonhoeffer, egocentric selfhood shuts persons out from reality. As Green explains, "Christ is the Mediator of human existence in that he negates the unlimited, self-established, isolated power of the dominating ego and justifies a person for a life of love for others."[27] Thus, Christ's kenotic subjectivity catalyzes our kenotic subjectivity as well. As Christ frees the person from the prideful ego, the person himself awakens to his subjectivity *pro nobis*. Green claims that Bonhoeffer's christology thus reveals that "true human being is being-for-others.[28]

---

[22] Bonhoeffer, "Lectures on Christology," 305, cf. 303.
[23] Green, 214, cf. 216.
[24] Green, 215.
[25] This idea of Bonhoeffer's resonates with the feminist work of Jessica Benjamin, who writes of being the other that survives one's own attempts to destroy that other, and of Luce Irigaray. See Benjamin's *Shadow of the Other: Intersubjectivity and Gender in Psychoanalysis*. London: Routledge, 1998 and Irigaray's *I Love to You: Sketch for a Felicity Within History*, trans. Alison Martin. New York: Routledge, 1996.
[26] See Green, 227, and Dahill.
[27] Green, 227.
[28] Ibid. Green demonstrates that though this early christology of Bonhoeffer's does not yet state Christ as "the one for others" in the manner of his later prison letters, the same metaphysics of self and God are already present (*Bonhoeffer: A Theology of Sociality*, 227).

Clearly Bonhoeffer's christology is based on the sort of theological anthropology that has been criticized by feminist theologians (starting with Saiving) in which the self is sinful because of its prideful ego. Lisa Dahill analyzes Bonhoeffer from a feminist perspective, summarizing that his "faith statements emerge not from some universally-valid human reality but from a specific psycho-social stance, namely that of the separative self, the traditionally-socialized male."[29] I suggest that after recognizing Bonhoeffer's problematically masculinist assumption that Christ's self-giving serves only to resist the power-over posturing of the self-aggrandized personality, one can also recognize in Bonhoeffer's christology a christic self that can also resist the dissipating power-drain of the profoundly soluble self.[30]

Though Bonhoeffer does not consider it, the soluble self may also be served by Bonhoeffer's self-giving Christ. This Christ is, after all, none other than that which is for her—the being for her being. And just as this Christ will not be absorbed into the domination of another, so also can this Christ's self-giving resist absorbing the diffusion of the soluble self. Christ's gravities flow in a different direction: as though in Christ's emptying out for you, there is no working upstream to hide away from yourself.

Christ's immanent transcendence presses the question of one's own subjectivity. It is as though, encountering another human with full attention on you, you ask yourself, "Who is this?" And then, "Who am *I* upon whom this other is so focused?" And thus Christ's presence—always a concrete human presence—brings the soluble one around to herself or himself. In this way Christ is the "*pro-me* Sein." Christ's kenotic self serves the multiple predicaments that stagnate us, separative and soluble alike. Christ stands as a guarantor of subjectivity. By insisting on difference, being the space of that difference, Christ serves the purpose of the other's well-being.[31]

I suggest that we, in our *kenosis*, may provide this space as well. Why? Not for virtue, for christic imitation, but because we, as ourselves, have room to want to move toward others—not to absorb them, not to hide away in them, but to encounter their transcendence with awe and passion. Here is the *eros* of our *kenosis*—for to be for others is also a self-serving posture. As Christ is Christ in *kenosis*, as God is God in devoting the holy self to you, so we become ourselves, over and over again, in the vulnerable play of our passionate trajectories toward others. By these we are known, and not as some abstract or stable self. In the specificities of our self-giving is the daily revelation of our own christic

---

[29] Lisa Dahill, *Reading from the Underside of Selfhood: Bonhoeffer and Spiritual Formation*. Eugene, OR: Pickwick Publications, 2009, 175. I discuss Dahill's argument again in chapter 5.
[30] See my further development of this reading of Bonhoeffer in my "Who Are You? Christ and the Imperative of Subjectivity," in *Transformative Lutheran Theologies: Feminist, Womanist, and Mujerista Perspectives*, ed. Mary Streufert. Minneapolis: Fortress Press, September 2010.
[31] Bonhoeffer explores the ways in which Christ creates space for relationship in his *Life Together*, vol. 5 of *Dietrich Bonhoeffer Works*. Minneapolis: Fortress Press, 1996.

subjectivity. Power for the others we move toward is also power for ourselves: this is the kinetic musculature of Christ in our world today.

Trinitarian Erotics

While subjectivity is a clear theme in Bonhoeffer's christology, a *kenosis* that brings together divine desire with subjectivity can be found in the work of several explicitly trinitarian theologians, and particularly in the theology of twentieth-century Swiss Roman Catholic theologian Hans Urs von Balthasar. Balthasar posits a fundamentally relational *kenosis*, presenting *kenosis* both as the foundation of relationship and the guarantor of difference in relationships. *Kenosis* assures connectedness *and* guards against collapse into uniformity. In Balthasar, *kenosis* requires a love between more than one (though joined as one in dependably complicated trinitarian theology), and thus his sense of *kenosis* seems to build from a dynamic less unilateral than traditional *agape*. Balthasar regards a reciprocal love as fundamental to the chemistry of *kenosis*, and for him this reciprocity flows between the members of the triune god. Accordingly, Graham Ward describes Balthasar's understanding of the kenotic trinity as "a community constituted by differences which desire the other."[32]

This reciprocal desire is productive; *kenosis* creates and enables subjectivity. For Balthasar, the primal kenosis of the Father "brings forth" a self of equal substance, and consequently brings forth the Trinity.[33] Triune subjectivity—and ultimately all subjectivity—is thus born through *kenosis*. Balthasar clarifies that this *kenosis* is not a self-abnegation, for "the Father, in uttering and surrendering himself without reserve, does not lose himself. He does not extinguish himself by self-giving, just as he does not keep back anything of himself either."[34] The "self-surrender" itself pulses with "the whole divine essence,"[35] pulsing with self. The "whole divine essence" is not spilling hopelessly in *kenosis*; rather, the kenotic act conveys the essence of what it is for God to be God.

Balthasar's understandings of *kenosis* cannot be depicted apart from the triune divine subjectivity he envisions, and which *kenosis* originally creates. Balthasar's depiction of trinitarian dynamism circulates between the "Father's original self surrender" and the Son's "eternal thanksgiving (*eucharistia*), to the Father, the Source" itself "selfless and unreserved" and equal to the Father's *kenosis*. In the shape of Balthasar's Trinity, the Spirit is the "we," automatic with the Son.[36] As Balthasar describes it, "Proceeding from both, as their subsistent

---
[32] Ward, "Kenosis," 45.
[33] Hans Urs von Balthasar, *Theo-drama: Theological Dramatic Theory IV: The Action*. San Francisco: Ignatius Press, 1994, 331 and 325.
[34] Ibid., 325.
[35] Ibid.
[36] Ibid., 331.

'We,' there breathes the 'Spirit' who is common to both: as the essence of love, he maintains the infinite difference between them, seals it and, since is the one Spirit of them both, bridges it."[37]

The Spirit's nature, then, is like a buffering current of desire; the Spirit is "the essence of love, both infinite difference and the union of one shared spirit, both of these sealed without end."[38] The triune desire is eternally satisfied, eternally unmet. The Spirit maintains and fuels the distance between Father and Son, but the Spirit also serves as "the realized union of this love."[39] So for Balthasar, always there is the breathy desire of the Spirit in the distance, at once holding and bridging divine difference. As Graham Ward describes it, "There cannot be true *kenosis* without hiatus, without true difference," for "hiatus fosters desire by opening the space for creativity, the stage for action, the yearning for unity; it fosters a spiritual *dunamis*, a theological *kinesis*, which is kenotic."[40] Or, as Aristotle Papanikolaou writes, "'Otherness' is constituted in and through 'distance,' which is the precondition for real communion."[41] This *kenosis* sets a distance between the Father and Son, an "infinite distinction," with the Spirit "spanning the gulf."[42] This distance enables the self to be not lost but instead realized in *kenosis*. As Papanikolaou explains, "Personhood, for Balthasar, is not a quality possessed, but a unique and irreducible identity received in relations of love and freedom that can only be labeled as *kenotic*."[43]

Kenotic subjectivity avoids the "sin" of self-diffusion by insisting on strength both of self and of the others to whom the self devotes itself. Kenotic subjectivity also steps aside from the powers of domination, of assuming others in the domain of one's own overpowering sense of self.

Though Balthasar's triune image may at first appear closed in on itself, as a cosmic dance between Father and Son across the breadth of the Spirit, Balthasar does not depict the Son's "eucharistia" as internal to God, closed in tightly as some divine eternal essence and sealed off from creation. Rather, the kenotic exchange between Father and Son necessarily opens out toward the furthest reaches of creation. As Balthasar understands it, the trinitarian kenotic exchange is "for us," exceeding Father and Son, such that, as he writes, "the ultimate form of this pouring-forth will be that of the Eucharist, which,

---

[37] Ibid., 324.
[38] Ibid., 331. Yet the Spirit "does not want anything 'for himself' but, as his revelation in the world shows, wants simply to be the pure manifestation and communication of the love between Father and Son" (*Theo-drama IV*, 331).
[39] Ibid., 326.
[40] Ward, "Kenosis," 44.
[41] Aristotle Papanikolaou, "Person, *Kenosis*, and Abuse: Hans Urs von Balthasar and Feminist Theologies in Conversation," *Modern Theology* 19.1 (January 2003): 41–65, this quote 51. Papanikolaou suggests Balthasar as a conversation partner for feminist theologians.
[42] Balthasar, *Theo-drama IV*, 326.
[43] Papanikolaou, 42.

as we know it, is intimately connected with the Passion, *pro nobis*."[44] Christ "manifests his Eucharistic attitude (which was always his) in the *pro nobis* of the Cross and Resurrection for the sake of the world."[45] Troubling the dichotomy of divine transcendent power over creation, this eternal *kenosis* circulates for the sake of the world. For Balthasar, *kenosis* is an expression of both omnipotence and release of power, for "here we see both God's infinite power and his powerlessness; he cannot be God in any other way but in this 'kenosis' within the Godhead itself."[46]

Thus for Balthasar, a desiring *kenosis* holds open the essential structure of both God and cosmos. Balthasar writes that God "*is* this movement of self-giving that holds nothing back"; *kenosis* is "an action he both 'does' and 'is'."[47] He quotes the Russian kenoticist Bulgakov: "The Cross of Christ is inscribed in the creation of the world since its basis was laid."[48] Here Balthasar does not mean to stress the preeminence of Christ particularly, but rather the nature of the triune god in self-exteriorization, seen at its greatest scope in the cross, a scope of exteriorization that was already there in the beginning.

And this is a vast exteriorization, a lengthy desire, an extended passion. For Balthasar imagines that the kenotic Trinity catalyzes human *kenosis*; the possibility of all acts of human *kenosis* is grounded in the trinitarian "substructure". Balthasar's "primal kenosis" of the Father—that is, the unfolding of the trinitarian substructure—"almost automatically" enables "all other kenotic movements of God into the world; they are simply its consequences."[49] All other *kenosis*, as in creation or covenant, comes in the sequence of the primal *kenosis*.[50] *Kenosis* is catalyzed in "ever-intensifying and ever more concentrated stages."[51] Ultimately, all subjectivity, divine and human, comes from divine, primal *kenosis*.

Balthasar's understanding of divine creation, in which holy self-release leads to triune self-realization, resonates with Luther's sense that God is made known in the beloved's encounter with God poured-out-for her. As Alyssa Lyra Pitstick has noted: "Balthasar's admiration of Luther is unmistakable."[52] By way of comparison, in Luther's thought, God's *kenosis* makes Godself known to a person. Thus, *kenosis* comprises at the same time a self-emptying and a self-realization or revelation. In Bonhoeffer, God's *kenosis* instigates a person's true knowledge of himself or herself. Thus again, *kenosis* concerns self-realization, now of the

---

[44] Balthasar, *Theo-drama IV*, 330.
[45] Ibid., 331.
[46] Ibid., cf. 335.
[47] Ibid., 323–324.
[48] Bulgakov, *Du Verbe Incarne: Agnus Dei* (Paris, 1943), as in Balthasar, *Theo-Drama IV*, 281.
[49] Balthasar, *Theo-drama IV*, 331–332 and 326.
[50] Ibid., 328.
[51] Ibid., 333.
[52] Alyssa Lyra Pitstick, *Light in Darkness: Hans Urs von Balthasar and the Catholic Doctrine of Christ's Descent into Hell*. Grand Rapids, MI: Wm. B. Eerdmans, 2007, 392.

human self. In Balthasar, kenosis brings forth self and other. Thus, self-*emptying* is at once relational and self-creative. All three of these theologians join a *kenosis pro nobis* with a concept of the creation or catalyzing of the self, whether God's, the human person's, or both.

In Balthasar's kenotic cosmology all the world is held in the stretch of divine desire and divine being. All creation resides in the spiritual space between Father and Son: "For where else is the creature to be found?"[53] But this also means that all creation's sin, which could also be described for Balthasar as creation's rebellion against passionately kenotic relationship, is held in God. All rebellion against *kenosis* hangs in the expansive distance between Father and Son, forever bridged and held fast by the Spirit, already resolved in triune dynamism.[54] While it seems that Balthasar's trinitarian structures risk erasing distance in this resolution, Balthasar seems to intend instead that God stretches to accommodate difference, as he insists that the *kenosis* of God grounds human freedom, creating the freedom of the creature and "taking it utterly seriously."[55] Just as difference is essential to divine subjectivity, necessary differentiation characterizes God's relationship to humanity in Balthasar's cosmology.

For Balthasar, the exteriorization necessitated by God's *kenosis* is vast, for "the greater the revelation of divine (ground-less) love, the more it elicits a groundless (John 15:25) hatred from man."[56] Indeed, "no end to this escalation can be envisaged, so the cross must be deferred to an endless end (since Jesus has atoned for all sin). The cross is raised up at the end of evil, at the end of hell."[57] The Son is positioned at the ultimate possible distance from the Father, spaced to accommodate all possibilities of sin.[58]

Balthasar's understanding of sinfulness, like Bonhoeffer's, falls into the traditional masculinist category discussed by Saiving. Balthasar describes a "rebellious, sinful, self-sufficient creature" that "tries to arrogate divine

---

[53] Balthasar, *Theo-drama IV*, 329, cf. 260.
[54] Balthasar theorizes that with human action, human *kenosis*, comes the possibility of human sin, sin that is therefore ultimately grounded in triune *kenosis*. Human refusal is "possible because of the trinitarian 'recklessness' of divine love" (*Theo-drama IV* 329). Thus, "there is something in God that can develop into suffering. This suffering occurs when the recklessness with which the Father gives away himself (and *all* that is his) encounters a freedom that, instead of responding in kind to this magnanimity, changes it into a calculating, cautious self-preservation." The paradigmatic (and again masculinist) sin of egotism "contrasts with the essentially divine recklessness of the Son, who allows himself to be squandered, and of the Spirit who accompanies him" (*Theo-drama IV*, 328).
[55] Balthasar, *Theo-drama IV*, 331. Balthasar also writes that "human freedom participates in the divine autonomy, both when it says Yes and when it says No" and that human freedom is "analogous to the way in which the Son receives the autonomy of the divine nature in the mode of receptivity (not, like the creature, in being created)" (*Theo-drama IV*, 328).
[56] Ibid., 338.
[57] Ibid.
[58] Referencing the reformers, Balthasar writes that "thus it is just as possible to maintain that Jesus' being forsaken by God was the opposite of hell as to say that it *was* hell (Luther, Calvin) or even the ultimate heightening of hell (Quenstedt)" (*Theo-drama IV*, 336).

nature to itself without sharing in the Person who is always endowing, receiving, pouring forth and giving thanks for that nature—and who embodies its self-giving."[59] The sinful person indulges in a "calculating, cautious self-preservation" rather than "allowing" himself or herself to "be squandered."[60]

Balthasar's sinful person tries for personhood without *kenosis*. In converse, can a person also depart from the flow of kenotic power by being overly self-effacing? If so, the distance fundamental to Balthasar's *kenosis* guards against the collapse of difference into utter solubility. The Spirit buffers our subjectivity. This efficacious distance again parallels the mediatory role of Christ in Bonhoeffer's soteriology.

For Balthasar the creature's "no" is "the lie, which only exists by courtesy of the truth and has already been overtaken by it."[61] Balthasar claims that God "is above the necessity to dominate, let alone use violence."[62] While the Son's "no" is "overtaken" and absorbed back into the matrix of the divine life, still Balthasar claims that the Son is not forced, for the Son "allows himself to be squandered."[63] Similarly, "God does not overwhelm man; he leads him to his goals . . ."[64]

In some ways, then, Balthasar's sense of *kenosis* offers a productive distortion of power over theologies, because between the members of the trinity and between the divine and the human, difference and distinction are enabled and survive due to the space *kenosis* creates. In other ways, however, Balthasar's triune system still remains closed and overpowering, absorbing and taking over the threat of sin. While Balthasar's God is kenotic, this God is not vulnerable to the influences of those God loves.

In contrast, Jürgen Moltmann and Michael Welker offer kenotic trinitarian visions that differ from Balthasar in the degree to which they posit vulnerability as a consequence of God's *kenosis*. Welker describes God's *kenosis* as a matter of passion: "In kenotic love God reveals a burning passion for creatures—not

---

[59] Ibid., 328–329.
[60] Ibid., 328.
[61] Ibid., 329. This "no" helps to explicate Balthasar's kenotic soteriology: "The creature's No, its wanting to be autonomous without acknowledging its origin, must be located within the Son's all-embracing Yes to the Father, in the Spirit; it is the refusal to participate in the autonomy with which the Son is endowed" (*Theo-drama IV*, 329). In other words, Christ actually bears the No—that is, the sin. Christ is "the sin-bearing Son," who is "made to be sin" (*Theo-drama IV*, 335–336). Or, more properly for Balthasar, Christ bears the sin very momentarily, because Christ's nature is as a Yes to the Father. Here Balthasar affirms Luther's understanding: "Luther says that this No at least begins to surface in Jesus but he 'swallows it down'" (*Theo-drama IV*, 336). In contrast Balthasar criticizes both Rahner and Anselm, who teach that Christ overthrows sin through "pure merit" (*Theo-drama IV*, 336). For Balthasar such soteriology is too external, for "The Crucified does not bear the burden as something external: he in no way distances himself from those who by rights should have to bear it. (Indeed, he is *in* them eucharistically!)" (*Theo-drama IV* 337–338).
[62] Balthasar, *Theo-drama IV*, 331.
[63] Ibid., 330 and 328.
[64] Ibid., 331.

just for their suitability to the divine plan for the world."⁶⁵ In fact, this burning love comes despite the creatures' lack of suitability to that plan. God's desire seeks to win over God's beloved.

Again preserving distance, this divine *kenosis* reveals "a passionate interest in the otherness of the other, a passionate interest in letting the other unfold himself/herself in freedom, a passionate interest to pave ways for the unfolding of his/her life." This passion, however, does not consume the beloved, but rather "it respects the depth and the mystery and the freedom of the loved one; it even keeps this depth and mystery and freedom alive and holds it open." This passion, then, is distinctly nonpossessive: "In this kenotic love, God really gives space for the individuality and depth of creatures."⁶⁶

Also "giving space," Moltmann's sense of *kenosis* echoes the *zimzum* of kabbalistic thought. In *zimzum*, the self "empties" in withdrawing, in contracting the self to make space for creation, for the other. Moltmann elaborates that "it is not just self-giving that belongs to creative love; it is self-limitation too; not only affection, but respect for the unique nature of the others as well."⁶⁷

Moltmann further portrays a God who *wants* to be with God's creatures. This wanting implies a vulnerability and dependency. Thus Moltmann writes that "in a certain way God thus becomes dependent on the response of his beloved creatures."⁶⁸ God is the desiring lover eager for response, yet able to wait and not seek to force love. Moltmann describes God's amorous waiting: "Waiting means expecting, expecting means inviting, inviting means attracting, alluring, and enticing. By doing this, the waiting and awaiting one keeps an open space for the other, gives the other time, and creates possibilities of life for the other."⁶⁹

Like Balthasar, Moltmann describes the "essential surrendering" of God—essential because *kenosis* is the very essence of God. Moltmann continually emphasizes the "unselfishness" essential to the Trinity, and yet he also stresses the synchronous "self-realization" of the Trinity: "It is the divine being of the Father, the Son, and the Holy Spirit to surrender entirely to the other persons and in this way to achieve self-realization only in the other persons."⁷⁰ Self-emptying is here again simultaneously the realization

---

⁶⁵ Michael Welker, "Romantic Love, Covenantal Love, Kenotic Love," in *The Work of Love: Creation as Kenosis*, ed. John Polkinghorne. Grand Rapids, MI: Wm. B. Eerdmans, 2001, 134.
⁶⁶ Ibid., 134.
⁶⁷ Jürgen Moltmann, "God's *Kenosis* in the Creation and Consummation of the World," in *The Work of Love: Creation as Kenosis*, ed. John Polkinghorne. Grand Rapids, MI: Wm. B. Eerdmans, 2001, 147.
⁶⁸ Moltmann, "God's Kenosis," 148.
⁶⁹ Ibid.
⁷⁰ Jürgen Moltmann, "God Is Unselfish Love," in *The Emptying God*, eds. John B. Cobb, Jr. and Christopher Ives, 116–124. Maryknoll, NY: Orbis Books, 1990, 119.

of the self. To the extent that it is desire, it is desire both for the other and for the self.

Moltmann appreciates much of Balthasar's conception of divine *kenosis*, in which he sees that "each person of the Trinity is in ecstasy out of itself in the other."[71] The appreciation is not mutual. Balthasar is critical of Moltmann, considering him to be ensnared in the mistakes Balthasar sees in process theology, or of any theology where God is "entangled in the world process."[72] For Balthasar, such theology "betrays a hubris, an exaggerated self-importance, on the part of creaturely freedom; it has succumbed to the illusion that man's ability to say No to God actually limits the divine omnipotence."[73] Though his trinitarian cosmology seems to suggest otherwise, Balthasar firmly denies that God needs the creation God loves.[74]

But while protecting God from the flux of the world, Balthasar also makes the claim that God "will not be God for himself alone."[75] In *Mysterium Pascale*, a later work perhaps aiming to clear up his untraditional claims in *Theo-drama IV*, Balthasar wants to clarify that he is not rendering God impotent. Rather "one can only agree with those Fathers who not only indentified the Kenosis—as God's self-limitation and self-renunciation—with the divine *freedom* . . . but went on to see in the powerlessness of the Incarnate and Crucified One the shining forth of God's *omnipotence*."[76]

Balthasar insists that although all things, including the tangle of sin, are caught up in God, "God cannot be entangled in some kind of tragic role . . ."[77] The distance that opens desire and the possibility of sin also "contains and surpasses all possible drama between God and a world."[78] In Balthasar, human toil and salvation are resolutely internal to the Trinity, and this trinitarian ontology safeguards God from tragedy.[79] Balthasar's God is the moved yet unshaken mover. His triune God does express ardent longing, and yet within perfect self-sufficiency.

For Balthasar, "no" does not mean no: "The creature's No is merely a twisted knot within the Son's pouring-forth." Whereas in process theology the "knot" would retexture the character of God, here "it is left behind by the current of love."[80] This love, then, is ultimately oblivious to the beloved; it is a power over

---

[71] Moltmann, "God's *Kenosis*," 141.
[72] Balthasar, *Theo-drama IV*, 322.
[73] Ibid., 326, cf. 322. Also see Catherine Mowry LaCugna, *God for Us: The Trinity and Christian Life*. New York: Harper San Francisco, 1991, 364.
[74] Balthasar, *Theo-drama IV*, 323.
[75] Ibid., 324.
[76] Hans Urs von Balthasar, *Mysterium Pascale*. Edinburgh, Scotland: T&T Clark, 1990, 33–34. For evidence of the way in which Balthasar has become a controversial figure in Roman Catholicism, see Alyssa Lyra Pitstick, *Light in Darkness: Hans Urs von Balthasar and the Catholic Doctrine of Christ's Descent into Hell*. Grand Rapids, MI: Wm. B. Eerdmans, 2007.
[77] Balthasar, *Theo-drama IV*, 331.
[78] Ibid., 327.
[79] Ibid., 332–333.
[80] Ibid., 330, cf. 322.

the beloved that ultimately forgets and absorbs the other. While Balthasar's use of *kenosis* portrays the role of divine *kenosis* in subjectivity—divine and human—it does not imagine that human *kenosis* could alter or renew divine subjectivity. Others come into being through God's self-giving, but as with the theologies reviewed in Chapter 1, God's overbearing power is reasserted through this sort of *kenosis*.

Human *Kenosis* and Divine Subjectivity

Marcella Althaus-Reid finds fodder for a kind of *eros* in the metaphor of the Trinity, though she writes much more explicitly than would Balthasar of a specifically "sexual kenosis." While she acknowledges the many ways in which feminist theologies have made use of the trinitarian metaphor, she finds that the doctrine of the Trinity remains inadequately sexual. Thus she claims that "the task of Queer Theology is precisely to deepen this reflection on the sexual relationship manifested in the Trinity and to consider how God in the Trinity may come out in a relationship outside heterosexualism."[81] For Althaus-Reid, the *kenosis* of God becoming flesh as described by Philippians does not just concern "God devolving itself in Christ but in the Trinity, and in the Trinity understood as an orgy . . ."[82] Queer theology is "theology in the image of our own Queer bodies,"[83] and thus God becomes incarnate in multifarious ways, led astray into the alleys where far more than two dichotomized gender identities are performed.[84] Queer theology seeks "to produce a post-colonial dislocation of God's (heterosexual) omnipresence,"[85] and this is a kenotic dislocation.

Though Althaus-Reid's emphasis on the Trinity makes her work resonant with Balthasar's kenotic trinity, Balthasar could hardly have written a queer orgy. His *kenosis* between the divine persons is quite clearly, as Lucy Gardner and David Moss have analyzed, gendered between masculine activity and female receptivity, despite the queer "Father and Son" language.[86] Whereas Balthasar's Trinity, kenotic though it is, ultimately holds on to its power and its control, Althaus-Reid imagines an erotic *kenosis* that tempts God to let go of power and control. In this way her theology destabilizes theologies

---

[81] Marcella Althaus-Reid, *Queer God* (London: Routledge, 2003), 46.
[82] Ibid., 57.
[83] Ibid., 51.
[84] For more on gender "performativity," see Judith Butler, *Gender Trouble: Feminism and the Subversion of Identity* (New York: Routledge Classics, 2006).
[85] Althaus-Reid, *Queer God*, 52. Althaus-Reid explains that practically the dislocation produced by Queer theology may function more as a pendulum than as a thorough dislocation.
[86] See Lucy Gardner and David Moss, "Something like Time; Something Like the Sexes—an Essay in Reception," in *Balthasar at the End of Modernity*, by Lucy Gardner, David Moss, Ben Quash and Graham Ward (Edinburgh: T&T Clark, 1999), 69–138.

of God's power over us, using *kenosis* to explicate the "coming out of God." For Althaus-Reid, "queering" is a theological vocation, and *kenosis* is central to the method by which the theologian queers. The queer theologian seeks to "lead God astray," a kenotic movement in that she is "facilitating God's own disempowering act . . ."[87] Althaus-Reid explains: "Using an image from the S/M [sadomasochism] scene we may ask, for instance, how can we lead God astray (consensually), and how could a theologian facilitate this God-in-relationship towards a kenotic self-betrayal?"[88] Althaus-Reid speaks of *kenosis* in terms of "dislocation," "letting go," being "led astray," and following "nomadic wanderlust."

She sees in doctrines of *kenosis* attempts "to explain unusual relationships, for instance, the way God relates to Godself, that is, God's own identity questioning (symbolized by the relationship between God and Christ) and the amorous dealings between God and people."[89] In pointing to kenoticism as a form of identity questioning, Althaus-Reid emphasizes the importance of *kenosis* in negotiating shifting subjectivities.

Showing similarity to Frascati-Lochhead's Heideggerian themes, Althaus-Reid laments "all the early closures of meaning" in Christian history.[90] She understands "theological originality" to mean, not newness, but rather, "the originality of visibility." It occurs when "forgotten, suppressed, unvalued, or underprivileged fragments of our lives get access to public theological discussion."[91] This new visibility is "necessary for the kenosis of God."[92] This sort of *kenosis* does not simply pull God to the margins, but rather shifts the center to queer spaces, as God joins in the passion of the theologically underprivileged spaces: the dark alley, or the bedroom, or impoverished spaces. While many other contemporary theologians could be said to join in her lament over Christianity's "early closures of meaning," Althaus-Reid uniquely stresses the way in which Christian God-concepts have been subjected to a specifically sexual orthodoxy. She writes, "If we wanted to reflect on a second coming of Christ, we should need to start by acknowledging that the second coming of the divinity is a sexual coming and a sexual kenosis."[93] Althaus-Reid warns that even in theologies sensitive to gender issues, a simplistic, dissembling "inclusion" may occur when the norms of heterosexual "equality" are assumed.[94] Althaus-Reid's overall project involves deconstructing the heterosexual brace

---

[87] Althaus-Reid, *Queer God*, 56–57.
[88] Ibid., 46.
[89] Ibid., 55.
[90] Ibid., 48.
[91] Ibid.
[92] Ibid., 50.
[93] Ibid., 46.
[94] Marcella Althaus-Reid, *Indecent Theology: Theological Perversions in Sex, Gender, and Politics*. London: Routledge, 2000, 89–91.

historically placed on conceptions of God. In this the queer theologian helps to free God, beckoning God to come out of the closet.

As queer theologians beckon God's *kenosis*, they display theological originalities that enjoin a shift in theological epistemology. Althaus-Reid insists that "we cannot think a Queer God without understanding different sexual ways of knowing."[95] She offers the following lucid example of the way in which "different sexual ways of knowing" can shift theological thinking: "It is not enough to open, for instance, a theological reflection on masturbation, using masturbation as the motive of an ecclesiastical or eschatological concern (are masturbators going to be amongst the elect?), but rather to think Christian eschatology from an epistemology derived from masturbation."[96] "Queer theology" is not simply a supplemental chapter in the enlarged territory of traditional androcentric, heterosexist, European theology, and it is not simply an effort "to induce oppressed multitudes to invest their identities in the center-defined theological exercise by a simple economy of inclusion."[97]

Instead, luring the *kenosis* of God into queer spaces involves rethinking heterosexual power dynamics, dynamics that have been a lens through which theologians have read, for instance, the Philippians *kenosis* hymn. Althaus-Reid is critical of the ways in which the *kenosis* motif has historically reinforced heterosexual power norms within theology. She sees traditional readings of *kenosis* as trapped within a dualistic relationship between God's power and Christ's vulnerability. In such traditional readings *kenosis* functions as "a transmutation from omnipotence to less (but not ineffectual) power."[98] Althaus-Reid explains, "In reality, this has been a 'power to power' kenotic understanding, that is, how to find in Jesus the imperial power of God which is not self-evident, and make of it a grandiose theological speech of power."[99] Althaus-Reid particularly accuses scholarship close to her own, including "liberationist and Feminist Theologies, which have striven to redefine power from the margins." She finds that "'empowering' the poor has been a difficult process of replacements, re-conceptualizations and other devices which could pragmatically deal with reality of empowering without giving any real power to anybody (in church or in society)."[100] Her observations

---

[95] Althaus-Reid, *Queer God*, 52.
[96] Ibid., 51.
[97] Ibid., 51.
[98] Ibid., 57.
[99] Ibid., 56.
[100] Ibid. In feminist theology particularly, Althaus-Reid points to the way in which "'power in vulnerability' has been stressed as positive not only for women but also for men (however women and men are defined here)." She mentions Ruether and the feminist appropriations of her work as key examples of this sort of interpretation of *kenosis*, but Coakley's insistence on omnipotence comes more quickly to mind for me. Althaus-Reid does not completely disregard feminist insights on "power in vulnerability" or on the *kenosis* of patriarchy, but for her these insights are overly simplistic, assuming two gender identities of "man" and "woman" and a dichotomy of power and vulnerability.

resonate with the thesis of Chapter 1, where I argued that doctrines of *kenosis* have often functioned to bolster theologies of God's power over us.

In deconstructing patriarchy and in explorations of power, Althaus-Reid's queer theology looks "beyond dual models of loving relationships," destabilizing the heteronormative dichotomy of power and powerless in the gender roles of "man" and "woman." Thus, while the queer theologian is "facilitating God's own disempowering act," she does so "without presuming to know what original power is there to let go" in an effort to destabilize the traditional "power to power" interpretation of *kenosis*.[101]

Embodied lovers court God's presence, but the courtship does not primarily intend a manipulation of power; rather, pleasure, fecundity, perversity, even curiosity and exploration, mark this interpretation of kenotic loving. Here Althaus-Reid helps me to express again my difference from Coakley's kenotic christology. Instead of securing all power conceptually in God and then trying to make power apparent in the submission of the human, kenotic christology may instead focus on a power that resides *in the kenotic action itself*, a power that does not start from certain power or end with certain power, but rather is in itself a power of momentum, of fecundity, of embodied transcendence, and of pleasure.

For Althaus-Reid human passions lure the *kenosis* of God, drawing God into the bedroom of queer desires, helping God to explore new identities. "The Voyeur God, for instance, may depend for God's own kenosis on what God sees and learns from our bedrooms or closets, for affective and sexual habits inform identity and inform God's own identity too."[102] She writes of "the theologian's nomadic desire for crossing frontiers made of theological condemnatory gossip" and emphasizes that this "nomadic movement of theology" enables God to "leave God's own closet."[103]

The vulnerable, creative "nomadic queer" who lures the self-emptying of God offers a strikingly reversed image of Bonhoeffer's christology. Whereas in Bonhoeffer, it is God in Christ who lures the human person out of his egotistical closet, in Althaus-Reid it is the human queer who beckons God. It is as though the voyeur God peaks into the queer bed and says, "Who are they?," thus turning the question *on God*, such that the divine is beckoned to new subjectivity and fresh *kenosis*. This queering of Bonhoeffer's christology emphasizes the true agency of the human subject, the power to lure and affect even the divine.

Kenosis and the Kinetics of Subjectivity

Catherine Keller describes feminist selfhood as involving "a series of retrievals," reclaiming body, particularity, emotion, imagination, connection

---

[101] Ibid., 56–57.
[102] Ibid., 53.
[103] Ibid., 49.

to the environment, and action against suffering. "And above all," she writes, a feminist selfhood "strengthens both the sense of attachment and the sense of self, seeking not to overcome self but to experience and to articulate an extensively relational self."[104] In the process of such retrieval, might a feminist discover, back at the pulsing heart of her sense of self, the swirling of kenotic energies, the circulation of her relational integrity?

This chapter has sought to demonstrate that *kenosis*, self-emptying, may function as a mechanism for renewed subjectivity—divine and human. Perhaps surprisingly, even while and perhaps because self-development remains a vital aspect of feminist activism, self-surrender may express a feminist's creative power, not her feminist shortcomings. Were feminists to sweepingly cleanse Christianity of its self-surrendering themes, we may in the process dam(n) our own desires.

Graham Ward claims that "there can be no kenotic love which is not erotic also—endless giving without reception announces a demonic and nihilistic logic. It is indifferent."[105] For Ward it is indifferent literally, in that there is no difference between. Here, then, Ward returns us to what feminists find problematic about *agape*: "endless giving without reception" is a problem. Incessant giving without the generation of power for ourselves would be—flatly—disempowering.

Indeed, any *kenosis* whose *eros* has gone flat reveals what Saiving may have considered a typically female sin of self-diffusion. At the end of her 1960 article, Saiving speaks prophetically of "the feminizing of society itself, including men as well as women."[106] Such a society would be what Audre Lorde names an "anti-erotic" society. In Lorde's analysis, "in order to perpetuate itself, every oppression must corrupt or distort those various sources of power within the culture of the oppressed that can provide energy for change." Sexism thus must distort the erotic within women's lives, and in men's as well, in different ways, causing "a suppression of the erotic as a considered source of power and information in our lives."[107]

Where *kenosis* has been construed as the doctrine of desire's sacrifice, the obedient self has dams set on its own desire and, stagnant, is easily handled in the rush of other people's desires. A ban on desire is an oppressive system's

---

[104] Keller, "Scoop Up the Water," 107.
[105] Graham Ward, "The Erotics of Redemption: After Karl Barth," *Theology and Sexuality* 8, 1998: 52–72, this quotation 71. Ward stresses in this article that "marriage is not a rite of synthesis" and thus "the church must sanctify difference" (71). Since "there is no desire without difference" (70), "true desire, that is, God-ordained desire can only be heterosexual," in which Ward includes all "so-called homosexual relationships whose structure of desire is heterosexual" but excludes "self-designated 'heterosexual relationships' whose structure of desire is homosexual" (71).
[106] Saiving, "Human Situation," 40.
[107] Lorde, "Uses of the Erotic," in Sister Outsider, 53–59. The connections between ownership of sexual desire and resistance to sexual abuse are explored in the recent anthology by Jaclyn Friedman and Jessica Valenti, *Yes Means Yes: Visions of Female Sexual Power and a World Without Rape*. Berkeley, CA: Seal, 2008.

way of stagnating persons' selfhood, and misinterpreted *kenosis* has served as just such a ban, a controlling tool wielded to serve the needs of patriarchal systems, distracting persons from their own becoming, and, I would claim, denying active participation in christic presence in the world. Perhaps Mary Daly speaks of a similar dynamic when she decries that "ontological impotence which is blockage of participation in Be-ing."[108]

Ward, reading both Balthasar and Luce Irigaray, invokes *kenosis* as he seeks to "deconstruct the dualism of agape and eros."[109] He writes of human love partnerships that "in our attraction-in-difference is reflected the difference-in-relation in our Trinitarian God."[110] Just as the Spirit holds necessary difference between Father and Son in Balthasar's Trinity, so for Ward human love relationships must be composed of distinct difference, such that "what is loved in love is difference." According to Ward, "such difference . . . operates according to the economies of both kenotic and erotic desire." Distinct subjectivity in relationship is maintained through both *agape* and *eros*, operating within one dynamic: "In fact, *agape* and *eros* can be seen as two perspectives within the same dynamic, moments of giving and receiving where giving is also receiving, and vice versa."[111] Though Ward seems to equate the kenotic with *agape* here, such that *kenosis* is "giving," he ceases the long tradition of opposing *eros* and *agape*.

Mostly in concert with Ward, then, I suggest that *eros* and *agape* blur in the flow of *kenosis*. I would stress, however, that *kenosis* need be no more closely aligned with *agape* than with *eros*. If it is to function as a power for ourselves and our subjectivities, *kenosis* will need to be more than the pure *agape* it has so often been connected with, and if our subjectivities are to be other than overpowering illusions of self-grandeur, then *kenosis* will, perhaps ironically, need to reveal our capacities to need and to want the caress of the other, our capacities for *eros*. Because our kenotic *eros* is self-emptying, it does not employ *eros* as a tool of acquisition and domination, and because our kenotic *agape* becomes us, it need not mean our disavowal of all we have to offer the world, or any flat surrender to the powers over us. It is, joyfully, a much more productive surrender.

In addition to blocking the fullness of kenotic powers within us, a predominately agapeic reading of *kenosis* overlooks some of the powers of God's *kenosis*. A uniformly agapeic reading of divine self-giving deflates the relational, *pro nobis* vector explored in the previous chapter, with results that are problematic both for feminism and for theology. While in the first chapter I argued that a totally nonkenotic divinity paired with kenotic humanity

---

[108] Daly, *Pure Lust: Elemental Feminist Philosophy*. Boston: Beacon, 1984, 35–36.
[109] Graham Ward, "The Erotics of Redemption," 52.
[110] Ibid., 55.
[111] Ibid.

constructs a potentially oppressive dynamic, the converse problem is that a totally kenotic divinity unmet by the agency expressed in human kenosis sets up a nearly identical hazard: again humans are totally passive beneath God, though God has now become the Master Kenoticist. It makes only a small difference whether people are humbly submissive beneath a nonkenotic God or overwhelmed by a sweeping divine *kenosis*: they play the receptive and stereotypically feminine role either way. More than a problem for human social relationships, such a stereotypical setup constitutes a problem *for God*, as God is left with little to love other than God's own self. No other subjectivity is ever given room or invitation to grow. It is a unilateral situation. And if no agency besides God's own is involved, then *kenosis* ceases to follow a for-others vector, and God's character collapses into itself, flattened out of the nature of an inherently for-you God. God's own nature collapses. Without partners, without relationality, no eccentricity is involved in self-emptying; instead, it is a closed, entropic system, and contrary to the character of christic *kenosis*.

And yet, were divine *kenosis* directly equatable with the currents of *eros*, it could be read as acquisitive in the extreme, not at all *pro nobis*, and potentially violent, or in Keller's words: "cruel as crucifixion when passion splits from compassion."[112] As I will explore further in Chapter 6, *eros* alone does not necessarily promote a power for ourselves or those we desire. Neither *eros* nor *agape* need fully chart the vectors of *kenosis*.

Kenotic flow is not unilateral; rather, *kenosis* desires for itself as well, such that *kenosis* becomes you: you the kenotic one, or you the one addressed by another's *kenosis*. Though *kenosis* is a passion, which, as Balthasar has it, "in its self-giving, observed no limits and had no regard for itself,"[113] it also depends on the survival of desire's exchange between points of difference. One can get so caught up in erotic desire as to forget one's own self-interests—is such a passion agapeic or erotic? Self-emptying surges and swirls for many reasons by which we find ourselves committed for the other, and in being so, find ourselves.

Kenotic passion may be both self-effacing *and* self-interested. Its generosity is generative. God's is not the *kenosis* of a diffusely and indifferently overflowing godhead. This is a relational connection: a God seeking after you, particularly, and seeking to *become God* in relation to you. As Melanchthon writes, "God desired to be known." Through divine *kenosis*, one encounters a God willing to become godless—and thereby God again—in order to be with you. And through the agapeic, erotic urges propelling us out toward the specific

---

[112] Keller, "Afterword: A Theology of Eros, After Transfiguring Passion," 366–374, in *Toward a Theology of Eros: Transfiguring Passion at the Limits of Discipline*, eds. Virginia Burrus and Catherine Keller. New York: Fordham University Press, 2006, 374.

[113] Balthasar, *Theo-drama IV*, 329.

others in our day, we lose hold of our self in the process of becoming our self, again and differently, in the context of others.

Yet such a possibility quickly raises the topic of masochism. As the next chapter will demonstrate, while some feminists see in the coalescence of desire and pain the lingering traces of patriarchal violence within the feminist subconscious, other feminist scholars also see in it creative strategy and a fruitful zone for the production of subjectivity. The latter demonstrate that desire leading through pain and self-surrender can be desire *for the self,* especially for the self made new.

Chapter 4

Beyond "Power-With": Martyrs and Masochists

"... all Christians, as well as many others, bear scars of sadomasochistic relations."
—Carter Heyward and Beverly Harrison[1]

The 1998 edition of the classic feminist health book *Our Bodies, Ourselves* reports two contrasting experiences of sexual sadomasochism. One woman reports: "S/M allows my partner and me to share a fantasy life, which is a deep kind of intimacy, very special and unique, which I would not trade for anything." But another woman writes: "I was a battered wife. My husband, a professional with a good job, said he was into bondage. I bought into it at first. Toward the end he said that he could relate to me sexually only if he tied me up. At the end he was threatening to kill me. For him, bondage had to do with low self-esteem and wasn't a healthy expression of sexuality."[2] This second woman's experience of sadomasochism as conflated with battering expresses the most direct reason why the topic of masochism has been controversial in feminist analysis. The continuing reality of violence against women problematizes any feminist approach to masochism that is not an outright criticism of its dangers.

Yet feminism has not univocally condemned sadomasochism. *Our Bodies, Ourselves*, for example, admits into its pages both of the aforementioned experiences, in their tension. Though other feminist publications and organizations have sought to cleanse the ranks, there are both anti-S/M and pro-S/M feminists. Especially since the "sex and culture wars" of the 1980s, feminism has a turbulent history with the topic of sadomasochism, with dramatic moments like burning of lesbian S/M fiction outside a women's bookstore in London in

---

[1] Beverly W. Harrison and Carter Heyward, "Pain and Pleasure: Avoiding the Confusions of Christian Tradition in Feminist Theory," in *Christianity, Patriarchy, and Abuse: A Feminist Critique*, eds. Joanne Carlson Brown and Carole R. Bohn. Cleveland, OH: Pilgrim Press, 1989, 155.
[2] Boston Women's Healthbook Collective, *Our Bodies, Ourselves for the New Century*. New York: Touchstone, 1998, 247.

1983.[3] The very book that was burned began by querying the ardent lesbian feminist resistance to S/M. It seems that even such a query had to be reduced to ashes. One wonders, looking back: why the violent gesture from feminists seeking to denounce a violent sexual paradigm? Lynda Hart suggests that "the issue has less to do with 'violence' and sexual practices and more to do with the way in which 'the Lesbian' became, ironically, positioned as the sign of purity in the liberal feminist agenda."[4]

This points to the way feminism can, with its alternatives to "power over" models of relating, establish other modes of power that, while configuring power differently, are presented as better than, as totally apart from, the model they dispute. Our power can "one up" your power: we've got a power over power over. The result is yet another dominating gesture. (As we saw in Chapter 2, feminists like Marta Frascati-Lochhead have worked to avoid such results). One way that this has happened is with arguments for mutuality or reciprocity: the "power with" of feminist theology. This power with is often imagined in erotic terms, and thus S/M practices appear as obvious rivals to the pure ideal of an erotic of mutuality.

Feminism has become more self-critical of its own attempts at purity since the 1980s. Feminist theology, too, has followed the diversifying currents of third-wave feminism, but with a few exceptions, has mostly remained either critical or silent on the topic of masochism. The Christian tradition's legacy of something like masochism is long; as Althaus-Reid writes, "God the master and the Christian as the submissive slave subject, the top/bottom relationship of S/M people, is a master sketch of Christianity done in a moment."[5] Such a master sketch still holds too much cultural sway, it seems, for most feminist theology to risk constructively engaging it: best to stay on guard against it, to criticize it, and to try to define ourselves apart from it. The defensive posture, though, does imply a subtly complicit engagement, if only in a willingness to rival for the most or best power. Meanwhile, with fascinating implications for theological discourse, historians and philosophers have explored masochism alongside the related concepts of martyrdom, renunciation, and asceticism, particularly as these appear in the lives of Christian saints. Their analyses indicate that amid the dangers of masochism, potent performances of the masochist's ironic agency transpire.

---

[3] The book was a publication of *Samois*, entitled *Coming to Power*, that explored lesbian S/M. For a brief chronology that encompasses the 1980s sex and culture wars see Nan Hunter, "Contextualizing the Sexuality Debates: A Chronology 1966–2005," in *Sex Wars: Sexual Dissent and Political Culture*, 10th Anniversary edn, eds. Lisa Duggan and Nan D. Hunter. New York: Routledge, 2006, 15–28.

[4] Lynda Hart, *Between the Body and the Flesh: Performing Sadomasochism*. New York: Columbia University Press, 1998, 52. On page 51 she also quotes the introduction to *Coming to Power*: "This turbulence is symbolic of a much deeper, more invisible and less-than-direct ideological power struggle."

[5] Althaus-Reid, *Indecent Theology*, 153.

In the previous chapter I explored desire as a valence of *kenosis*. In this chapter I give attention to the possibility that such desire may sometimes coalesce with a desired experience of pain. I will define masochism here as the desired experience of pain. In this chapter I will explore both feminist theological critique of masochism and the recent Christian scholarship that has found something complexly attractive in the masochistic trends of the Christian past. With regard to the latter, I will particularly draw upon the work of Karmen MacKendrick and Virginia Burrus, though I will also refer to the work of Judith Perkins. The primary theological text I will employ is the 1989 article "Pain and Pleasure: On Avoiding Confusions of Christian Tradition in Feminist Theory," by Carter Heyward and Beverly Harrison.[6] Their title already reveals their emphasis: the complications of S/M are confusions to avoid. In contrast, I seek to demonstrate here that theology may also creatively court these confusions. It may be that all Christians "bear scars of sadomasochistic relations," but some of these scars, rather than a source of regret, may serve as *productive* sites, the marks of powerful, shifting subjectivity.[7]

I should be clear from the outset that I do not intend in this chapter to flatly equate *kenosis* with masochism. A person might give of, "empty," or even surrender herself without actively desiring pain. Yet it would be irresponsible to recommend a kenotic christology without addressing the feminist theological suspicion toward masochism: irresponsible in failing to respond to the abuse that women daily face and the ways that women's so-called masochism is blamed for eliciting such abuse. While I will discuss abuse at more length in the next chapter, in this chapter I seek to bring the creative possibilities of masochism into the feminist theological consideration of *kenosis*. As I imagine it, *kenosis* may indeed merge into or make use of masochism, but this need not be the point at which such *kenosis* ceases to be "feminist." The creative use of

---

[6] For other feminist theological criticisms of sadomasochism see Sara Maitland, "Passionate Prayer: Masochistic Images in Women's Experience," 125–140, in *Sex and God*, ed. Linda Hurcombe. New York: Routledge and Kegan Paul, 1987; Alison Jasper, "Reading for Pleasure/Reading for Pain: Feminist Reflections on the Passion Narrative in John's Gospel," in *Religion and Sexuality*, eds. Michael A. Hayes, Wendy J. Porter, and David Tombs. Sheffield, Eng: Sheffield Academic Press, 1998, 203–212; and Susanna Heine, "Female Masochism and the Theology of the Cross," trans. Fredrick J. Gaiser, *Word & World* 15 (1995): 299–305. In contrast, for a criticism of Heyward's understanding of masochism, see K. Roberts Skerrett, "When Yes Means No: The Passion of Carter Heyward," *Journal of Feminist Studies in Religion* 12.1 (1996): 71–92.

[7] For some Christian feminists, as with Brock and Parker in their conclusion to *Proverbs of Ashes*, the resurrection may stand for survival hard and vigorously won. For others, survival may be sought precisely through masochistic practice. For these, even the most painful memories of their crucifixions may brand them with a mark of new life, a resistance that was in itself resurrection. "Here is one of the most important sources of the senses of masochistic power," writes Karmen MacKendrick: "the subject, oneself, retains *in the body* the memory of this transgressive rupture," in the marks of bruises, cuts, piercing, brands (*Counterpleasures*, 118).

masochistic pain is something with which feminists may trust themselves, and perhaps on occasion something with which those who have survived abuse will be intimately familiar. Like *kenosis*, and at times in synchrony with *kenosis*, masochism carries a capacity for subversion and resistance in a paradoxical yet vibrant experience of one's own agency. Constructing situations luminous in their liminality, masochistic self-emptying sheds new light upon whom a person is becoming and where her desires are leading her, rather than simply outing an insufficiently developed or pathological sense of self.

Feminism and Masochism

The essentializing of women as fundamentally self-giving and nurturing, as—in Virginia Burrus's words—"(alas) merely *natural* masochists,"[8] has long come under the critique of feminist theology. Valerie Saiving's analysis of "the human situation" already points in this direction in claiming that women's tendency is the sin of diffusion and lack of care for the self. Such neglect of the self is not necessarily the choice of pain for the self, but Saiving's "feminine" sin and masochism parallel one another in their seeming inattention to personal pleasure. This masochistic posture therefore appears as something to subvert or as something from which to liberate women, rather than a stance that could be *in itself* a subversion or an exercise of liberation, even a pleasurable one. Speaking of this latter possibility, Karmen MacKendrick writes in her study of sadomasochism that "rather than being only something to be resisted, restraint itself is a strategy of resistance."[9]

Perched on the shifting sands between second- and third-wave feminisms, Heyward and Harrison's 1989 article affirms that "theories that oversimplify the constructive feminist agenda or challenge the troubling dualisms of patriarchal culture in an overly reactive way merely feed the divisiveness among women that political repression seeks to sow."[10] Heyward and Harrison's article tries to avoid the pitfalls of the "overly reactive"; they account for views that differ from their own and proceed sympathetically and even pastorally, advocating for just and powerful relationships. However, in light of more recent studies of Christian renunciations, their analysis does appear too simplistic, if still important.

Heyward and Harrison acknowledge that "the threat of violence and the objectification of women's bodies create genuine barriers to women's

---

[8] Virginia Burrus, *Sex Lives of Saints: An Erotics of Ancient Hagiography*. Philadelphia: University of Pennsylvania Press, 2003, 12, also 52, quoting Hart's summary of theories of women as ontologically masochistic.

[9] MacKendrick, *Counterpleasures*, 107. Restraint of self need not equate to loss of self. Rather, "the masochist finds restraint and pain against which to push herself past herself" (107).

[10] Harrison and Heyward, "Pain and Pleasure," 148.

realization of the erotic," and that women, for that reason, therefore seek sexual fulfillment in dangerous, non-neutral settings. They acknowledge that one cannot proceed to develop a feminist *eros* "as if our desires were homogeneous or untouched by the disordered power dynamics of patriarchal eroticism,"[11] but they do not therefore see these ambivalent dynamics as available for engagement in the name of resistance. Instead they focus on emphasizing the ways in which Christianity has been complicit in disordering the desires of women into sadomasochistic form: into "a social (not only sexual) relation—in which pleasure is available chiefly through pain."[12] Contemplating Christian accounts of martyrdom and asceticism, of atonement theologies and sexual repression, they conclude that "the primary architect of the identification of pain with pleasure in Western culture has been the Christian church with its basically dualistic anthropology."[13]

Heyward and Harrison find that the Christian sadomasochistic worldview has implications for subjectivity that are in particular conflict with the relational commitments of feminist theology. In their analysis, the effects of deeply embedded heterosexist patriarchy include the ramification that "the self/other relation which elicits strong erotic desire frequently is one of domination and submission," and "as such, sex is often experienced as a dynamic of conquest and surrender rather than as power in mutual relation."[14] "Power in mutual relation" is a key vision for Heyward and Harrison, explored particularly by Heyward in other writings.[15] In this article the vision of mutuality functions as an alternative to the distorted experience of relationship available through a sadomasochistic society.

For Heyward and Harrison, sadomasochism limits to two the options available for a person in sexual relationship: "In such 'eroticization of domination,' sexual desire is linked with either self-oblivion or self assertion."[16] In contrast, Heyward and Harrison aim for "self-and-other-empowering relations"[17] and accordingly, "a theological reconstruction of the terms of divine-human interaction predicated by Christian patriarchal imagination."[18] They envision, in keeping with many other feminist theological voices, "a thoroughgoing social theory of selfhood."[19] They see relationality at the heart of things—but theirs is a specifically mutual and reciprocal kind of relationality, a power with.

---

[11] Ibid., 150.
[12] Ibid., 151.
[13] Ibid.
[14] Ibid., 150.
[15] See Heyward's *The Redemption of God: A Theology of Mutual Relation*. Lanham, MD: University Press of America, 1982.
[16] Harrison and Heyward, 150.
[17] Ibid., 151.
[18] Ibid., 160.
[19] Ibid., 165.

Heyward and Harrison see little room for women's desires in sadomasochism. They analyze the Christian metaphysics of power as dualistically male/male. Christian men, as sons of God, relate to the divine as the disobedient sons of a powerful father. "The son's pain is merely in proportion to what they deserve for the sin of their disobedience . . . Masochistic sons will enjoy the discipline because it will set them into right relation with their father, whose love they seek."[20] Rather than an experience of mutual relation, the experience is primarily sadistic, focused on the power and reprimand of the father, rather than the active obedience of the sons, who are active only in their disobedience. Sexual sadomasochism, specifically, exemplifies for Heyward and Harrison "a sexual politic of male-male relations—even when the participants include females."[21] But they are not seeing some liberating break from heterosexism here, only another example of what I have been calling power over. Heyward and Harrison link the practice of celibacy to this male-male dynamic: "We believe that Christianity has intensely eroticized male-male transactions of subordination and dominance, obedience and defiance. In the face of this we interpret much male fear of sexuality as a defense against these desires and interpret the lure of celibacy within Christianity as a fragile defense against them."[22] They do not recognize the renunciations of celibacy as possible practices of an active, if sometimes masochistic, agency.

Heyward and Harrison see not agency but powerlessness in masochism. They define the core of sadomasochism as follows: "the embodied, sensual appropriation of absolute power, or abject powerlessness, in relation to others."[23] This rigid dichotomy of omnipotence and depravity allots no power to the masochistic stance. In their analysis influences of patriarchy, Enlightenment, and capitalism fuse such that "power-in-relation, if not antagonistic, is at least competitive such that either self *or* other must prevail."[24] In patriarchal metaphysics, personal power is understood as fundamentally "nonmutual."[25] Affirming instead mutual relation as the erotic aim, and as their model of power in relation, Heyward and Harrison hypothesize that very few individuals encounter this ideal because of "the widespread cultural entanglement of violence and sex" that has created a context in which "few people experience tension-free relationships as erotic."[26]

In her own book from the same year as her joint article, Heyward gives slightly more credit to masochistic or even sadist practices as forms that people

---

[20] Ibid., 156.
[21] Ibid., 158.
[22] Ibid., 156.
[23] Ibid., 167.
[24] Ibid., 161.
[25] Ibid.
[26] Ibid. This is expressed somewhat differently in a monograph of Heyward's; cf. Carter Heyward, *Touching Our Strength: The Erotic as Power and the Love of God*, San Francisco: Harper & Row, 1989, 105.

may, and indeed must, move through on the way to mutuality. "Only from this present place, broken and battered as we may be, can we reach toward one another and ourselves and be really in touch with the knowledge and love of God, our power in right relation."[27] As in her work with Harrison, Heyward presents sadomasochism as a societal deformation. Yet here she makes greater concession to the need for engaging this problematic context in the process of redemption. "We cannot journey entirely beyond sadomasochism because the culture breeds it faster than we are able to imagine expunging it from our midst, either as a people or as individuals."[28] Thus Heyward concedes that S/M fantasies may not always be a moral wrong, as people "struggle together in the tensions and pathos of being more or less in control of our lives, dreams, and destinies."[29] She distinguishes between experiences of mutuality and the *yearning* for as-yet-unrealized mutuality.[30] That unmet yearning necessarily involves a nonmutual context, which she understands to be paradigmatically sadomasochistic. As such, "sadomasochistic sensibilities need not be denied. They are the raw material out of which are formed relationships in which people, slowly and partially, are able to experience—share and feel—love without pain."[31] Thus Heyward does not unilaterally condemn masochism, though she does understand it to be a component of a society based in wrong relation and at best a step toward the more ideal situation where S/M is entirely "expunged." She writes with compassion, acknowledging that "we cannot simply lift our embodied feelings out of a world that has alienated us, broken us, and *at best* given us conflicting feelings about ourselves and others . . ."[32] Nonetheless, this acknowledgement remains a statement about the unfortunate condition of masochism.

Since 1989 when Heyward and Harrison issued their critique, feminist theology has largely remained wary of experiments with masochism. An unspecified "masochism" has served as the boundary marker at the edge of appropriate feminism. For instance, Cynthia Crysdale, in her 2001 book powerfully reclaiming the cross for feminism, nonetheless makes it clear that she is not encouraging masochism: "Imitation of Jesus is not sweetness and light. Nor is it masochism. It involves choosing to be a Self oriented to God and abiding in God's love in a way that courageously confronts evil as woundedness and evil as sin."[33] This hesitancy to admit masochism among the possibilities of Christian practice is understandable considering the strong feminist critique of theologies of redemptive suffering. Yet in some readings of masochism in

---

[27] Heyward, *Touching Our Strength*, 108.
[28] Ibid.
[29] Ibid., 109.
[30] Ibid., 105.
[31] Ibid., 106.
[32] Ibid.
[33] Crysdale, *Embracing Travail*, 154.

the lives of the ancient saints, to which I now turn, masochism does not neatly match the atonement theology of Anselm.[34] One need not suffer in order to gain the eternal reward. The practiced suffering is, not unproblematically, instead *itself* the reward, as the masochist revels in his own desire. Masochism can be its own courageous confrontation.

Reading Masochism in Christian Asceticism

In her philosophical exploration of the "counterpleasures" of sadism, masochism, and asceticism, Karmen MacKendrick consistently refers to these precisely as *pleasures*.[35] She insists upon wider options than a choice between "normal" and "neurotic," and asserts that these counterpleasures, while not the norm, need not therefore be neuroses. MacKendrick describes masochistic practices as "strategically deployed forces of power through which the body resists, not the trivial and momentary restraint nor even, in the case of the saintly ascetic, the entire life of the flesh, but rather . . . the social restraints that constitute the good subject."[36] In her analysis, masochism serves the purposes only of pleasure, but in such a refusal of teleology, perhaps also of transgression.[37] "Transgression isn't normal";[38] neither need it be pathological.

Though Heyward and Harrison write that "early Christian anthropology required that *pain*—the *deprivation of sensual pleasure*—be accepted as an important element in attaining the joy of salvation,"[39] this understanding of pain as deprivation of pleasure is complicated by MacKendrick's reading of Christian asceticism. On one hand, one can surely find evidence of deprivation in the lives of the saints: they deny themselves food; they refuse rescue from death. Accordingly MacKendrick writes that "asceticism would seem to be the very opposite of excess, a defiance even of the more moderate demands of one's bodily and social selves, certainly a defiance of hedonistic extravagance.

---

[34] Heyward and Harrison directly link atonement christology to sadomasochism: "As the classical portrait of the punitive character of . . . divine-human transaction, Anselm of Canterbury's doctrine of the atonement (1093–1109) probably represents the sadomasochism of Christian teaching at its most transparent." And as Rita Brock and Rebecca Parker conclude in their book *Proverbs of Ashes* (249), "Western Christianity claims we are saved by the execution, that violence and terror reveal the grace of God."

[35] For example, see MacKendrick, *Counterpleasures*, 14: "However they appear initially, all of the counterpleasures discussed here are ultimately modes of asceticism. That is, all defy pleasure as we have come to know it; all are *strategies* of pleasure against the simple gratification of desire."

[36] MacKendrick, *Counterpleasures*, 109. Unlike Jessica Benjamin, MacKendrick argues that S/M disrupts differentiation of the self rather than reinforcing it (MacKendrick, 117).

[37] Ibid., 12–13: "[P]leasure is not subversive if we make of it something useful, even if that use is to subvert."

[38] Ibid., 20.

[39] Harrison and Heyward, "Pain and Pleasure," 152.

Yet it is in this *defiance* that we find not only the *pleasure* of asceticism, but its *excessiveness*: it is a denial beyond all moderation."[40] Thus she stresses that "no one should assume . . . that the denial inherent in restraint is predicated upon the *repression* of desire . . . "[41] An ascetic may experience pain, not as deprivation of pleasure, but as intensity and oversaturation. Rather than "antisensual pain,"[42] ascetic pain can be read as *super*sensual.

Further, the desire of the masochist points to her agency. The agency of the masochist is more clearly recognized when the concepts of sadism and masochism are unbound from one another. Like the distinct works of the eighteenth- and nineteenth-century literary figures Marquis de Sade and Leopold von Sacher-Masoch, which MacKendrick analyzes and from which S/M finds its name, the concepts of sadism and masochism each have their own intentions. They are not necessarily polarized and do not rely on each other to function in tandem.[43] Instead, masochism can function on its own, with its own strength. Though associated with passivity, it strategizes and *chooses* its own passivity, thus compromising that passivity. MacKendrick's study of masochism repeatedly emphasizes an active will in the masochist.[44]

MacKendrick, however, presents no clean, docile sense of agency. Rather, she emphasizes the undeniable reality of pain in masochism: "Pain makes it hard to present a picture of mere self-discipline and strong character, or of ironic simulation, innocent role-play . . . any sort of healthy normality. Whatever else may be purely simulated, the *pain* remains real, and as it increases the order of the ego is broken."[45] This very real pain is a desirable dynamic serving the transgression of subjection: "As pain continues, repeats, and builds (and desire . . . explodes), there is a sense of being slammed, repeatedly, into the wall of oneself, against one's own ego boundaries until these break, and, with them, shatter the descriptive capabilities of language."[46] Surely many feminists take pause at the image of a person slammed into a wall. Yet MacKendrick is responsive to the feminist criticisms of sadomasochism. Where these criticisms often determine sadomasochism to be a paradigmatic example of patriarchal power structures, as with Harrison and Heyward, MacKendrick instead demonstrates that sadism and

---

[40] MacKendrick, *Counterpleasures*, 65–66. MacKendrick points to the *eros* in asceticism: "Startlingly, we also find in asceticism—pure, chaste asceticism—the paradox of Eros, the movement between desire's furtherance and its cessation, taken to violent extremes, with satisfaction removed from the picture . . . The ascetic courts temptation and raises desire *in order to* do violence against it (Counterpleasures, 78).

[41] Ibid., 108. She continues: "This desire is precisely the desire of (or inherent in) power, power's desire for expansion."

[42] Harrison and Heyward, "Pain and Pleasure," 152, italics theirs.

[43] MacKendrick, *Counterpleasures*, 52–53.

[44] For instance see MacKendrick, *Counterpleasures*, 156: "This is no passive willingness; oneself is not so easily exposed to the outside; it is hard even to *think* of exposing the self to its own loss with joy, carelessness, impatience (which is not to say without fear)."

[45] MacKendrick, *Counterpleasures*, 119.

[46] Ibid.

masochism may each enact an unraveling or reworking of oppressive structures. "Sadomasochistic eroticism intensifies relations of control and subordination by fundamentally (that is, at the very beginning or foundation) altering their meaning, removing power from its orderly binarism of oppression . . ."[47] MacKendrick presents masochism as "a sense of power as *strength,* and extraordinary relation to one's own self, flesh, and subjectivity, to a world as a space of possibility, an openness to the outside."[48]

MacKendrick understands that feminist critics read in masochism "an excess of cultural conditioning *denying an authentically free subjectivity.*"[49] She writes that "opponents of restraint's excesses often point to the claims of lost self among ascetics as well as submissives and masochists," but for her this loss is "less a disappearance than a giving over of the self, a voluntary enslavement, whether this takes the form of an impassioned Augustinian insistence that freedom comes in turning the will over to God, or the less transcendent form of leather collars with rings for leads."[50] Reflecting their feminism, Heyward and Harrison also understand authentically free subjectivity to be relational, and thus not quite "free." They do not advocate the struggle for sheer autonomy, but rather autonomy joined with dependence, a selfhood correspondingly self-legislating and other-reliant, but a theory of self they do not picture in leather. Their vision seems so radically *other* than the dominating power over structure of patriarchy that they do not consider any feminist possibilities of pleasurably engaging patriarchy's forms in any but a provisional way. Yet MacKendrick's reading of masochism points toward another feminist alternative. She writes that "a sufficiently impassioned desire turns the body against the restraint of subjection, yanks the body beyond the subject—institutes the body's rebellion against its subjection to subjectivity . . ."[51] Perhaps much of feminism's problem with voluntary restraint is that it seems to lack agency, and to be, as Heyward and Harrison propose, a position of abject powerlessness. Feminist theology has overlooked the expressions of agency and resistance that are generated through masochism. Similarly, as we saw in the previous chapter, *kenosis,* where it has seemed a masochistic imitation of Christ, has also been read as a disimpassioned *agape,* rather than a "sufficiently impassioned desire," with an *eros* as unexpected in masochism as in *kenosis.*

---

[47] Ibid., 14, also see 16.
[48] Ibid., 103.
[49] Ibid., 120.
[50] Ibid., 119–120. She continues, "If we assume—and as good rational subjects we would have to assume—that freedom and autonomy are to be desired, this is pretty clearly not a good thing." For more from MacKendrick on Augustine see "Carthage Didn't Burn Hot Enough: Saint Augustine's Divine Seduction," in *Toward a Theology of Eros: Transfiguring Passion at the Limits of Discipline,* eds. Virginia Burrus and Catherine Keller. New York: Fordham University Press, 2006.
[51] Ibid., 120. Also see pages 120–121 for discussion of the political import of masochistic subversion.

Historian Virginia Burrus draws on MacKendrick's study as she emphasizes the *eros* expressed in Christian hagiography. Burrus finds in the lives of the saints something akin to a feminist, masochistic strategy, writing that "hagiography radically denaturalizes the feminine as the unstable and queerly reversible site of a decidedly *perverse*, even effectively *feminist*, masochistic subjectivity that actively resists patriarchy from within the very structures of misogynistic discourse."[52] She reads this "unstable and queerly reversible site" particularly in three women's lives: Gregory of Nyssa's *Life of Macrina*, Augustine's Monica, and Jerome's account of Paula. She introduces her reading of those texts by emphasizing the *agency* of passivity in Jerome's description of the torture of a woman accused of adultery. Burrus finds that "here as in other ancient Christian accounts of torture and resistance, the plot pivots on the subject's consent: the perverse extravagance of her passivity is the source of her power."[53] The function of this perversity is to transmute the victim into an active practitioner: "Martyrdom is thereby construed as an ascetic practice, and submission is converted to defiance, subverting the fraudulent script of 'self-betrayal' insinuated by the ritual of forced confession and further underwritten by the body's betrayal in pain."[54] The woman (or rather Jerome) scrambles the label of "sexual sinner" that has been cast upon her and rewrites her identity as strong and self-assured. Thus the dichotomized choices of either domination or powerless submission to domination, the options Heyward and Harrison see in sadism and masochism, fail to adequately describe Jerome's accused woman, for whom extravagant passivity generates power.[55]

In the stories of Monica, Macrina, and Paula, stories only barely *theirs*, written as they are by the pens of other men—son, brother, and friend—Burrus hears the assertion of these women's subjectivities, even and especially in their deaths. Each woman dies, "but 'she' also lives on (she gets a Life), even as 'he' (the writer) surrenders to a memorial of what he has become."[56] Paula, as Burrus explains, "has a near-Life experience in Jerome's over-long letter."[57] And Monica, dead, nonetheless "*demands a strong reading*," through the texts of her son's grief, texts in which Augustine's own masculinity is destabilized: "he mourns a much-loved woman—grieves like a woman—reluctantly, and also excessively, with ambivalence," and he admonishes "that his reader not despise such womanish behavior but rather imitate it."[58] Masculinity and femininity are likewise destabilized in Gregory of Nyssa's account of his sister's death.[59]

---

[52] Burrus, *Sex Lives*, 12.
[53] Ibid., 55.
[54] Ibid.
[55] Ibid.
[56] Ibid., 87.
[57] Ibid., 68.
[58] Ibid., 82, on Augustine's *Confessions* 9.12.
[59] Ibid., 72.

Macrina, described both as athlete and bride, ascends into ecstatic death, while her brother falls in with the wailing of the surrounding virgins and even assumes the womanly task of dressing the dead, following his sister's bidding. Burrus explains that "such reversibility is not incidental—far less a sign of sexual indifference—but rather is crucial to a text that relocates, or rather persistently dislocates, eroticism in the continual inscription and reinscription of a difference that resists the fixity of identities and is most lively in the passages in between."[60] Pain, whether the memory of pain in Macrina's cancerous scar or the pain of grief, serves as the pivot around which the slippery identities vacillate. "From the start, it is Macrina's physical pain and the power manifested in her conversion of pain into joy that draws Gregory's attention."[61]

Similarly, in Jerome's grief for Paula, he describes the extremity of her painful ascetic commitments. Yet her asceticism and her forgoing of former marriage and family do not signal an abstinence from desire itself: "face furrowed by grief, body practically a corpse, her mortal flesh betrays an immense desire."[62] Paula's incessant weeping is too much for Jerome, who warns her to "spare her eyes."[63] Yet Paula (or rather Jerome as author) asserts her agency, insisting on her desire for Christ and the disfigurations and mortifications that convey that urgent desire. "Resisting Jerome," as Jerome resists himself in his text, disfiguring his own authorial authority, "Paula claims her ascetic practice as her own. Seeming to swap beauty for ugliness and pleasure for pain, she is making herself over as the bride of Christ."[64]

Considering more contemporary "makeovers," Burrus ponders the feminist dilemmas surrounding the subjection of women's bodies through sexual objectification: is cosmetic makeup, for instance, permissible for the feminist? Burrus writes, "I used to think being a real woman (and a good feminist) meant being 'natural'—at all costs resisting being made a 'sex object.'" But now she wonders, "Is it possible for me to be *sexual at all* without flirting dangerously with the terms of my own objectification—playing at the 'feminine' so as to make myself 'femme' so as to become *someone other* than either a 'man' or his desired 'object'?"[65] Indeed, while Heyward and Harrison point to cosmetics as an example of women's ambivalence toward their own bodies that is symptomatic of the male-male culture of sadomasochism,[66] Burrus describes the savvy application of this same tool now as a means by which to come out of that masculinist dyad.

---

[60] Ibid., 76.
[61] Ibid., 72.
[62] Ibid., 64.
[63] Ibid., 63.
[64] Ibid., 64.
[65] Ibid., 88.
[66] Harrison and Heyward write that "a more female embodiment of sadomasochism originates not in our desire to control others but in an ambivalence toward our bodies" ("Pain and Pleasure," 158). They list cosmetics and eating disorders particularly.

In her *Sex Lives of Saints*, cosmetics can serve as an analogy for Burrus's overall presentation of ascetic masochism: both may seem against the grain of feminism, but the transgressive employment of either may instead work against the grain of the oppressions feminists (and others) wish to counter. The asceticism of the saints may too easily be read as repression, and particularly sexual repression, because the reader is expecting victims of a hierarchal, sexist religion. But the hagiographical portrayal of active passion in these saints betrays such a reading. Burrus traces a "powerful crosscurrent of asceticized eroticism," a "countererotics," challenging the heterosexist regime that would develop as part of Christian hegemony, seeing "within Christianity a distinctive *ars erotica* that does not so much predate as effectively resist and evade the *scientia sexualis* that likewise emerges (derivatively) in late antiquity and eventually culminates in the production of the modern, western regime of 'sexuality'."[67]

Elsewhere, Burrus further demonstrates the powerful fluidity of ascetic identity (and the further transgression of orthodox sexuality) through a "queer reading" of Gregory of Nyssa. "By destabilizing the ontological hierarchy inscribed by active and passive sexual roles, Gregory also queers the mimetic economy of pederasty, in which a beloved 'son' is erotically reproduced as the perfect image of a mature, paternalized lover." Gregory's masochism is too full of willful desire to conform as a perfect reproduction of the pederastic economy: his own agency, in choosing so ardently his submission, betrays that same submission. "Feminized as a soul 'wounded by the arrow of love,' Gregory is an ardent Divinity's receptive beloved, playing the 'Bottom' almost (but not quite) as a Platonist would expect—*because playing it too well*."[68] Not surprisingly then, Burrus also explains how Gregory allows himself to also enact the "top." He plays the switch, "oscillating between discipleship and domination."[69] Burrus concludes, "Beaten, wounded, stripped—there is no limit to what can be suffered in love, the Cappadocian suggests. Gregory of Nyssa is a queer Father not because he is purified of passion but rather because he is purely passionate, nothing more (or less) than the abysmal creature of divine desire."[70] The way in which the bottom gets so good at being a bottom so as to slip into more of a top, thus pulling down the transcendence of the top (or the God), is here reminiscent of Althaus-Reid's depiction of how the queer theologian beckons God out of the closet through "perversion."

The saints' lives engage the terms of their own subjection with agency *on their own terms*. Their ascetic resistance to the norms of marital sexual

---

[67] In so doing, Burrus offers her own volume to Foucault's unfinished *History of Sexuality*. See the introduction to her *Sex Lives of Saints*.

[68] Virginia Burrus, "Queer Father: Gregory of Nyssa and the Subversion of Identity," in *Queer Theology: Rethinking the Western Body*, ed. Gerard Loughlin. Malden, MA: Blackwell, 2007, 147–162, these quotes 158. See also Burrus's earlier *Begotten Not Made: Conceiving Manhood in Late Antiquity*.

[69] Burrus, "Queer Father," 158.

[70] Ibid., 159.

regulation persistently holds open the increasingly fortified enclosure of desire's control. The cloister opens the enclosure.[71] "There is a sense of being slammed, repeatedly, into the wall of oneself," against the limits of the scripted self, not in repeated victimization but in steady resistance to the terms of that victimization.

Other scholars of late antiquity, though not framing their inquiries in terms of masochism, have also considered the agency that inheres in some forms of passivity and vulnerability. Averil Cameron reads an expression of desire in early Christian abstinence. She writes that "paradoxically, in the context of the discourse of abstinence, the true knowledge at which the signs pointed was defined in terms of desire."[72] The language of desire intimates self-expression at work in the sacrifices of deprivation. Carlin Barton's study of martyrdom in Roman culture again emphasizes agency. Barton explains that "in Roman (as in early Christian) sacrifice the victim was conspicuously central and active. The more actively voluntary, the more effective the sacrifice."[73] It was essential to this sacrificial economy that the martyr desire her own sacrifice. "The Roman physics of sacrifice was more ambiguous than our notions of sacrifice allow because depriving oneself was a commonly understood way of increasing one's own vitality."[74] Willful desire offered the means by which a victim could transgress her own limitations and politically rewrite the limiting script of the criminal: "The laughing, joyous submission to the rigamarole of the arena, the tranquil accommodation to brutality, and the apology that publicized their motivations were meant to forestall the perception of them as mere *ludibria* [criminals], ridiculous, weak, and humiliated."[75] Redemptive self-sacrifice in the Roman arena was a means by which the victim claimed power for herself, restoring her honor, and even realizing consecrated or divine status.[76] Again, expression of desire for the sacrifice was essential to redemption.

---

[71] Similarly, at least in my reading, Burrus writes that "asceticism and queerness are, arguably, heavily overlapped terms: both designate practices that center on *resistance* to normative discourses on sex and sexuality" ("Queer Father," 147).

[72] Averil Cameron, *Christianity and the Rhetoric of Empire: The Development of Christian Discourse.* Berkeley: University of California, 1991, 228.

[73] Carlin A. Barton, "Savage Miracles: The Redemption of Lost Honor in Roman Society and the Sacrament of the Gladiator and the Martyr." *Representations* 45 (1994): 41–71, this quotation 53.

[74] Ibid. Barton continues by footnote: "This is an assumption that is also implied in modern Christian notions of sacrifice but which is difficult to articulate because, in Christian thought, all sacredness derives from the godhead" (68).

[75] Ibid., 57. Gender inequality was involved in that females had less chance of finding an apologist ("Savage Miracles," 58).

[76] Ibid., 53. This self-realization involved divining, in keeping with sacrifice as "sacralizing." Also, Barton points out that from a contemporary perspective there is a tendency to see the proud Roman in opposition to the humble Christian: "Caesar and Christ are, for us, the archetypical heroes of two antithetical cosmologies" (59), but this means "we fail to see the degree to which the proud Roman *animus* was already turned against itself, nor how deeply in love with victory and glory was the humble Christian" (60).

As Barton describes Roman perception of willfulness, "the sensation of volition was one of energy and enhanced existence, an experience often described by the Romans in terms of growth and expansion . . . The end of volition was self-realization, an expansion of the self, and required the meeting and overcoming of opposition, the transgression of boundaries."[77] A narrative of volitional or desired self-sacrifice could thus function as self-expansion through a reclaiming of power in the face of victimization.

The Suffering Self

Historian Judith Perkins analyzes the "discursive climate" of the early Roman Empire and determines that "from a number of different locations, narratives were projecting a particular representation of the human self as a body liable to pain and suffering."[78] Christians, and others, chose to present themselves under a *pained* identity. In addition to her study of this discursive production, Perkins stresses the emerging Christian empire's use of the rhetoric of pain and suffering.

The image of the "suffering self," Perkins claims, effectively "challenged another, prevailing, more traditional Greco-Roman image of the self as a soul/mind controlling the body."[79] Overall, this construction of the self offered a rivaling contrast to the body and mind dichotomy of Stoic philosophy. Thus, though Heyward and Harrison see a "dualistic anthropology" serving as the framework undergirding Christian sadomasochism, in that spiritual pleasure is achieved at the expense of the body,[80] Perkins suggests that the Christian embrace of pain was actually a *challenge* to that dualism (it was a challenge without yet being a complete antithesis).[81]

Elizabeth Clark's writing on renunciation further complicates Heyward and Harrison's claims. Clark writes that "the standard textbook approach to asceticism that dualistically pits soul against body is in urgent need of nuance, for early Christian ascetics usually claimed that soul and body were tightly connected, that the actions and movements of one had a direct effect upon

---

[77] Ibid., 54–55.
[78] Judith Perkins, *The Suffering Self: Pain and Narrative Representation in the Early Christian Era.* London: Routledge, 1995, 3.
[79] Ibid., 3.
[80] Harrison and Heyward, "Pain and Pleasure," 151.
[81] In addition, Averil Cameron also writes that "the sign system of early Christianity did not, surprisingly perhaps, form itself around eating (as in the Last Supper) or death (as in the Crucifixion) but . . . around the body itself." Thus, accounts of martyrdom and asceticism, while masochistic in their approach to the body, were not separated or split off from the body. Masochism seated desire *in the body* in a unique way. See Cameron, *Christianity and the Rhetoric of Empire: The Development of Christian Discourse.* Berkeley: University of California, 1991, 228.

the other." While Heyward and Harrison may rightly note the connection of bodily pain with spiritual pleasure, Clark stresses "a certain optimism" at play in asceticism that Heyward and Harrison miss. "Despite the obvious ways in which asceticism can appear as a pessimistic movement in its alleged flight from 'the world'," Clark writes that it can also work to "cultivate extraordinary forms of human existence."[82]

Perkins stresses that the construction of the self as a subject of pain was not only a Christian project. As Perkins emphasizes, "Christianity found a subject for itself already being prepared in the Greco-Roman world of the early empire."[83] The depiction of the "sufferer" was popular not only in religious circles,[84] but was particularly evident in medical discourse, and apparent even in children's play. For example, as Perkins recounts, "Theodoret describes a group of young girls in fourth-century Syria playing a game; some girls dressed in rags as monks while others acted as sufferers seeking exorcism. In other words, one group played at being poor and the other at being possessed."[85] It is in the midst of such a social milieu that "Christian texts of the late first and second centuries almost without exception assiduously project the message that to be a Christian was to suffer and die,"[86] such that "if Christianity was known at all, it was known for its adherents' attitude toward death and suffering."[87]

The trope of "suffering" could serve to demarcate "orthodox" subjectivity from other Christian subjectivities, as is clear in Irenaeus's writing "against the heretics." Irenaeus teaches that "all those on whom the Spirit of God should rest . . . should suffer persecution and be stoned and slain."[88] Here martyrdom marks orthodoxy. Constructing the Christian community as a community of sufferers, Irenaeus stresses that God sends forth through time a multitude of martyrs.[89] He presents this theme in the context of his letter against other Christians he considered to be heretical, particularly those with Gnostic views less focused on the body. And "though Irenaeus surely . . . exaggerates the infrequency of martyrdom among the 'heretics'," Elaine Pagels explains that these other Christians do seem to have experienced less frequent martyrdom.[90] For Irenaeus, intensity of suffering epitomized in martyrdom proves one's Christian status.

---

[82] See Elizabeth A. Clark, *Reading Renunciation: Asceticism and Scripture in Early Christianity*. Princeton, NJ: Princeton University Press, 1999, 17.
[83] Perkins, *Suffering Self*, 142.
[84] See Clark, *Reading Renunciation*, and Daniel Boyarin, *Carnal Israel: Reading Sex in Talmudic Culture*. Berkeley: University of California Press, 1995.
[85] Perkins, *Suffering Self*, 12, on Theodoret's *Historia Religiosa*, *Patrologia Graeca* 1384.
[86] Ibid., 24.
[87] Ibid., 20.
[88] Irenaeus, *Against Heresies* 2.22, as quoted in Perkins, *Suffering Self*, 24.
[89] Irenaeus, *Against Heresies*, 4.33.9.
[90] Elaine Pagels, "Gnostic and Orthodox Views of Christ's Passion: Paradigms for the Christian's Response to Persecution?," in *Rediscovery of Gnosticism*, vol. 1, ed. Bentley Layton. Ithaca, NY: Snow Lion Publications, 2002, 271.

The presentation of Christians as sufferers was also a way of attracting converts. Perkins finds that "Christian narratives . . . testify to a genuine confidence in the efficacy of persecution in attracting members with their repeated representation of their group as a sect of sufferers."[91] Likewise Tertullian testified, "We multiply whenever we are mown down by you: the blood of Christians is seed."[92]

Perkins acknowledges that when viewed with a contemporary lens early Christian texts can seem problematically fixated on death, with "an inordinate fixation on bodily pain and suffering,"[93] and that the tendency can thus be to detect "the pathology of aberrant individuals" in these texts. Yet Perkins repudiates such a focus on individual pathology and cautions that "such a reading prevents the recognition that their emphasis on pain and suffering reflects a widespread cultural concern, which during the period was using representations of bodily pain and suffering to construct a new subjectivity of the human person."[94] Again, there is something more than neurosis in early Christian portrayals of suffering: a new and subversive subjectivity is at stake.

Perkins further notes that the shift away from self-mastery was ceding to the divine—even in non-Christian texts like that of Aelius Aristides. Perkins sees a relocation of the self through "relinquishing control and regulation to the divine."[95] She compares the Stoic *Meditations* of Marcus Aurelius to two texts representing the loss of self-control (but *not* of self): Ignatius of Antioch and Aelius Aristides. She finds the *Meditations*, with its Stoic message of self-control, to be "the least joyful of the three."[96] Perhaps this joy serves as an example of what MacKendrick calls "subject-breaking joy"[97] found in "m-powerment" and "the pleasure and power of pain and restraint."[98] Masochistic agency, though expressive of the self, remains distinct from self-control, which is perhaps why this form of subjectivity does not register on Heyward and Harrison's radar, despite their commitment to relational subjectivities. Agency could now be attained by giving over control rather than striving to maintain it—but still it was *agency* that was attained through this sacrificial economy. As MacKendrick observes, "Self-mastery can itself be transcended in a self-defiance that overcomes the self in the discipline of restraint and the delight of pain."[99]

---

[91] Perkins, *Suffering Self*, 35.
[92] Tertullian, *Apologia* 50, as in Perkins, *Suffering Self*, 35.
[93] Perkins, *Suffering Self*, 173.
[94] Ibid., cf. 192.
[95] Ibid., 199.
[96] Ibid.
[97] MacKendrick, *Counterpleasures*, 158.
[98] Ibid., 101.
[99] Ibid., 108.

Perkins further suggests that the "representational coup"[100] of the self as sufferer sought to articulate a site of revelation and transcendence. Perkins shows that like the non-Christian Aristides (again demonstrating that "the suffering self" was not limited to Christianity), Ignatius "projected the suffering body as the meeting place of human and divine."[101] This meeting place also became the site of subjectivity: "In Ignatius," Perkins determines, "the 'self' did not really come into being until it suffered; suffering was not simply something that happened to a person. Rather, it was the means of achieving real selfhood."[102]

The prevalence of the representation of "the Christian as sufferer"[103] might be more easily understandable if it came from a time during which Christians were undergoing extensive persecution. But instead, as Perkins demonstrates, Christians had established their reputation as sufferers before "any concentrated, general persecution of Christianity."[104] Indeed, as Heyward and Harrison say, "To be Christian was to accept or even to seek pain."[105] But this was not only the negative phenomenon that they suspect. In conjunction with the wider culture, Christianity was discursively presented in this way and indeed was attractive and alluring because of this presentation.

As Perkins writes, "After all, the one thing everyone knows about Christianity is that it centers on suffering in the exemplar of the crucified Christ." But Perkins stresses that "the acceptance of Christian representation as obvious has concealed its effect and the workings-out of its achievement."[106] Perkins urges contemporary readers to look beyond what now seems obvious in Christianity and to ponder "why groups of Christians in the Greco-Roman world chose to foreground their own suffering in their early texts and why they picked the suffering in their founder's life to emulate."[107]

To their credit Harrison and Heyward state that within the scope of their article they can only speculate about how and why Christians came to accept pain as "a source of spiritual satisfaction."[108] They suggest the influences of morality: "Without pain, pleasure was immoral; whereas by pain, with pain, and through pain, pleasure became a happy consequence of the Christian pilgrimage."[109] Perkins's study, as well as the work of most of the others surveyed in this chapter, came after Harrison and Heyward in this article, shedding

---

[100] Perkins, *Suffering Self*, 201. In agreement with the type of work Burrus and MacKendrick have done, Perkins writes on the same page that "quite clearly the writers of hagiography would have agreed with contemporary literary theorists on the important consequences in actual human lives of narrative representation."
[101] Ibid., 189.
[102] Ibid., 190.
[103] Ibid., 16.
[104] Ibid., 23.
[105] Harrison and Heyward, 152.
[106] Perkins, *Suffering Self*, 13.
[107] Ibid.
[108] Harrison and Heyward, 153.
[109] Ibid.

new light on the cultures in which Christian connections between pain and subjectivity formed.

In light of this newer scholarship, we can now supplement feminist theological claims about the place of death and suffering in early Christianity. We know that later atonement theologies will be problematic, and we know that early Christian rhetoric around martyrdom and asceticism raises alarms for contemporary feminists. But rather than repudiating these stages of Christian doctrine, or allowing martyrdom and renunciation only as necessary realities in juxtaposition and resistance to empire, we can recognize the complicated cultural productions in which these Christian persons may have taken pride, and in which they may have found themselves. While this production would not have been free of tensions with imperial power, neither was it likely to have been wholly a resistance strategy against it, at least in part because, as Perkins shows, the strategy was such a wide cultural phenomenon, and also at least in part because, as I will discuss later, the same discursive strategy was later used to bolster Christian imperial power.

Rita Brock and Rebecca Parker explain in their book *Saving Paradise* that Christian martyrdom could make a statement of resistance to empire, a desire to manifest "paradise to earth," not through death but by refusing to live by the empire's standards.[110] But the cultural production of the self as sufferer in late antiquity points to the possibility that for some Christian martyrs their persecution itself may have been a sort of paradise, in the realization of themselves as persons—that is, as persons in pain. This recognition does not render Brock and Parker's claim invalid, but it does trouble their feminist efforts to present Christianity as a life-loving, rather than death-affirming, movement. For some early Christians (and perhaps some later ones as well) the affirmation of pain and suffering may have merged with an affirmation of vivacity. For instance, Perkins tells us that "Ignatius was the first writer to use the word *pathos* (suffering) to describe Christ's death, and its choice underlines his focus. Christ's suffering was his essential message, and Christians' acceptance of suffering was the sign of their commitment to his message."[111]

Perkins ultimately demonstrates that through this rhetorical strategy—in the claim that "to be Christian was to accept or even to seek pain"—a creative and successful project of constructing social status was underway. This strategy was integral to the way in which specific forms of Christianity eventually came to power in the empire. Thus, the discourse of suffering became a means of political power, and "the triumph of Christianity was, in part at least, a triumph of a particular representation of the self."[112] While contemporary feminism is needfully concerned with ways in which the powerful deploy rhetoric

---

[110] Rita N. Brock and Rebecca Ann Parker, *Saving Paradise: How Christianity Traded Love of this World for Crucifixion and Empire.* Boston: Beacon, 2008, 56–83.
[111] Perkins, *Suffering Self*, 189.
[112] Ibid., 11.

of suffering in order to *disempower* their subjects, it is notable that in nascent Christianity a disorganized and originally disempowered group employed this rhetoric in order to lift itself to power. There was creativity and discursive power in suffering subjectivity.

However, just as the production of "the suffering self" in early Christian discourse at first functioned to produce an alternative subjectivity, this discursive identity also made way for ecclesial control of the suffering masses, control that threatened to undercut subversive potential, and perhaps mostly succeeded in doing so. Perkins asks, "Whose power was in [the] new knowledge of the self as sufferer?" and answers, "Christianity's power." She explains that "the effects of this new knowledge of sufferers can be seen in the institutionalization of the Christian church. From its earliest periods, Christianity's growth correlated with the constitution of a category of sufferers, in particular, with the poor and the sick."[113] While the churches' affiliation with the poor may seem unremarkable from contemporary standpoint, historian Peter Brown emphasizes that the poor were "a newly created constituency."[114] Perkins summarizes that "the bishops' authority thus rested on their connection with a category whose visibility in the Roman cities derived from the perception of the subjectivity of 'the sufferer'."[115] For example, Perkins notes Ignatius's emphasis on ecclesial control as he contemplates his own martyrdom: "A main focus of Ignatius' *Letters* was to urge the obedience of each Christian community to the church structure" with "his death, in fact, as the emblem of his commitment to the structural integrity of the community."[116] Perkins finds that "there is very nearly a correlation between submission to suffering and submission to the bishop."[117] This was the case already in the pre-imperial time of Ignatius, and, as Brown has shown, grew only stronger once Christianity began to merge with imperial power.

Brown traces the church's rise to power in his study of fourth-century bishops as "lovers of the poor." He demonstrates that growing ecclesial power relied upon the *economic* relevance of suffering subjectivity. The ecclesial leaders presented themselves to the emperor as better able to care for the masses

---

[113] Ibid., *Suffering Self*, 8. Susanna Elm writes that "asceticism began as a method for men and women to transcend, as virgins of God, the limitations of humanity in relation to the divine. It slowly changed into a way for men as men and women as women to symbolize the power of the Church to surpass human weakness" (*Virgins of God: The Making of Asceticism in Late Antiquity*. Oxford: Clarendon, 1994, 384, as in Clark, *Renunciation*, 16.)

[114] Brown, *Power and Persuasion*, 78.

[115] Perkins, *Suffering Self*, 10. Perkins summarizes that "in the representational calculus of hagiography, suffering was the new riches. The body wasted by suffering had become more desirable than one covered in jewels" (211, cf. 213). This again strikes an interesting contrast with Rita Brock and Rebecca Parker's study in *Saving Paradise*, where they demonstrate that Christian art did not become fixated on a suffering Christ on the cross until much later, around the time of the Crusades. In the earlier church the image of a cross covered with jewels was much more common.

[116] Perkins, *Suffering Self*, 191.

[117] Ibid.

than the traditional system of urban patronage. Christian leaders "consistently presented their claims to prominence" by emphasizing their "particular concern" for "a category of persons that had no place in the traditional model of urban community,"[118] that is, the poor. The churches gained power as "they claimed to speak for the populations of troubled cities at a time of mounting crisis."[119] As Rebecca Lyman describes them, the bishops became "architects of both social and doctrinal unity" as "the pivot between government and those who were largely unseen in Late Roman society: the poor and women."[120] Eventually the "poor" were concretely transcribed through enrollment on the official lists of their particular local bishop. They could not then move to another city and expect care. They needed the bishop's signature even to beg.[121] Thus, as Brown concludes, through control of the newly articulated "poor," "the Christian bishop and his clergy claimed an ever-increasing share in the exercise of the authority in the city."[122] Perkins summarizes that "Christianity formed around this subjectivity of the sufferer, not only conceptually, but also actively—collecting funds, acquiring power, administering hospitals and poorhouses to succor various categories of sufferers."[123]

As the church began to use the rhetoric of suffering as its tool for domination of others, the strategy of the "suffering self" furthered the church's power. Through the "suffering" of (the bishops of) Christ, seen in their Christ-like condescension to care for the poor, freedom from suffering for the masses could be hypothetically achieved (and simultaneously maintained). This resonates with Althaus-Reid's critique of power-to-power kenotic contortions, where no power is really shared under the name of *kenosis*. The bishops play at self-giving and simultaneously achieve power over "the poor"—now defined externally rather than through a self-empowering title. It is also during this time, as I discussed in Chapter 1, that Christ is theorized as one who plays at suffering. Christ becomes an increasingly remote figure whose human suffering was never out of control. It is as though with imperial power Stoicism merges with the alternate discursive strategy of the suffering self. Suffering is not lack of control—rather charitable "suffering" from on high is control. Christ's suffering becomes symbolic, like the "suffering" of the bishops in stooping to care for the poor. How condescension hurts! How Christ could take it like a man!

In taking suffering from Christ, and in the shift from suffering as resistance to "suffering" as ecclesial control, theologians mute the "bottom's" agency

---

[118] Brown, 91.
[119] Ibid., 78.
[120] Rebecca Lyman, *Christology and Cosmology: Models of Divine Activity in Origen, Eusebius, and Athanasius*. New York: Oxford University Press, 1993, 125.
[121] Brown, 98.
[122] Brown, 77.
[123] Perkins, *Suffering Self*, 202.

in masochism. The top appropriates the agency of the masochist, and the masochistic strategy is effectively deflated. The good Christian should now surrender her agency to Christ's (church). Here perhaps is the strand of theology against which Harrison and Heyward's claims are most appropriately leveled: a powerful ecclesial patriarchy that feigns masochism itself and meanwhile manages to prescribe it.

Considering this disempowering consequence of imperial christology, it is particularly problematic that Coakley, in her construction of *kenosis*, advocates a christology in which only the human nature of Christ suffers while the divine nature remains truly impassible. The historical collusion of this sort of christology with imperial control signals that it may be a problematic fit for the human "power-in-vulnerability" that Coakley wishes to construct for feminism.

Contemporary theologians rightly continue to decry the ways in which the elements of christology are misused to violently subjugate peoples. Renunciation, sacrifice, and pain are far from benign elements in the chemistry of christology, but feminist theologians particularly need not therefore forego the use of these elements altogether. As a strategy that can be deployed between the sheets of power difference, feminism may recognize the creative power in masochism. But as Burrus writes, "modern discussions of Christian asceticism remain unavoidably haunted by the specter of a widely discredited 'masochism' (associations both typically dismissive and difficult simply to dismiss) . . ."[124] Should *kenosis* also be dismissed from feminist theology because of its potentially masochistic character, the strategy of resistance possible in *kenosis* will be overlooked, along with the lived experience of women who have exercised this strategy. The strength of *kenosis* cannot be appreciated fully without understanding something of the masochistic power of the saints and martyrs. Rather than only or necessarily a means by which Christianity's powerful reinforce oppression, masochistic strategy is also in the hands of those on the bottom of Christian hierarchies, directed by their own agency toward creative potential. Constructive masochism honors a realm of lived experience that cannot simply be consigned to the neurotic, even if it transcends normality.

Virginia Burrus and Stephen Moore write in their commentary on the *Song of Songs* of "the potential, indeed the propensity, of erotic fantasy not merely to resemble but also dissemble, and thereby reassemble, reality, engaging in a transgressive mimicry rather than a compliant mimesis."[125] They note that "the line between the female masochist and the battered woman may continue to blur troublingly" even *necessarily* so, "because s/m is characterized by a subtle play of resemblance and dissimilarity" that "lends it much of its subversive

---

[124] Burrus, *Sex Lives*, 9.

[125] Virginia Burrus and Stephen D. Moore, "Unsafe Sex: Feminism, Pornography, and the Song of Songs." *Biblical Interpretation* 11 (2003): 48. They footnote Linda Hart's term "dissonant displacements" (Hart, *Between the Body and the Flesh*, 86).

potential."¹²⁶ Mimicry and mimesis may vary vastly in significance but only slightly in kind.

MacKendrick insists upon pleasure as a characteristic distinguishing "m-powerment"¹²⁷ from abuse, writing that "pleasurable restraint, restraint that *provokes* the power of joyous resistance, cannot be identical with the power that seeks to *forestall* resistance. Starting in pleasure, masochism is wholly unlike oppression."¹²⁸ It may be wholly unlike, yet not wholly distinguishable. Similarly, Kathleen Sands, in her examination of the use of *eros* as a theme in feminist theology, says of lesbian S/M: "Obviously, the power of such scenarios has something to do with a social world in which women are forcibly humiliated around sex. But for a woman to *use* these feelings, in a deliberate, bounded and often humorous way, for the sake of her own pleasure, is to defy the intent of that socialization and also perhaps to remove the sting from the humiliation itself."¹²⁹

As discussed earlier, in the growing power of the church, the same rhetoric of suffering that had been a resistance strategy aimed to forestall resistance. And yet, persons in the Christian empire would still sometimes practice masochism as an exercise of agency, subverting the rhetoric aimed against them. As makeup can mark one woman's constraints within patriarchy while marking another woman's restraint against it, distinguishing between oppression and empowered acts of integrity—realities that can occur together—is difficult, perhaps necessarily so. There are no clean-cut separations here, which is part of what makes masochistic strategies potentially effective.

MacKendrick's emphasis on agency helps to reframe the paradigm of domination so problematic in Heyward and Harrison's analysis. Contemplating the divine image portrayed by sadomasochistic Christian theology, they write, "In this erotic fantasy, the father is turned on by his absolute power over another."¹³⁰ However, in contrast, if the masochist or "bottom" (construed in Heyward and Harrison's analysis as the human) is actively aroused and empowered, the strength of her own masochistic desire compromises both the "absolute power" of the top ("Father") as well as the passivity of the bottom's experience of love. Burrus and Moore write that "the patriarchal sexual order is, arguably, already disrupted when a woman constructs herself

---

[126] Burrus and Moore, 48–49. Burrus also writes that just as ascetic disruption of subjectivity should not be "conflated" with similar attempts in contemporary S/M, neither should either of these be "*conflated* with oppressive acts of violence designed to 'break' the psyche" (*Sex Lives*, 9). Burrus writes that "erotic 'self-shattering' differs dramatically from the 'unmaking' of the self effected by techniques of torture that *intensify*—rather than *disrupt*—the isolation of the subject" (*Sex Lives*, 14).
[127] MacKendrick, *Counterpleasures*, chapter 6.
[128] Ibid., 107.
[129] Kathleen Sands, "Uses of the Thea(o)logian: Sex and Theodicy in Religious Feminism," 31.
[130] MacKendrick, 156.

as an actively desiring subject . . ."¹³¹ For the masochist, empowerment turns on desire and agency.

Heyward and Harrison analyze sadomasochism as a lack of health, a sign that a person is still trapped in patriarchal options for selfhood, "'turned on' by a sense of being *either* self-possessed *or* belonging to another."¹³² For them S/M implies the dualism of autonomous selves in an intensely polarized bind: "In the context of this dualistic eroticism, *for a woman to feel that she belongs both to herself and to another is rare*. To do so involves breaking the tension generated by the split between oneself and other."¹³³ They decry "the association of eroticism with the split between self and other that is endemic to the patriarchal view of reality,"¹³⁴ and emphasize the warped situation in which we come to feel pleasure in the very splits that cause us pain, in "our alienation from one another, as people who have difficulty *feeling* power by *sharing* it."¹³⁵

Yet, considering the agency of the masochist, is not the masochist precisely *sharing* power, in a perverse form of power that reworks that power's use? His is not the pleasure of mutual or reciprocal power. Rather than a dance of corresponding power, he engages himself in a "delicate collusion" of power difference. As Burrus and Moore write, "s/m *marks the difference* between an intricate transaction, on the one hand, in which the power and overpowering of resistance delicately collude, each deriving its pleasure from the other; and a sheerly oppositional imposition of the will, on the other hand, that is at once repressive and oppressive."¹³⁶ In the alchemy of this power difference, the masochistic strategy can be empowering ("m-powering"). MacKendrick describes the potency of self-transgression: "Restraint is, in fact, a manipulation of the power of desire, a manipulation that neither denies nor undoes that power, but maximizes it to maximize the body's improbable if unlasting triumph against its subjection—its subjectivity . . ."¹³⁷ In contrast to the atomistic dyad Heyward and Harrison imagine in S/M, MacKendrick sees instead a momentary freedom from such constraints: "we are beyond the freedom of autonomous subjects (even gods); we are abandoned to the infinite generosity that cuts across our own limits, and with infinite generosity we abandon those limits."¹³⁸

---

[131] Burrus and Moore, "Unsafe Sex," 48.
[132] Harrison and Heyward, "Pain and Pleasure," 162.
[133] Ibid.
[134] Ibid.
[135] Ibid., 162–163. Harrison and Heyward work toward "relationships in which dependence and autonomy are realized simultaneously through the erotic" (165). Here they critique the idea of a balance between self and other in Jessica Benjamin. Benjamin's work, however, has grown more complex than their summary indicates. See Benjamin's *Shadow of the Other: Intersubjectivity and Gender in Psychoanalysis*. London: Routledge, 1998.
[136] Burrus and Moore, "Unsafe Sex," 49, intentionally resonating with MacKendrick,129.
[137] MacKendrick, *Counterpleasures*, 107, cf. 106, 109, 120.
[138] Ibid., 160.

In MacKendrick's self-abandon it would seem that the goals of Heyward and Harrison are (transgressively) met.[139] Here power is felt through excessive extension of power and the lover experiences herself as beyond autonomy, more than a subjected self, while also in a volitional relationship of dependence, as she "needs an other: reader, god, top, bottom."[140]

Opening a space within feminist theological discourse for the use of masochism without weakening feminism's protest against abuse remains a delicate challenge. Yet where it considers masochism to be simply "off limits" to its field, feminist theology cuts itself off from the creative uses of willed and pained self-abandon, and thus ignores a form of resistance that may in fact *strengthen* feminism's protest of abuse. Though masochism may seem a subversion of feminism, feminists may deftly employ it in their own acts of strategic subversion, or at least in the experience of their own pleasure: a pleasure that is itself a subversion.[141]

---

[139] MacKendrick uses the term "abandon" to describe a dynamic of intensely pleasing deferral. She refers specifically to the philosophical sense of God after Nietzsche (resonating therefore with Vattimo's reading of *kenosis* after Nietzsche, and Frascati-Lochhead's reading of Vattimo, as in Chapter 2); cf. MacKendrick's use of "sacrificial expenditure" (*Counterpleasures*, 120) and Burrus, *Sex Lives*, 18.

[140] MacKendrick, *Counterpleasures*, 156, cf. 158 and 107.

[141] On female pleasure as morally relevant, see Mary Pellauer, "The Moral Significance of the Female Orgasm," in *Sexuality and the Sacred: Sources for Theological Reflection*, eds. James B. Nelson and Sandra P. Longfellow. Louisville, KY: Westminster/John Knox Press, 1994, 149–168.

Chapter 5

Power for Resistance: Abuse and Self-Giving Care

Christianity has been a primary—in many women's lives the primary—force in shaping our acceptance of abuse. The central image of Christ on the cross as the savior of the world communicates the message that suffering is redemptive. If the best person who ever lived gave his life for others, then, to be of value we should likewise sacrifice ourselves. Any sense that we have a right to care for our own needs is in conflict with being a faithful follower of Jesus. Our suffering for others will save the world.

–Joanne Carlson Browne and Rebecca Parker[1]

Theologians Rita Brock and Rebecca Parker have collaboratively and powerfully written about the intimate entanglement of theologies of redemptive suffering and their own experiences of abuse.[2] For example, Rebecca records the experience of her friend Pat, who like Rebecca is a United Methodist minister. Pat tells Rebecca about the women who have come to her church for help: "Almost every woman who's come here for refuge has gone back to her violent husband or boyfriend. She thinks it's her religious duty." Pat always counsels otherwise.[3]

One day Rebecca receives a knock on her own office door. "I haven't talked to anyone about this for a while," Lucia begins. Indeed, it had been two decades: "I went to my priest twenty years ago. I've been trying to follow his advice. The priest said I should rejoice in my sufferings because they bring me closer to Jesus . . . He said, 'If you love Jesus, accept the beatings and bear them gladly, as Jesus bore the cross.'" Rebecca could see in Lucia's eyes that this strong woman already knew that such a theology was faulty. With Rebecca's

---

[1] Brown and Parker, 2, "For God So Loved the World?", *Christianity, Patriarchy, and Abuse: A Feminist Critique*, eds. Joanne Carlson Brown and Carole R. Bohn. Cleveland, OH: Pilgrim Press, 1989, 1–30.
[2] Rita N. Brock and Rebecca Ann Parker, *Proverbs of Ashes: Violence, Redemptive Suffering, and the Search for What Saves Us*. Boston: Beacon Press, 2001.
[3] Ibid., 17.

affirmation of Lucia's own intuition, Lucia was strengthened in her plan to separate herself and her children from abuse.[4]

Though Rebecca and Pat respond in empowering ways to the abused persons who come to them, the Christian clergy's overall record in responding to abuse has been less positive.[5] Several studies emerging from the feminist movement in the early 1980s demonstrate that clergy have far too often failed to stand in solidarity with abused persons, and have instead furthered their suffering, often counseling them to bear their abuse with a "Christ-like" humility. From her experience of working with abused women, Marie Fortune stresses that many persons are therefore hesitant to come to clergy to report abuse, fearing "the disbelief, judgment, and ostracism that so often characterizes church officials' responses."[6] Mildred Pagelow's research shows that when abused women turn to clergy, the response they receive from them is then either unhelpful or harmful: "the primary responses of the clergy to these women were to (1) tell them to do their duty, forgive and forget; (2) avoid involvement and make a referral; and (3) give useless advice, sometimes based on religious doctrine instead of the needs of the women."[7]

Thirty years later, and thanks to the second-wave feminist movement, more clergy are now receiving training about abuse, and there are some indications that more ministers are now responding like Rebecca and Pat. For instance, Nancy Nason-Clark's 1999 study of specifically evangelical churches finds, in contrast to past studies, "no evidence that pastors sent physically battered

---

[4] Ibid., 21.
[5] See Monica Coleman, *The Dinah Project: A Handbook for Congregational Response to Sexual Violence*. Cleveland, OH: Pilgrim Press, 2004; and Pamela Cooper-White, *The Cry of Tamar: Violence Against Women and the Church's Response*. Minneapolis: Fortress Press, 1995. Other resources on church response to abuse include Toinette M. Eugene and James Newton Poling, *Balm for Gilead: Pastoral Advocacy for African American Families Experiencing Abuse*. Nashville, TN: Abingdon Press, 1998; Al Miles, *Domestic Violence: What Every Pastor Needs to Know*, 2nd edition. Minneapolis: Fortress Press, 2011; Nancy Nason Clark, *The Battered Wife: How Christians Confront Family Violence*. Louisville, KY: WJKP, 1997; J. M. Alsdurf, "Wife Abuse and the Church: The Response of Pastors," *Response to the Victimization of Women and Children* 8.1 (1985): 9–11; Anne Horton and Judith Williamson, eds. *Abuse and Religion: When Praying Isn't Enough*. New York: D.C. Heath and Company, 1988; and the studies by John M. Johnson in *Violence against Woman and Children: A Christian Theological Sourcebook*, eds. Carol J. Adams and Marie M. Fortune. New York: Continuum, 1998, 413–427.
[6] John M. Johnson, "Church Response to Domestic Violence," in *Violence against Women and Children: A Christian Theological Sourcebook*, eds. Carol J. Adams and Marie M. Fortune. New York: Continuum, 1998, 418.
[7] Lee H. Bowker, "Women and the Clergy: An Evaluation," *The Journal of Pastoral Care* 36.4 (1982): 227. Here Bowker is summarizing Mildred Daley Pagelow, "Secondary Battering and Alternatives of Female Victims to Spouse Abuse," in Lee H. Bowker, *Women and Crime in America*. New York: Macmillan, 1981, 277–300. Also see Mildred Daley Pagelow, *Woman Battering: Victims and Their Experiences*. Beverly Hills, CA: SAGE Publications, 1981. Bowker's study shows a slightly more positive review of pastoral response than Pagelow's, while still indicating a mix of pastoral help and pastoral harm, with some women still sent back to abusive situations in fulfillment of their Christian duty.

women home to pray that the violence would cease, or that they would become better wives or mothers."[8] But this does not mean that the churches had transformed into safe places for abused persons. The researchers instead found the evangelical clergy reluctant to fully acknowledge the abuse as *abuse* and also extremely unlikely to counsel separation or divorce. Thus, though the words "go home and suffer" are not spoken, the clergy's "family values" convey the overall message that abuse should be endured. The message is effectively, "I won't tell you to go home and bear your cross, but certainly don't leave your marriage." As Nason-Clark describes the situation, "By default the issue is silenced. A pervasive *holy hush* occurs."[9]

Theologian Monica Coleman's recent experience confirms that many clergy are still perpetuating the sexism that increases suffering rather than promoting healing. When Coleman went to clergy to speak about her own rape, the first clergyperson dismissed her story flippantly while watching a television behind her, the next blamed her, asking, "Well, what was he [the man who raped you] doing in your apartment anyway?," and the third told her that "depression was a tool of the enemy and [she] should cast it out in the name of Jesus."[10] Coleman went on to organize with others to found "The Dinah Project" and seek to break the churches' "holy hush" around abuse.

In reading Coleman's *The Dinah Project* with my own students—young adults born in the early 1990s—it became clear that while few if any of them have been told that they should endure abuse in the name of Christian humility, many of them have been given the message that "good" sexual morality will protect them from abuse.[11] In other words, if they practice abstinence, they will be safe, and if they don't, well, what could they expect? "What was he doing in your apartment anyway?" In addition to learning that victimization will be their own fault, they learn that good Christians hold their intimate longings in check until they are in a mutually committed relationship. This message fails these young people in at least two ways: it ignores the likelihood that a "committed" intimate partner, not a stranger, will abuse them, and it contradicts other Christian themes they have been taught, such as prodigal love, countercultural boldness, and risky care for others. However, as much as some Christian theologians have wanted those themes neatly tucked away from anything sexual, tidily contained within the rubrics of *agape* love, the

---

[8] Nancy Nason-Clark, "Shattered Silence or Holy Hush? Emerging Definitions of Violence Against Women in Sacred and Secular Contexts," *Family Ministry* 13 (Spring 1999): 48. Also see Nancy Nason Clark, *The Battered Wife: How Christians Confront Family Violence*. Louisville, KY: WJKP, 1997.

[9] Ibid., 49. On this point, Nason-Clark also references Vicky Whipple, "Counseling Battered Women from Fundamentalist Churches," *Journal for Marital and Family Therapy* 13.3 (1987): 251–258.

[10] Coleman, *The Dinah Project*, x.

[11] My current students are mostly Midwestern, upper-middle-class European Americans.

Christian call to passion for others remains, for many of us, larger than such boundaries.

Without denying the many ways in which Christianity has been and continues to be vastly abusive, and instead clearly in the context of such a history, this chapter seeks to explore the ways in which Christian doctrines of self-giving may also shape violated persons' protest of abuse—may in fact be part of their care for themselves. Brown and Parker have solid grounding for their claim that "Christianity has been a primary—in many women's lives *the* primary—force in shaping our acceptance of abuse."[12] The prevalence of ecclesial, patriarchal, domestic, and colonial abuses of power rightly raises the question of whether self-emptying ethics can ever be more than a program enforced by oppressors in order to control the abused.[13] The history of unjust clergy response to abuse gives solid grounding to the question of whether feminist theology can responsibly advocate *kenosis*. I will argue here that self-giving can in some cases reveal the tenacity and resilience of a person facing abuse, rather than her pathological, self-abnegating condition or her capitulation to the demands of her abuser (or her church). Rather than an ethics applicable only from a dominant status or from safe positions, self-giving persists in the lives of some abused persons as a form of their resistance and a method for moving their families and communities toward

---

[12] Brown and Parker, "For God So Loved the World?," 2.

[13] For studies of churches' response to violence see footnote 5. For a theological exploration of the impact of church response to abuse see Rita Brock and Rebecca Parker, *Proverbs of Ashes: Violence, Redemptive Suffering, and the Search for What Saves Us*. Boston: Beacon Press, 2001. For academic readers on the topic see Adams, Carol J. and Marie M. Fortune, eds. *Violence against Woman and Children: A Christian Theological Sourcebook*. New York: Continuum, 1998 and Brown, Joanne Carlson and Carole R. Bohn, eds. *Christianity, Patriarchy, and Abuse: A Feminist Critique*. Cleveland, OH: Pilgrim Press, 1989. For detailed suggestions for appropriate and helpful church responses see Pamela Cooper-White, *The Cry of Tamar: Violence Against Women and the Church's Response*. Minneapolis: Fortress Press, 1995; Monica Coleman, *The Dinah Project: A Handbook for Congregational Response to Sexual Violence*. Cleveland, OH: Pilgrim Press, 2004; and Mary Pellauer et al., eds. *Sexual Assault and Abuse: A Handbook for Clergy and Religious Professionals*. San Francisco: Harper and Row, 1987. Brief suggestions can be found in Carol J. Adams, "'I Just Raped My Wife! What Are You Going to Do About It, Pastor?': The Church and Sexual Violence," in *Transforming a Rape Culture*, rev. ed., eds. Emilie Buchwald, Pamela R. Fletcher, and Martha Roth. Minneapolis: Milkweed, 2005), 75–104 and Marie M. Fortune and James Poling, "Calling to Accountability: The Churches' Response to Abusers," in *Violence against Women and Children: A Christian Theological Sourcebook*, Carol J. Adams and Marie M. Fortune, eds. New York: Continuum, 1998, 451–463. Also see Joy Bussert, *Battered Women: From a Theology of Suffering to an Ethic of Empowerment*. New York: Lutheran Church of American, Division for Mission in North America, 1986.

For the role of spirituality in resistance to and healing from abuse, see Tameka Gillum, Cris M. Sullivan, and Deborah I. Bybee, "The Importance of Spirituality in the Lives of Domestic Violence Survivors," *Violence Against Women* 12 (March 2006): 240–250; and Pellauer, Mary D. with Susan Brooks Thistlethwaite. "Conversation on Grace and Healing: Perspectives from the Movement to End Violence Against Women," in *Lift Every Voice: Constructing Christian Theologies from the Underside*, eds. Susan Brooks Thistlethwaite and Mary Potter Engel. New York: Harper Collins, 1990, 169–185.

nonviolence. In this chapter, I will draw specifically upon the increasing psychoanalytic discussion of survivors' strength and resistance even amidst their victimization.[14] I seek to highlight here the kenotic tendencies already present *as strengths* in the lives of abuse survivors.

I contend that the same theological rhetoric of self-sacrifice and suffering that may cause abused persons to "accept" abuse has also functioned to inculcate *resistance* to that abuse. I explore here ways that care for others may function as an assertion of the self or, said differently, ways that we—or even God—may discover ourselves in the flow of care for others. Thus I do not argue for a different set of Christian doctrines for women, as though theology should offer women a curriculum based in self-development and men a study of self-giving. The aim of such balanced work would perhaps be for all of us to arrive at a place of sturdy selfhood, with those who have been culturally conditioned to think for themselves (often, men) now caring for others, and those who have been culturally conditioned to think of others (often, women) now thinking for themselves—arriving at some hypothetical equilibrium of the sturdy self. That may be good societal work, but it is not clear that the goal of Christian theology need be the development of sturdy selfhood. In the biblical texts and in the Christian traditions there is also a call to a passionate subjectivity whose longings are often vulnerable, a self that is always gesturing beyond itself: a kenotic selfhood, conveying power.

Self-Giving Care as a Resistance Strategy

Psychoanalytic literature about abused persons has shifted in the last two decades to include emphasis on the creative resistance of the persons themselves, rather than the multiple factors that victimize them.[15] This shift importantly alters not only outsider perception of abused persons but also shifts the abused person's perception of herself or himself.[16] For instance, both the detrimental social tendency to "blame the victim" for her supposed inaction

---

[14] For more reading on the concepts of "victims" and survivors see Liz Kelly, *Surviving Sexual Violence*. Minneapolis: University of Minnesota Press, 1988, chapter 9; Traci C. West, *Wounds of the Spirit: Black Women, Violence, and Resistance Ethics*. New York: New York University Press, 1999; and Sharon Lamb, ed. *New Versions of Victims: Feminists Struggle with the Concept*. New York: New York University Press, 1999. And Hoeft 162–163.

[15] For an overview of this development, see Jocelyn A. Hollander and Rachel L. Einwohner, "Conceptualizing Resistance," *Sociological Forum* 19 (December 2004): 533–554 and Cook, Sarah L., Jennifer L. Woolard, and Harriet C. McCollum, "The Strengths, Competencies, and Resilience of Women Facing Domestic Violence: How Can Research and Policy Support Them?," in *Investing in Children, Youth, Families, and Communities: Strength Based Research and Policy*, ed. Kenneth Maton. Washington, DC: APA Books, 2004, 95–115.

[16] Allan Wade, "Small Acts of Living: Everyday Resistance to Violence and Other Forms of Oppression," *Contemporary Family Therapy* 19 (March 1997): 23–39.

and the abused person's internalization of that message are undermined by a recognition of active resistance strategy. Further, knowledge of and conversation about resistance strategies also increases the likelihood that a person will resist and helps her to reconstruct her agency.[17] Recognizing the ability of abuse survivors to help themselves and others, even if only in small ways, deflects the label of "learned helplessness" away from them such that one can recognize their power. As psychologists Warner, Baro, and Eigenberg conclude, research on stories of resistance "asks us to shift our perception of women in violent relationships from passive victims to resourceful actors who resist assaults on their dignity and safety."[18] Many abused persons are able, through resistance, to maintain their sense of integrity; to find creative ways to protect their children, siblings, or even parents; and, in some cases, to shift their relationships to nonviolence.[19] Most often, women's resistance in violent relationships conveys their determination to transform their relationships rather than end them.[20] Thus their resistance shows their disapproval of the violence committed against them alongside a continuing valuation of relationship. Even where a relationship cannot be maintained, such women's goals of nonviolent relationship speak to their integrity.

A focus on resistance, however, need not mean that scrutinizing energy is no longer placed on the wrongfulness of abuse, the larger society supporting abusers, or the effects of their abuse. Warner, Baro, and Eigenberg stress that "it would be simplistic to suggest that merely taking notice of, supporting, or building on women's resistance is a sufficient political, cultural, or therapeutic response to the endemic problem of male violence in intimate relationships." Rather, they explain that their research investigates only one resource in the struggle against domestic violence, a resource particularly important because "it

---

[17] See Kate Warner, Agnes Baro, and Helen Eigenberg, "Stories of Resistance: Exploring Women's Responses to Male Violence," *Journal of Feminist Family Therapy* 16.4 (2004): 21–42; Jocelyn A. Hollander, "Challenging Despair: Teaching about Women's Resistance to Violence," *Violence Against Women* 11 (June 2005): 776–791; and Wood, Gale Goldberg, and Susan E. Roche. "Representing Selves, Reconstructing Lives: Feminist Group Work with Women Survivors of Male Violence," *Social Work with Groups* 23.4 (2001): 5–23.

[18] Warner, Kate, et al., 37.

[19] Judith Wuest and Marilyn Merritt-Gray study twenty-seven relationships that women have successfully shifted to nonviolence. See their article: "A Theoretical Understanding of Abusive Intimate Partner Relationships That Become Non-violent: Shifting the Pattern of Abusive Control," *Journal of Family Violence* 23 (May 2008): 281–293.

[20] "In response to the violent relationship, most women initiated a process of achieving nonviolence rather than necessarily leaving the intimate relationship. This process of achieving nonviolence was not linear with easily identifiable stages. The women described going back and forth, both in external acts such as leaving and returning but also in their internal thinking and feeling processes," write Jacquelyn Campbell, Linda Rose, Joan Kub, and Daphne Nedd, "Voices of Strength and Resistance: A Contextual and Longitudinal Analysis of Women's Responses to Battering." *Journal of Interpersonal Violence* 13 (December 1998): 743–762.

is often the one most overlooked: the courage, strength, and resistance of the women themselves."[21]

Also, emphasis on abused persons' resistance would defeat its own purposes if it then became another way to blame victims for having not properly resisted vigorously enough or not having physically left the abusive context. An abused person's resistance, on its own, may not and often does not halt the violence; nonetheless, *resistance is rarely ever lacking*. As Allan Wade, a practicing family therapist and scholar writes, "Alongside each history of violence and oppression, there runs a parallel history of prudent, creative, and determined resistance."[22] These creative resistance strategies, which I argue are sometimes surprisingly kenotic, are one way that abused persons *leave* abuse and begin to wash their hands of its cycle, even before they ever walk out the door, and even if they never do.

Not all resistance strategies can be compared to self-giving or kenotic behavior. Abused persons resist in a wide variety of ways, perhaps, for example, punching the abuser in the face.[23] Yet more "kenotic" forms of resistance may be particularly undervalued because they do not reflect the violent aggression that is culturally acknowledged as a form of resistance. Wade writes that part of the challenge in recognizing resistance in oppressed persons is that "what counts as resistance, at least in North American popular culture, is typically based on the model of male-to-male combat which presumes roughly equal strength between combatants. Unless a person fights back physically, it is assumed that she did not resist."[24] Similarly, if a person does not leave an

---

[21] Warner, et al., 40. Also, Wade claims that because the resistance strategies of abused persons have been underemphasized in psychoanalytic literature, there has been a tendency to wrongly identify resistance strategies as signs of disorder, such that "many of the ways in which persons spontaneously resist . . . have been either ignored or recast as pathology" ("Small Acts," 24). Further, "the word resistance has a well established meaning in psychoanalysis, where it refers to the supposed tendency of persons to erect psychological defenses against unconsciously threatening material," especially in defending oneself against the advice and suggestions of the therapist. Wade explains that "these narrow and quite pathology-oriented meanings of the word have made it more difficult to initiate a discourse concerning healthy resistance to violence and oppression" ("Small Acts, 25").

[22] Wade, "Small Acts," 23. Wade, for example, defines resistance broadly as "any mental or behavioral act through which a person attempts to expose, withstand, repel, stop, prevent, abstain from, strive against, impede, refuse to comply with, or oppose any form of violence or oppression (including any type of disrespect), or the conditions that make such acts possible."

[23] However, as Wade explains, "open defiance is the least common form of resistance" because of the danger such open defiance entails. The one resisting is not careless with her safety; to the contrary, it is her own integrity she is seeking to protect in the subtle self-assertions of her resistance. Often a series of "subtle and rapid, micro-level communicative behaviors," conveying "disguised or indirect expression of protest," most resistance strategies sit "between the extremes of open defiance on one hand, and completely disguised activities on the other" (Wade, "Small Acts," 30–32).

[24] Wade, "Small Acts," 25.

abusive relationship, one can too easily assume that she consents to it. And like the clinicians seeking to help them, oppressed persons may also be culturally influenced by the combat mentality and feel that they have done nothing to protest abuse if they have not resorted to the violent tactics of their abusers. But when oppressed persons are helped to recognize their own various methods of resistance, even the tactics that may appear passive, they differently appraise their own strength. Accordingly Pam, one of Wade's clients, reports: "To think that I actually fought back, I could get through from that, that feeling. Then I can have a bit of pride, have more self-worth. Then I started to get back some of the things I didn't have before, like feeling some dignity or having some value as a person."[25]

On the surface, kenotic behavior may seem the opposite of resistance, conjuring instead an image of passivity. Yet a sort of *kenosis* can be seen in at least two ways in the resistance strategies of abused women. First, self-emptying parallels in somewhat troubling ways the psychological dissociation seen in many abuse survivors, behaviors some researchers have specifically labeled as "subordination of the self." Second, and more vividly, survivors may also show an impassioned dedication to other people, particularly in caring for them justly. This ethics of care reveals a kenotic energy insistent on working against the currents of abuse. Both these forms of kenotic activity, in the subordination of the self and in an ethics of care, bear implications for theological response to abuse.

Resistance can be subtle, including even the intentional submerging of one's own feelings for the sake of protection and survival. Subordination of the self is only one among the spectrum of resistance strategies that abused persons employ, but it is a prevalent choice. In their 1998 study of battered women, Campbell, Rose, Kub, and Nedd specifically recognized this strategy as "a critical component of the active problem-solving process."[26] Subordinating included accommodating the partner's wishes, silencing their own feelings, and choosing passivity or docility.[27] Nonetheless, these researchers categorize it as *active*, because it involves the volitional choice of passivity: "It was classified as active because it resulted from a conscious choice, a proactive decision, to try a strategy to address a problem that had been recognized as abuse or controlling behavior."[28] Wade particularly asserts that resistance of this type, involving sublimating of the self, is too often devalued. He finds instead that though these behaviors "are often referred to as dissociation, meaning badly associated," "this is an unfortunate and misleading characterization . . . since

---

[25] Ibid., 37.
[26] Jacquelyn Campbell, Linda Rose, Joan Kub, and Daphne Nedd, "Voices of Strength and Resistance: A Contextual and Longitudinal Analysis of Women's Responses to Battering," *Journal of Interpersonal Violence* 13 (December 1998): 754.
[27] Campbell, et al., 756.
[28] Ibid., 755.

they often involve the construction of imaginative associations which are truly life-saving."[29]

None of these scholars view sublimation of the self as an ideal strategy; rather, they are able to see the creativity and strength within a nonideal situation. Accordingly Bonnie Burstow describes the labeling of such resistance behaviors as psychotic as "not so much wrong as horrendously limited." As an example, Burstow writes that "the woman who 'always has a headache' and the housewife sitting listlessly on the couch are in their own way 'going on strike'."[30] While listlessness and headaches are not in themselves desirable, they attest to the woman's refusal to consent to her abusive situation. She is on strike. Wade writes that "it is important not to romanticize such forms of resistance, or exaggerate their effectiveness in stopping violence. They are the desperate acts of persons living in extreme pain, fear, and isolation, and are no substitute for a life of equality and respect."[31] Campbell's coauthors conclude that "in the face of potential danger to both herself and her children, such decisions [of subordination] were clearly intelligent, courageous, and healthy, rather than passive." These same researchers find it important to simultaneously emphasize that "the subordinating strategy, although entered into purposively, may over time result in the disappearance of the self . . . and contribute to depression," as other researchers have found.[32]

It would be irresponsible to write about *kenosis* and resistance while omitting discussion of the self-subordinating behaviors observable in the lives of abused persons, and I concur with the psychoanalytic scholars who have recognized such actions as ambiguous strengths. Of more relevance to the current project, however, and with more resonance to Gospel stories of resistance, are the kenotic resistance strategies *that demonstrate an ethics of care*. These strategies resonate most strongly with the kenotic powers discussed in previous chapters. While self-subordinating resistance demonstrates an internalizing of the self, the resistance of persons in abusive situations takes more outgoing forms as well, especially in dedication to others. In protest of the violence

---

[29] Wade, "Small Acts," 30. Pamela Cooper-White shows her recognition of the creative strengths of "dissociation" when she writes that to know a person with multiple personalities resulting from extreme ritual abuse is "to enter a twilight zone of formerly unimaginable questions about the meaning of personality, identity, even soul, but also to become acquainted with the creativity and ingenuity of the human mind for survival" (*Cry of Tamar*, 190).

[30] Bonnie Burstow, *Radical Feminist Therapy*. Newbury Park, CA: Sage, 16, as quoted in Wade, 34.

[31] Wade, "Small Acts," 31.

[32] Campbell, et al., 758, citing here T. Mills, "The Assault on the Self: Stages in Coping with Battering Husbands," *Qualitative Sociology*, 8 (1985): 103–123; K. Landenburger, "A Process of Entrapment in and Recovery from an Abusive Relationship," *Issues in Mental Health Nursing*, 3 (1989): 209–227; D. C. Jack, *Silencing the Self*. Cambridge, MA: Harvard University Press, 1991; and J. C. Campbell, L. Kub, R. A. Belknap, and T. Templin, "Predictors of Depression in Battered Women," *Violence Against Women*, 3.3 (1997): 271–293.

shown them, abused persons sometimes dedicate themselves to a markedly different way of life. They become passionate about advocating just relationships and caring for others: they commit themselves to an ethic of care.

I will include examples from several researchers. Allan Wade's work is particularly strong in that he considers not only abused women but any persons who have endured oppression.[33] He emphasizes resistance in therapeutic sessions by choosing to "ask persons to describe how they responded to the violence rather than how they were affected by the violence."[34] This simple turn leads the abused person to articulate the strengths within himself or herself. Similarly, Gale Wood and Susan Roche describe a group process in which the facilitator seeks to draw out protest strategies by striving in each session "to identify at least one story of protest by each member" and to then "develop it as a story of personal agency."[35] Again, the abused person's strength receives emphasis through this method.

One of Wade's clients, Joanne, articulates the way in which she chooses an ethic of respect for others in protest of the violence her father has inflicted on her. In her case, her maintaining of respect, even alongside her own pain, reveals her resistance to abuse. Wade explains:

> I then asked Joanne a number of questions which I hoped would make it possible for her to articulate the beliefs, values, and commitments she had initiated in response to her father's violent conduct. For example: "Based on how you were raised, on all the things you were made to experience and witness as a kid, what kinds of decisions did you make about what sort of a person you wanted to be?" Joanne told me in so many words that it was very important to her that people be treated with respect, and she described how respectfully she treated others (even her father, when he was behaving reasonably). She had become a devout anti-racist. She had great fun with her nieces and nephews, and always made certain to listen to them.[36]

Joanne resists her father's culture by respecting others, combating racism, and befriending and listening to children. Wade describes Joanne's resistance as "pervasive and everyday, in the sense that she resisted not only at times when her father was violent or abusive, but rather, constantly subverted his status as the authority in the family and protested his exaggerated sense of entitlement."[37]

---

[33] Allan Wade, "Small Acts," 23–39.
[34] Ibid., 25.
[35] Wood and Roche, 13.
[36] Wade, "Small Acts," 27.
[37] Ibid., 29; cf. Ivone Gebara's theology of "everyday" salvation in her *Out of the Depths: Women's Experience of Evil and Salvation*, trans. Ann Patrick Ware. Minneapolis: Fortress Press, 2002.

Though Joanne's commitments to just relationships hardly seem objectionable on any feminist grounds, women who "love too much"[38] are too often blamed for making themselves doormats or "accepting" abuse. A person who dedicates herself to caretaking may on one hand appear inured to an oppressive and gendered conditioning toward others before self. Yet, as Joanne's narrative indicates, care for others can also be an expression of self-determination, a passionate dedication of the self, perhaps especially in the face of abuse.

Abused women's resistance to their own degradation may particularly appear through their determination to honor the dignity of their children. The protest strategy within this determination to care for dependents may too easily be misinterpreted by feminism as a woman's entrapment within patriarchal family values. In studies of abused women's resistance, however, maternal care witnesses to these women's dissent from the violence of patriarchy.

For example, Wood and Roche describe a group session that brought out the strength of Maria, who was being abused by her husband. Maria trusts the group with a poignant story: one night, she had almost killed her sleeping children and herself, because as she describes it, "it seemed like the only way I could get him to leave us alone." But then the intensity of her love for her children pulled her back from the edge, and that night she instead resolved to start hiding away money to eventually secure a safe living place.

> Thelma had tears in her eyes as she noted, "You hit bottom, and then you chose life for you and your children." Karen asked Maria what it took for her to make that choice. Maria said "Loving my children and then realizing I'm all they have. I vowed to be the mother I never had." "What does this tell you about yourself?" Karen asked. "Maybe that I have more guts than I give myself credit for," Maria replied. "Yeah, you're the mother bear who's fierce if she needs to be," Thelma said.[39]

Maria's story not only emphasizes the courage and capability she has, even in the context of abuse, but it also emphases the role that self-giving love carries in securing her self-confidence. Hers is not "doormat" love or sentimental love; it is fierce and vital. Her awareness of her own integrity, strength, and importance comes together with her concern for her children. In theological terms, her *kenosis* is also the foundation of her self-revelation. In Maria's case, her *kenosis* saves her life.

---

[38] On the "women who love too much" movement, Pamela Cooper-White finds that "there is still a subtle form of victim-blaming inherent in this trend, namely, that the focus is still on what the victim should or could do to change, rather than on the perpetrator's responsibility" (*Cry of Tamar*, 112). Cooper-White offers extensive references for this claim; see particularly Laura Brown, "What's Love Got to Do with It: A Feminist Takes a Critical Look at the Women Who Love Too Much Movement," *Working Together* 7/2 (December 1986), Center for the Prevention of Sexual and Domestic Violence, Seattle, WA.

[39] Wood and Roche, 14.

Another of Wade's clients, Katie, protested the violence of her childhood through dedicating herself to just relationships. She "told herself that she would be a good mother and always protect her children, stuck up for friends, confronted unfair teachers, and finally disclosed the abuse despite enormous pressure from family members."[40] For Katie, these were not incidental commitments; rather, she "readily agreed that these were different ways of fighting back or opposing her father's and uncles' abuse of her." Importantly, Katie also understands her desire to care for and about others and to speak out for justice as signs of her own self-respect, for she "agreed that these were definitely not the actions of a person who did not esteem herself, lacked assertiveness, or behaved passively toward men."[41] Katie's gift of self is a dignified, assertive choice.

Theological Recognition of Power for Resistance

Theologian Mary Pellauer writes that in her work with abused women she has come to realize that strategies for healing "are perfectly ordinary propensities that anyone can use, and that people *do* use every day."[42] Pellauer describes how she "learned slowly to claim more than victimization" and to "respect simple coping mechanisms . . ."[43] Based on the studies mentioned earlier, I suggest that these mechanisms can include care for others, even though such care may at first seem to be an indication of an abused person's inability to see beyond their abusive situation.

Theological studies have begun to recognize the resistance of abused women instead of only their victimization. In her work in theological ethics, Traci West seeks to identify resistance strategies in the lives of black women who are "victim-survivors."[44] In doing so, she refuses to "blame the victim," instead committing herself to recognizing the strength of these women. For West, "resistance involves any sign of dissent with the consuming effects of intimate and social violence."[45] West shows how abused women are too often

---

[40] Wade, "Small Acts," 36.
[41] Ibid.
[42] Mary D. Pellauer with Susan Brooks Thistlethwaite, "Conversation on Grace and Healing: Perspectives from the Movement to End Violence Against Women," in *Lift Every Voice: Constructing Christian Theologies from the Underside*, eds. Susan Brooks Thistlethwaite and Mary Potter Engel. New York: Harper Collins, 1990, 183.
[43] Paralleling the recognition of self-subordinating, Pellauer continues "and even to make room for denial" (Pellauer with Thistlethwaite, 169). West similarly writes of a need to protect oneself from racist assault, a protective splitting-off.
[44] West's focus on resistance does not indicate a denial of real pain and real victimization. Accordingly, West uses the language "victim-survivor," indicating both woundedness and strength as simultaneously possible realities.
[45] Ibid, 151. She continues: "When a woman survives, she accomplishes resistance. It occurs when a community leader publically contests through words and actions the male-centered notions of power, authority, and status that appear to authorize violence against women."

misunderstood as helpless victims, quoting a study that "documented the profoundly false nature of learned-helplessness theories of women in long term battering relationships." West emphasizes that "the depiction of women as paralyzed by the trauma of male violence is a gross misrepresentation," for "women do engage in resistance."[46]

Pastoral psychotherapist Pamela Cooper-White proposes the phrase "learned hopelessness" rather than "learned helplessness." She does recognize the potential of "learned helplessness," but proposes that "the mounting frustration and despair that are described by the theory are accurate and have much more to do with a woman's conviction that she *should* be able to save the relationship, out of a position of strength, than any stance of weakness."[47] Thus, she writes that "perhaps 'learned hopelessness' is a more accurate term and one that not incidentally names the theological dimension of her plight."[48] Cooper-White stresses the person's experience of despair while also affirming the presence of continuing strength.

Similarly West maintains that "while it is important to describe the possible, potent destructive impact upon victim-survivors of heterosexist, sexist, and racist cultural norms, any such analysis needs to be nuanced with consideration of the range of tactics available to women for coping with and stymieing this impact."[49] The point, then, is not the ungrounded construction of abused persons as superheroes who can free themselves from any danger, but rather the acknowledgement of the strong and even deeply spiritual other-centered commitments to which abused persons sometimes dedicate themselves. This acknowledgement of strength in self-giving is a complex acknowledgement for feminists to make, since the care of others and the seeming diffusion of selfhood have been highlighted as strictures patriarchal society imposes on women. Commitment to others may appear to be symptomatic of a weak sense of self, but this determination may miss the resistance effort at work.

As an example of resistance, West recounts the courageous testimony of one victim-survivor after her rape, speaking out in concern for some other woman who "needs my witness."[50] West names this a "self-giving, silence-breaking act."[51] In this example, it is precisely concern for others that reveals

---

[46] West, 158, on Edward Gondolf with Ellen R. Fisher, *Battered Women as Survivors: An Alternative to Treating Learned Helplessness*. New York: Lexington Books, 1988.

[47] Cooper-White, *Cry of Tamar*, 116. Cooper-White explains here that learned helplessness develops in a woman when "over time, her ability to mobilize her own defenses is eroded and her capacity for hope is numbed."

[48] Ibid.

[49] West, 153. West affirms that "resistance must encompass a broad-based movement for social change that pays particular attention to the intense anguish generated by the violence" (West, 160). Similarly, Pellauer writes, "I affirm both the existence of wounds and the existence of healing" (Pellauer with Thistlethwaite, 170).

[50] West, 180.

[51] Ibid.

this woman's resistance. Here self-giving action expresses this woman's resistance to the culture of abuse; it serves to undermine societal violence.

Similarly, in her work at the intersections of sexuality, abuse, and spirituality, L. J. Tessier notices "the life-affirming activities in which survivors engage as part of the healing process often reveal a new awareness of life's value as reflected in other living things." As a microlevel example, one survivor recounts, "It's a small thing, but I never had plants before. It's just my way of trying to keep something other than me alive. It gives me a lot of pleasure . . . I was scared about it at first. But now I know I can nurture them and keep them healthy."[52] For this survivor, her successful care of "something other than me" proves her own strength. The choice to care for another living thing, though potentially frightening, demonstrates the person's decision to live out a different sort of ethics than has been practiced upon her. Outgoing care for others can protest abusive culture.

As West writes, "the suppression of selfhood is one of the most profound and complex areas in women's struggle for visibility. In response to intimate violence, women usually learn a range of methods for dissociating from the immediate incident of abuse as well as from memories of the experience."[53] The result is that "for the victim-survivor, intimate violence can establish a lifelong pattern of dutifully polarizing and silencing many of her emotional responses."[54] In this light a woman's reemergence into the expression of her emotional responses is itself resistance.

And as discussed in previous chapters, the expression of desire belies sheer self-abnegation in self-giving. Tessier emphasizes the affirmation of sexual desire integral to the transformation of many survivors of sexual abuse. She writes that "women recovering from sexual abuse seek a new understanding of themselves as sexual beings, free of fear." Rather than asserting a strong self through protective boundaries, the survivors of whom Tessier writes express their strength in their pursuit of sexual abandon. "Certainly, there is always an element of acknowledgement here, a nod to the past, almost a memorial, for what has been lost," writes Tessier, "but my own experience assures me that deep, sweet sexual/spiritual celebration may well be part of this transformation process."[55]

Tessier's affirmation that desired sexual union, especially when such union has been "crushed or bruised,"[56] may lead to transformation and healing offers a parallel for *kenosis*: desired self-emptying, abandon, release—especially when these have been previously met with abuse—may testify to a person's

---

[52] Tessier, L. J. *Dancing After the Whirlwind: Feminist Reflections on Sex, Denial, and Spiritual Transformation*. Boston: Beacon, 1997, 186.
[53] West, 63. She also describes a "splitting behaviour," which is not only in response to domestic abuse but also the racist abuse of white supremacy (65).
[54] Ibid., 63.
[55] Tessier, 190.
[56] Ibid.

resistance, to her transformation and her healing. Tessier acknowledges that for her "sex is never safe. I risk everything here, dancing the shedding dance. Still, even as my skin peels back, just as I brace for the pain of air and light against raw flesh, I can feel the softest brush of lips against this brand-new surface of myself, and I let you in."[57] With a tinge of possible masochism in her account—risking everything, bracing for raw pain—Tessier may speak to the transformative *kenosis* of survivors of abuse. Though she is not addressing a traditionally agapeic self-giving, she articulates a self-release by which abused persons refuse subjection to victimization and claim the "brand new surface" of the self. She testifies that "to fully enter into this transformative process in community with survivors is both a challenge and an opportunity for those who relish the joys of resistance."[58] The joys of resistance can open even on the ground of pain, even when abuse is still occurring, even when there is much healing yet to be done.

When Wade asks Katie "how it felt to finally recognize her own history of resistance," Katie responds, "I feel like I could lift up my fucking car."[59] Theological recognition of the assertiveness and strength of kenotic acts might similarly help persons feel the power to lift cars, or move mountains. In contrast, well-intended feminist critique of the ways in which Christian theology teaches persons to be self-sacrificial might inadvertently *disempower* persons whose kenotic commitments are marks of their own integrity and expressions of their resistance to oppression. It is her fierce love for her children that reveals in herself what Maria describes as "more guts than I give myself credit for." Instead of highlighting all the "guts" *kenosis* requires, a shaming of an abused person's kenotic tendencies may only emphasize how deeply victimized a person has been, stressing the extent to which they have been abused. They may be well aware that they have been physically beaten, but then an overly simplistic feminist analysis may show them that they have also been beaten into psychological form by cultural and spiritual patriarchal gendering that has inculcated in them a self-sacrificial personality. In such cases feminism inadvertently produces more guilt than liberation. In contrast, the recognizing of kenotic resistance strategies not only as strengths but also as examples of Christian ethics may offer abused persons who are Christians a sense of renewed and holy dignity.

Yet this sort of recognition is far from common in wider culture. Building upon therapeutic research, Linda Coates and Allan Wade conducted a study analyzing the discourse of public figures concerning violence.[60] They

---

[57] Ibid., 190–191.
[58] Ibid., 189. Tessier's language of *joy* in resistance sheds light on a felicity possible in the vulnerability of passionate *kenosis*. *Kenosis* may be, as Balthasar has it, our "bliss," a "mode of our divine joy." Balthasar, *Theo-Drama IV*, 252–257, 268; cf. Pitstick, 340.
[59] Wade, "Small Acts," 36–37.
[60] Linda Coates and Allan Wade, "Language and Violence: Analysis of Four Discursive Operations," *Journal of Family Violence* 22 (2007): 511–522.

demonstrate how the public rhetoric around violence consistently conceals resistance strategies, downplays violence, and blames the victim rather than the perpetrator. They propose that all public and scholarly work on the topic of violence should seek to "expose violence . . . b) clarify offenders' responsibility . . . c) elucidate and honor victims' responses and resistance . . . and d) contest the blaming and pathologizing of victims by obtaining accounts of victims' prudent, determined, and creative resistance."[61]

Warner and her colleagues find that emphasis on resistance in therapeutic practice is especially important because current methods for working with abused women center on two models, both of which emphasize the ways in which abused people are controlled, thus highlighting their passive position. "Both models intend to teach clients and clinicians the ways abusers have taken advantage of women's powerlessness and vulnerability." Thus Warner and her colleagues refer to these prominent methods as "'pathology' based intervention models." They find these models to be particularly problematic because "deficit focused models of intervention may also further invigorate or inflate women's ideas about why they cannot leave while suppressing the potentially liberating narratives about the ways they are already succeeding at resisting violence and empowering themselves."[62]

I suggest that pastoral caregivers might succeed in unleashing "liberative narratives" by helping abused persons to recognize their resistance strategies and perhaps even the Christian resonance in these strategies. A clergy person might helpfully repeat back to an abused woman those pieces of her own narrative in which she has described any self-giving or outgoing urges she continues to feel. The clergy person can further name those self-giving urges as potential strengths, signs of life, even christic virtues, even if there are also health concerns to work through, even if there are also situational dangers that need immediate attention.[63] Alongside the clinical or legal referrals that a pastor will need to make, her priestly role may involve affirmation of a person's strengths, and indeed the way in which her actions are vivaciously reflective of her self-giving baptismal identity: "I see life in you! Look how much you are already doing to build the kind of life you want!" Such a pastoral response does not say, "Go home and bear your cross—be a good wife," but nor does it say, "In your case, self-sacrifice is a sin." Rather, a pastoral response mindful of the possibility of self-giving resistance might say something like the following: "You have described to me so many ways that your heart really goes out to others, even while you're hurting so much yourself. This concern for others

---

[61] Coates and Wade, "Language and Violence," 521.
[62] Warner, 39. Also see Traci West, *Wounds of the Spirit*, 55 and 159.
[63] As Jeanne M. Hoeft writes, "Acts of resistance need not be based on unambivalent clarity but can simply be tentative acts of uncertainty in the hope of more life" (*Agency, Culture, and Human Personhood: Pastoral Theology and Intimate Partner Violence*. Eugene, OR: Pickwick, 2009), 161.

doesn't have to mean that you've been weak and let others walk all over you. Taking care of others doesn't always mean that you're neglecting your own self-care. To me it sounds like your persistent concern for others is how you say 'no' to the kind of brutality you have experienced. You don't let that sort of cruelty characterize who you are as a person." Not all abused persons will resist in self-giving ways, and to pastorally prescribe such strategies can be violently counterproductive, but pastoral recognition of strategies already at work may help a person recognize not only her own strength but also the holy presence that her tenacious care makes manifest.[64]

In her feminist appropriation of Bonhoeffer, Lisa Dahill draws important critical attention to Bonhoeffer's understanding of Christ as the person-for-others. Dahill writes that for women in abuse, "'being there for others' manifestly fails to redeem. It is not a window opening into the experience of transcendence." Rather, "what for Bonhoeffer was the liberating experience of surrender, joy, and solidarity with others is, for these women, a grinding day-to-day suffocation" and the "pattern of sin."[65] Thus, for his position, she understands the appeal of "self-surrender, a process simultaneously sacrificial and redemptive."[66] For Bonhoeffer, Dahill explains that "relinquishment of the loud and coercive demands of the ego was the blessed way forward into life, i.e., into ever fuller friendship with and transparency to Jesus Christ himself, who is the very reality of all that is."[67] However, in accord with Saiving's analysis of diffusion as a form of sin, Dahill concludes that for survivors of abuse, focus on others can be "the shape of an excruciating life."[68]

The churches have such a deeply harmful record in responses to abuse: as West writes, "The church's neglect of issues of male violence, combined with its insistent demands for female labor and self-sacrifice, can exact an excruciating emotional and spiritual toll."[69] And as Catherine Keller writes, "In a social situation of women's subordination, when the male preachers and teachers exhort the predominately female flock to deny themselves and practice obedience, they reinforce woman's already unhealthy dependency upon men for spiritual, cultural, and economic identity."[70] Keller goes on to claim, invoking *kenosis* specifically, that "the politics of kenotic humility incarnates itself all too clearly in the willingness of most male ministers, especially but not exclusively within theologically conservative churches, to deal with situations of physical, often

---

[64] In the work of Melissa Raphael it is the care women gave each other in the Holocaust camps, which she names as resistance, that undermines a theology of absence and attests to the presence of God in the midst of the camps. See *The Female Face of God in Auschwitz: A Jewish Feminist Theology of the Holocaust*. London: Routledge, 2003.
[65] Dahill, 176.
[66] Ibid., 174.
[67] Ibid., 83.
[68] Ibid., 176.
[69] West, 141.
[70] Keller, "Scoop up the Moon," 105–106.

life-endangering abuse by counseling the woman to remain and submit." In the context of such a harmful history, Dahill's critique offers healing; it raises awareness of the ways in which theological rhetoric, like that of Bonhoeffer, has different embodied affects based on gender and social location. However, heeding the psychoanalytic literature on abused person's resistance strategies, feminist theologians may also recognize that for a woman in abuse the gift of herself may be a strategy of protest against the abuser's attempts to suffocate her spirit. Even for abused persons, "being there for others"[71] can be a mark of vivacity. Rather than needs that are "opposite" to those that persons caught up in ego might need, some abused men and women may express their strength through other-centered commitments.

The pastoral language appropriate for people experiencing abuse may also invoke some of the Christian tradition's most painful stories and images, though feminists have been wary of the dangers here. Resistance can be "perfectly ordinary" and "everyday," to borrow the language of Pellauer and Wade. It can also be gritty and tough. Maria's story, reaching for a gun as she beholds her sleeping children, testifies to the visceral despair with which victim-survivors are familiar. Perhaps theology need not always cushion and soften its themes when responding to abused persons, as though looking for a contrast to the theologies appropriate for hypothetically nonabused persons. Tessier emphasizes the gore of survivors' resistance:

> Survivors are rarely drawn to images of pretty buds opening or sweet little butterflies emerging from cocoons. Theirs is the country of Inanna, scourged and slaughtered by her shadow-sister and hung on a hook to rot. Theirs is Tiamat, silenced, skewered, and split asunder. These are the creation stories, the stories of death, dismemberment, and rebirth, that survivors recognized. This is chaos, coming apart, going to pieces, dying to the old self.[72]

Though Tessier finds that many survivors have trouble appropriating traditional religious symbols,[73] of which the Christian cross would certainly be one, I offer that the tradition of the kenotic Christ crucified does offer a "silenced, skewered, and split" re-creation story that feminists should not quickly erase from our theologies. Tessier continues, "As for transformation, that is what happens in hell. If we emerge, and many of us do, we are not the same on the return journey. When Inanna descends into the underworld, she is stripped naked, destroyed, and hung on a hook. Survivors know the feeling."[74] Beholding

---

[71] For a reading of Bonhoeffer's "being for one another" in relation to his "being with one another," see Cynthia Moe-Lobeda, "A Theology of the Cross for the 'Uncreators'," in Trelstad, ed. *Cross Examinations*. Minneapolis: Fortress, 2006, 300, note 36.
[72] Tessier, 189.
[73] Ibid., 185.
[74] Ibid., 190.

the cross, where a Christ who, though powerful in his resistance to imperial oppression, nonetheless hung on a hook, some abused persons may nod and "know the feeling." In this sense the cross does not mandate further suffering, but rather appears as utterly familiar in the midst of pain, and perhaps even as a sign of holy solidarity, offering a still small voice "for us" from the storm.

Melinda Contreras-Byrd calls for the scrutiny of self-sacrifice in theology, writing that "women who stay in abusive relationships are willing to suffer in the hopes that their suffering might somehow become redemptive . . . These women bring new meaning to the admonition of Romans 12:1: 'Offer up your body, a living sacrifice'."[75] Contreras-Byrd points to theology as one example of the wider culture surrounding and supporting domestic abuse. Similarly Pellauer notes that the culture and theologies of our churches often fail to support victim-survivors: "The patriarchy of traditional theological categories systematically distorts the experience of survivors of rape and battering and abuse in childhood" such that "unless you bracket many of those traditional categories, it's almost impossible to understand the experience of survivors theologically."[76] *Kenosis* is surely one such doctrine with patriarchal distortions that blur the theological understanding of survivor experience. Recognizing self-giving only as some nullification of the self in the name of another's power, one fails to focus on the many resistance strategies of the incarnate Christ. The many acts of resistance on the part of those forced into oppression by culture, spouse, and church then fail to register on the theological radar as christologically significant activity. The final chapter will explore ways in which our powers for resistance may also be powers for the continuing incarnation of Christ among us.

---

[75] Contreras-Byrd, 22–23.
[76] Pellauer with Thistlethwaite, 176, cf. West, 141.

Chapter 6

Power for Christ: Self-Giving and Incarnation

Feminists have always known that the personal is political and Christians have always known that incarnation changes the world; if we combine the two we have a powerful mix.

—Lisa Isherwood[1]

I wrote in the introduction about the genesis of my queries into the doctrine of *kenosis*. My own experience had demonstrated to me the vulnerability of self-giving commitments, and my growing acquaintance with feminism had an ambivalent effect: empowering in some ways, as I learned of the extent of sexism, but also disempowering, as I came to feel guilty for the generosity toward others I had adopted as a Christian. My newborn feminism indicted my *kenosis* and declared me guilty of my own suffering. Worse, the *kenosis* woven through my whole sense of life purpose now seemed to be one of the oldest tricks in sexism's book. How naïve I had been!

And yet, I couldn't quite accept the whole blame, on myself or my religious tradition. If my as yet simplistic feminism was teaching me to above all else develop my own sense of self, it seemed counter to that project to give up a major component of my overall spiritual framework. Without *kenosis* I felt like I would go dry, like there would be no oil left between the gears: a real self-abnegation. An elusive urge (feminist as much as it was Christian) reassured me that I did not have to take a path away from *kenosis*.

The urge had something to do with September 11, 2001, or more specifically with the Bush administration's response to the violence of that day.[2] The towers and the Pentagon were hit at a time when my own more private woundedness

---

[1] Lisa Isherwood, "The Embodiment of Feminist Liberation Theology: The Spiralling of Incarnation." *Feminist Theology* 12.2 (2004): 140–156, this quotation 153.
[2] See my "A Christian Politics of Vulnerability," in *The Sleeping Giant Has Awoken: The New Politics of Religion in the United States*, Jeffrey W. Robbins and Neal Magee, eds. New York: Continuum, 2008.

had left me with a heightened sense of vulnerability. One might think that my own vulnerability would have led me to scream to my government: "Don't be a doormat." But instead, I was phoning the White House answering service and adding my voice to a chorus of others: "Don't go to war. I don't support the war."

In my analysis, *kenosis* seemed like just the thing for my nation, not just because it was powerful, but importantly also *because* it was now in a vulnerable position. I could not have explained it this way at the time, but I feared that in going to war and choosing violent defense rather than hospitality and generosity, the United States would be forgoing a major resistance strategy. I wanted the Christian majority in my nation to stand up and speak for our ancient heritage in Jesus' practice of passionate nonviolent resistance. And some of us did. Our resistance to war was real and important, if in the end ineffectual in preventing more violence. Our resistance helped to establish a new sense of self for the American people, fostering a movement toward new political identities that are still taking shape and growing in power. The previous chapters have sought to demonstrate something of the power generated by *kenosis*—power both for the kenotic subject and also potentially for the ones toward whom the *kenosis* is drawn. Depletion of the self quite obviously has different implications for a feminist analysis than does empowerment.

As Chapter 1 explored, doctrines of *kenosis* can also serve to disempower, or at least to bolster, a unilateral image of God's own power, as a power hoarded over. While this mode of power will still be compelling for many Christians, it rightly concerns many feminist theologians. Doctrines of God's power over us not only serve to diminutize all human agency but also potentially shame God by conveying a sort of subjectivity God does not choose to inhabit. In this latter way doctrines of God's power over, especially when expressed through concepts of *kenosis*, may also short-shrift christology, a realm of theology with so much potential for conveying forms of divine power beyond power over.

I argued in Chapter 2 that Luther and Melanchthon, read side by side, express interpersonal experience as the essential element of christology. Luther casts such experience in terms of the cross, and Melanchthon in terms of the benefits of Christ: we know Christ is present where we experience Christ as intimately efficacious for us. Outside that intimacy there is for these figures no Christian God.

In the third chapter I explored the self-interested and self-expressive contours of *kenosis*. I argued that the type of self-giving at work in christic *kenosis* can be more than a unilateral *agape*: *eros* is part of *kenosis*, too. As feminists have recognized desire as a potent vehicle for self-exploration and development, so, too, may *kenosis* generate subjectivity, pleasure, and power.

As discussed in Chapter 4, feminist theologians have written of a "power in mutual relation," in contrast to the "power-over" of patriarchal domination, and yet other possibilities can be explored. Presenting a vivid image of patriarchal "power over," Althaus-Reid writes that "the logic of theology follows models of spermatic flow, of ideas of male reproduction which defy modern science but are established firmly in the sexual symbolic of theology." She thus chastises theological norms, which are perpetually reduplicated without recognition of otherness, always relying on the passive receptivity of others and lacking desire for the theological expression of those others. Althaus-Reid determines, with a characteristically "indecent" image, "The question is, how can we cool down this erection of the *logos spermatikos* in theology?"[3] Althaus-Reid claims two possible paths: "giving privilege to the subordinated part of the binary compositions, what 'leather' people would call the prevalence of 'bottoms' (submissive partners) over 'tops' (dominant partners)" and "trying to find the different (not belonging to the binary pair in conceptual opposition)."[4]

I have suggested "kenotic power" as another possible method of "finding the different," for locating a practice that does not belong to the "binary pair" of the dominant and the submissive, but also does not require pure distinction or separation from these positions. As in *Verwindung*, kenotic power heals and engages these positions rather than presenting itself as a pure alternative.

Thus in Chapter 4 I explored how the "submissive" masochist claims her desire and thusly demonstrates herself to be something more than submissive. She may ultimately *also* enact submission, but her submission burns with a vigorous agency. This agency itself will sometimes be enough, I suspect, to "cool down" the erection of domination, for if domination has fueled itself on unchallenged power, the presence of a desiring other may ruin the mood. Rather than the hoarding of power, in kenotic desire, it is the release of power that is invigorating: the slipping of power, fluid and pleasurable, between the layers of ever-shifting power difference, the play of power as a thing not to be exploited or grasped.

With christic self-giving, which may overlap with masochism or asceticism but may take many other forms as well, the differences between vigor and victimization may be similarly crucial and subtle. *Kenosis* navigates a slippery slope: not only might a person's *kenosis* be mistaken for sheer victimization, but the kenotic person may herself encounter confusion as to the strength of her actions. Witnessed in another, *kenosis* is easily misread as a mark of oppression when the vital margin of agency is overlooked on the fine line between suppression and subversion. But even for the one involved in *kenosis*, ambiguity remains: leaving the stratosphere of familiar subjectivity, can anyone maintain a balanced tally between emphasis on self and other? *Kenosis* carries one beyond balance, beyond safety, and certainly beyond certainty.[5] It is an act of faith.

---

[3] Althaus-Reid, *Indecent Theology*, 155.
[4] Ibid.
[5] As to moving beyond safely, "There is no *safe* sex with Jesus but there may be some good sex in the split-space of transcendent flesh, the passage between (gendered) natures, the suffering of sacred eros," writes Virginia Burrus ("Radical Orthodoxy and the Heresiological Habit," 53).

It may be easy to miss the subjectivity of a self-giving agent and instead diagnose the kenotic posture as more evidence of soluble personality, and especially when a Christian woman is the agent, as more evidence of the problematic dictate that "*women in Christianity are meant to live for others*."[6] Heyward and Harrison hypothesize that "the inability of so many women even to imagine that they should be well-treated in a relationship with a man or that they deserve physical and emotional pleasure is conditioned by the demand that we have our being for others."[7] Yet to a large extent the "failure" of so many women to imagine that they should be well treated by men, or to realize that they deserve pleasure, is conditioned by the violent society in which they seek to love. Why must "being for others" be responsible for a lack of pleasure and for abuse?[8] In failing to see the agency that may adhere in *kenosis*, feminist theologians may also miss the creativity of women's and men's transgressions of subjection, moves that are sometimes subtle and easily misread. They may inadvertently blame persons for the wounds they suffer in the course of their desires, while meanwhile their desires may, as explored in Chapter 5, comprise *resistance* to rather than *collusion* with the oppressions that deserve the blame.

As we have seen, kenotic power can serve the perpetuation of subjectivity, and can work to resist abuse and exploitation. It may also serve Christ, and specifically the ongoing incarnation of Christ in our contemporary lives. In this final chapter I examine the texture of power for, in contrast to powers over and with, and I wonder at the chrism passed between us on the edges of our gestures *for*.

A Yielding Power

Surely not just any use of power incarnates Christ: power for christic incarnation will take particular forms, rooted, perhaps, in what we remember of Jesus. Among these forms, kenotic power need not be the best or only vehicle toward christic incarnation. Rather, it offers one possible venue, one sought

---

[6] Harrison and Heyward, "Pain and Pleasure," 157, italicized in the original.
[7] Ibid.
[8] In her *Wounds of the Spirit: Black Women, Violence, and Resistance Ethics*. New York: New York University Press, 1999, Traci West writes: "Since the entire community is morally culpable for the deleterious consequences of male sexual and physical assault on women, women's anguish is a communal problem . . . By assuming this responsibility we can grasp how we participate in socially constructing this painful phenomenon, and equip ourselves to dismantle its societal reinforcement" (55). She also claims that "the appreciation of women's moral agency is dramatically increased when the psychosocial issues that prolong and perpetuate long-term cycles of abuse are reframed as community deficiencies, rather than as flaws embedded in the psyches or moral characters of the women who are abused" (159). Also see Melinda Contreras-Byrd, "A Living Sacrifice?" *The Other Side* 38.2 (2002), 20–23.

more for the pleasure and empowerment of the way itself than for the specific and elusive goal of particular incarnation.

As I have discussed, the fluidity and intimate relationality of kenotic power challenges any fixing of *kenosis* into a "power over" model. But perhaps less obviously, kenotic power also exceeds the balance of "power with." It does not rely on cooperation or on equality, and may want more than mutuality has to offer. Alloyed with residues of unbalanced relation, *kenosis* bends ahead as *power for*: power for specific others, power for the self made new, and power for the Christ made new, as chrism trickles through the intervals we transverse, lending the glimmer of festival to the contours of our thick complexity.

Pamela Cooper-White summarizes feminist writers' proposals about power with in writing that "*power-with* carries the dignity of power-within into relationships. Power-with is the power of an individual to reach out in a manner that negates neither self nor other. It prizes mutuality over control and operates by negotiation and consensus."[9] But Cooper-White is dissatisfied, as am I, with the idea that power-with is defined by another's recognition of mutuality. Using the biblical example of Tamar, Cooper-White writes that "Tamar's exercise of power-with fails if judged by the response of the men around her, if power-with is defined only as the power to be listened to and to have influence. Tamar was not received, and yet her approach was one of mutuality."[10] Tamar exercises power, but not in the context of mutuality (though, for Cooper-White, Tamar nonetheless aims for mutuality). Cooper-White explains that in Tamar's story "the rupture of right relationality lay in the refusal of these men to meet her power-with stance in mutuality. Where she brought power-with, they met her with power-over."[11]

As Cooper-White's appraisal of feminism's "power with" shows, models of power-with strain to recognize empowerment that functions beneath the radar of dominant power. Thus Cooper-White suggests that "the exercise of power-with is an intention and commitment to mutuality, which is not wholly contingent upon the response or lack of response of the other."[12]

This remodeling helpfully qualifies some of the mutuality required for a desire for mutuality to be operative. Still, I find that the language of "with" too overtly suggests that the other is *with* you: on board, joining in, recognizing. Because there are forms of healing and newness of life that do not end in a unified community or in mutual recognition, it seems to me that the situations

---

[9] Cooper-White, *Cry of Tamar*, 33. Cooper-White notes that "this departs somewhat from Starhawk's original definition of power-with as 'the power of a strong individual in a group of equals, the power not to command, but to suggest and be listened to, to begin something and see it happen" (271, f42).

[10] Ibid., 271.

[11] Ibid., 33–34.

[12] Ibid., 271. Carter Heyward also recognizes a striving toward mutuality as functional before mutuality has been achieved; this is Heyward's "already/not yet."

considered in the previous two chapters are inadequately recognized by the language of "power with."

Cooper-White, in her dissatisfaction with power with, suggests her own model of "power-in-community," which accounts in a more thoroughgoing way for the impact of social construction and social sin. Cooper-White's model helpfully allows for power difference in community, and specifically for forms of authority and leadership as distinct from coercive domination.[13] In discussing the way in which leadership functions productively in power in community, Cooper-White draws on Martha Ellen Stortz's earlier reference to "power-for" in Stortz's *PastorPower*. Stortz's use of "power-for" is different from my use here because of the specific context Stortz considers: her "power-for" describes a leadership power, a healing modification of exploitive power over. Leadership power-for allows for power that is, as Cooper-White explains, "authorized by those who are served by that leadership and is accountable to them."[14] In Cooper-White's model of power-in-community, power-for remains linked to leadership and to a type of power-over: "Those who are authorized to serve in a power-over/power-for capacity do not *have* the power; it is on loan from the community."[15]

While I find Cooper-White's and Stortz's visions of leadership productive, the power for I am exploring here is not necessarily any exercise of power over. Christic power for may function as leadership or flow from leadership in some circumstances, but it need not start from there. Power for carries its own sort of yielding, desiring vector, and may be functional for persons in any number of social positions. Thus, my use of power for does not necessarily entail leadership, though it does not exclude it, either. It can function from whatever starting place a person finds herself or himself. And it does not hinge on the recognition or welcome of the other.

Like Cooper-White I want to allow for levels of power difference that quite practically exist and that also need not always be inherently problematic. And even when levels of power difference are deeply problematic, as in the situations of abuse explored in the previous chapter, the kenotic power for that I am advocating here can still function, which is part of what makes its power all the more remarkable.

In further contrast from power with, however, power for is not necessarily guided by the goal of mutuality.[16] The word mutuality itself implies reciprocity, a giving by each. As noted earlier, Cooper-White wisely distinguishes between

---

[13] Ibid., 38–39.
[14] Ibid., 38.
[15] Ibid., 39.
[16] This would be so even if mutuality remains distinct from equality. Cooper-White explains that "mutuality is not equality, not sameness. Mutuality involves empowering each other to find and express what each can truly know and do, each one's unique contributions, not the dulling uniformity of the lowest common denominator" (*Cry of Tamar*, 30), cf. Heyward, *Touching Our Strength*, 34.

the achievement of mutuality and the commitment to it. But power for, as I am using it here, releases the aim for any return; it devotes itself *for*. The pleasure of the for is its only aim. It is in this devotion that the felicity of empowerment adheres, and not in a desired or subsequent exchange.

Thus, power for is an energy that contrasts with exploitive power-over, but not necessarily by choosing mutuality. Mutual empowerment may felicitously occur along the kenotic way, but it need not be the goal. Power for leans toward another or others; its focus and its desire remain for the thriving of this particular other or others. In this sense it is very much a self-giving, a self-emptying. That the self empowers itself in so desiring and comes into a new incarnation of self in the kinetics of self-giving may resonate with the aim of "mutual empowerment," while the self is able to risk itself more deeply, and pleasure itself more immediately, than mutuality may allow.

Though self-giving may appear as the *loss* of power, kenotic outpouring may also, as the preceding chapters have sought to demonstrate, bear a mighty current: opening a revelation of oneself, beckoning the becoming of another, resisting oppression, and redefining subjection. Though feminist theology has been powerful in its message *against* sacrifice, suffering, and negation, one also sees in the work of third-wave feminism a growing embrace of limits and pain and an acceptance of ambiguity between those strategies which clearly may serve a feminist agenda and those which may not. This acceptance is no mere concession to the inevitable diversity of feminist opinions; rather, the ambiguity can become a fertile site for theological construction.

The kenotic as power for pulses with strength and weakness, assertion and yield, enlivening hybrid incarnations of "self" and "other." It muddies pure distinction, as a fluid movement between power difference rather than a proud siding with one or the other pole of a power dichotomy: strong/weak, active/passive, rich/poor, male/female, transcendent/immanent, colonizer/colonized. Rather than a static quality that could be the possession of any one group, the power that is kenotic generates and regenerates itself in motion, propelled by desire for the neighbor as for the self, embodied in, with, under, and beyond the identities we have already known. Currents of kenotic power erode the idealized futures that would guide our dreams, caught up instead in particular attractions and local desires. Fluid rather than static, vigorous emptying grows bored with unlikely states of perfection and cannot guarantee its next outcomes. Yet it carries a "greening power,"[17] as Hildegard of Bingen envisioned, productive and generative. It emerges as an urge toward vivacity, toward, as Ivone Gebara writes, "a human vocation to pleasure, beauty, and largesse."[18]

---

[17] Hildegard of Bingen, *The Book of Divine Works*, chapters 1, 2, 4, 9, and 10; cf. Shawn Madigan, "Hildegard of Bingen," in *Mystics, Visionaries, and Prophets*, ed. Shawn Madigan C.S.J. Minneapolis: Fortress, 1998, 95.
[18] Gebara, *Out of the Depths*, 90.

Heyward and Harrison speak of the difficult attempt "to disentangle, at the level of personal erotic experience, a clear difference between what hurts and what gives pleasure."[19] Kenotic power, unlike mutually shared power, can slide within such a tangle. *Kenosis* even *elicits* confusion, desiring the pleasure of this entanglement and willing to be surprised by its productivity, like the twisting of live wires: dangerous yet available for creative use. Rather than theorize the benefits of clear distinction between, for example, pain and pleasure, hypothetical clarities which seem unlikely in social context, one can develop capabilities for working productively with the confusion of categories. A possibility opens for pleasure *in the meanwhile*, in the thick of it all, in between power differences and even contrasting intentions. Pleasure, strength, and agency can be claimed though mutuality and reciprocity have not been achieved.

In comparison to feminist models emphasizing power with, kenotic power for does not rely on an extremely rare social context in order to function (as in the mutually "woman-identified" context of an *idealized* lesbian loving, which Heyward also criticizes[20]). Most human contexts—lesbian or otherwise!—involve variances of power. *Kenosis* can function productively within the multivalent power structures in which human lives are embedded.

For example, in her proposals for sexual ethics, Karen Lebacqz emphasizes that women face a particular power struggle in heterosexual relationships within patriarchal societies; in Lebacqz's formulation, women's love for men is akin to their "loving the enemy." Lebacqz writes that "heterosexual women must formulate our sexual ethics within the context of understanding the ironies of searching for intimacy in an unsafe environment."[21] Thus, though Heyward and Harrison claim that "feminism ought to affirm an eroticism that grows from the soil of nonalienated relationship as a profound source of an experience of transcendence,"[22] I argue that feminism also needs a way forward in love that grows in the inhospitable soil of alienation. We need the possibility of claiming our own ways to refertilize our land, and to claim those powers of re-creation even when others would deny them.

The expression of kenotic desire often walks a fine line between subversion and suppression: *kenosis* is risky. But even when it is not received or reciprocated, even in loss or pain or crucifixion, *kenosis* garners strength from its own gesture, and not by the final outcomes of society's (mis)appropriation of it.

---

[19] Harrison and Heyward, "Pain and Pleasure," 161.
[20] Heyward, *Touching Our Strength*, 108.
[21] Karen Lebacqz, "Love Your Enemy: Sex, Power, and Christian Ethics," in *Feminist Theological Ethics: A Reader*, ed. Lois K. Daly. Louisville, KY: Westminster/John Knox Press, 1994, 246. Also see Shere Hite, *Women and Love: A Cultural Revolution in Progress*. New York: Alfred A. Knopf, 1987, 292.
[22] Harrison and Heyward, "Pain and Pleasure," 166.

Lynda Hart writes of her conviction to search for different ways to love, rather than, as Hart quotes Luce Irigaray, engaging in "the exhausting labor of copying, miming. Dedicated to reproducing that sameness in which we have remained for centuries." Considering Irigaray's proposal, Hart concludes: "Utopian? Yes, perhaps. But I cannot stop seeking it. I do not expect to find it through 'sadomasochism,' but I don't expect to find it by avoiding what I think is a certain, inevitable power struggle within any erotic relationship."[23]

Also in search of different ways to love and live, though perhaps not utopian, I suggest that some might experience *kenosis* as a vehicle toward shifting the strictures of prevailing orders. And I suspect that, even in its potent utility, passionate *kenosis* will be best when experienced first as pleasure: undertaken for the sake of its own hearty, gritty bliss. Then, in the currents of that pleasure, may we experience a regeneration and reorganization of power: letting go in a satisfying peal of laughter and effort, at once transcendent and embodied, feeling the tension slip, knowing that things, if momentarily, imperfectly, impurely, have been made new.

Chrism Conveyed

Power for offers one way to describe the power of Christ. And our exercise of power for may also serve Christ, as our kenotic pleasures flow in a sustaining pulse of Christ's presence among us: extending holy chrism, bringing Christ to flesh again and again.

Christ's ongoing presence among us suggests that the embodied power of the incarnation has bearing on us, and in us. Christ's ongoing presence suggests that incarnation is an ongoing thing, active now, and active in conjunction with present human bodies. Yet, this way of thinking incarnation will still be foreign to many Christians.

Christians have become accustomed to thinking of "the incarnation" rather than "incarnation." Many may feel that it is a betrayal of the particularity of Jesus to imagine that Christ's incarnation is still happening today. But as John Cobb and other process theologians such as Monica Coleman have shown, it is possible to think the particularity of incarnation in Jesus while still maintaining that the incarnation of God in Christ continues now.[24] While some Christians will maintain that a theology of ongoing incarnation shames Jesus the Christ by stealing his uniqueness, others will maintain that a theology that neglects such a possibility shames Jesus by denying a major power of his movement.

---

[23] Hart, 3.
[24] See John B. Cobb, Jr., *Christ in Pluralistic Age, Making a Way Out of No Way*. Eugene, OR: Wipf and Stock, 1999 and Monica A. Coleman, *Making a Way Out of No Way: A Womanist Theology*. Minneapolis: Fortress Press, 2008.

Feminist theologians have often asserted the ongoing nature of Christ's incarnation. They have vividly asserted Christ's incarnation as a present-day reality, with relevance to our embodied selves. Many of these theologians have done so with particular reference to erotic power.

A central example comes from Rita Brock as she elaborates a "christology of erotic power."[25] Brock powerfully writes erotic intimations into christology, insisting that "we are called not to dependence on a power outside ourselves, but to an exploration of the depths of our most inner, personal selves as the root of our connections to all others."[26] Brock develops an erotic christology that posits desire as power, leading to "self-possession, profound relationality, and the emergence of creative caring."[27]

In doing so, Brock makes it clear how incarnation extends into our present lives. Hers is "a christology not centered in Jesus, but in relationship and community as the whole-making, healing center of Christianity." She names christic presence "Christa/Community." Christa/Community includes but is more than Jesus. Though "Jesus participates centrally" in Christa/Community, "the reality of erotic power within connectedness means it cannot be located in a single individual." Thus Brock casts christology into present tense, for "what is truly christological, that is, truly revealing of divine incarnation and salvific power in human life, must reside in connectedness and not in single individuals."[28]

However, Brock's christology can also serve as an example of the way in which *kenosis* has seemed to be the inverse of *eros*. For example, she criticizes the understanding of Jesus as a "model for self-giving." Under such a model, "the question a Christian must ask is, 'What would Jesus do or have me do in this situation?' Such a question leads the focus of feeling and action away from self-awareness, away from our inner selves . . . because we are not compelled to ask 'How do I feel right now, how are others feeling, and what can I do to lessen all our pain and suffering in this context?'" For Brock, imitation of Jesus' self-giving "focuses on reality external to us," whereas focus on one's own feelings, or erotic guides, "moves toward heart . . . ."[29] For Brock, in contrast to indoctrinated imitation of Christ that requires denial of feelings, true Christ-like caring stems from listening to one's own heart, from being "self-aware" in giving.[30] In contrast,

---

[25] Rita Nakashima Brock, *Journeys by Heart: a Christology of Erotic Power*. New York: Crossroad, 1988.
[26] Ibid., 16.
[27] Ibid., xiv.
[28] Ibid., 52.
[29] Ibid., xiv.
[30] Brock's christic vision aligns the active sharing of heart in community with the real presence of Christ; she writes, "Christa/Community is a lived reality expressed in relational images. Hence Christa/Community is described in the images of events in which erotic power is made manifest" (*Journeys by Heart*, 52). Where desire flows from the heart in relationship, "christ" is present.

I suggest that self-giving may also offer a generation of embodied power, which is not imitation as much as fully embodied continuation of Christ's self-giving, now claimed as our own, self-aware and self-propelling.

Offering another example of incarnation through erotic power, Carter Heyward envisions that in our bodily revelations of mutually shared power, we are "godding."[31] Like Brock, Heyward invokes a "Christa," here as "a transitional christian symbol of sacred power" that "may help christians envision more clearly our power in mutual relation as *christic* power—the radically mutual power by which, through which, and with which we participate in creating and blessing, healing and liberating, one another."[32] As will not seem surprising after the analysis of Heyward's work in Chapter 4, her vision of redemptive power is one of mutuality. Christa "moves among us in our right relatedness, the power in our connectedness," and her name "can be a christian name for *eros*."[33] Thus, Heyward again sees *eros* and mutuality as fundamentally related. Christa can be "both ground and figure of our lovemaking," the "power between us, in our relation, as well as in the persons we are and are becoming, you and I, together."[34]

In her *Touching Our Strength*, Heyward explores *eros* as a simultaneously creative and liberating process.[35] She explains how "the erotic fabric of our lives in relation has not been treated affirmatively in the history of christian life and thought," and she does restorative work in considering "the sense in which God is erotic power."[36] Heyward has a very high appraisal of *eros*: "The erotic is our most fully embodied experience of the love of God." For her this *eros* shows the inadequacy of traditional categories of love, for this *eros*, this sacred power, is a love that "is agapic, philial, and erotic." Sacred *eros* is loving and, it would seem, ideal, and therefore Heyward explains that it is needfully different from some instances of physical intercourse and some instances of social charity. It is distinguished again by mutuality, by "our shared experience of power in relation."[37]

---

[31] Carter Heyward, *Touching Our Strength: The Erotic as Power and the Love of God*. San Francisco: HarperCollins, 1989, 150.
[32] Ibid., 92, cf. 116. Christa must be a transitional concept because "we cannot get stuck on her as *the* redemptive image, even for those of us who are Christians. To reify one symbol is to give ourselves permission to stop growing and changing" (116). Thus, Christa can never be one particular woman or man, and Heyward affirms Brock for speaking of "Christa/Community" in emphasis of Christa's fundamentally relational nature.
[33] Heyward, *Touching*, 116.
[34] Heyward, *Touching*, 117–118. Heyward also insists that Christa cannot be a uniquely Christian power. Rather, "hers can be merely a Christian name for the universal body of diverse peoples, religions, nations, and species-beings being formed and re-formed by the sacred and erotic power of mutual relation" (117).
[35] Heyward, *Touching*, 91.
[36] Ibid., and 94 and 91.
[37] Ibid., 99.

Another confluence of *eros* and incarnation comes from Lisa Isherwood, who advocates "radical" or "raw" incarnation.[38] This radical incarnation is seated in our skin, for we must "dare to believe that the human and the divine dwell in one flesh and that flesh is ours."[39] Otherwise, "Christ becomes an old fashioned redeemer and we can go back to sleep in the comfort of those all-powerful arms." This sleep, however, is a betrayal: "betrayal because as we sleep we give up our power, becoming disembodied and dependent."[40] For Isherwood, incarnation occurs in our own bodies, in our own power; thus, she makes her assertion that "feminists have always known that the personal is political and Christians have always known that incarnation changes the world; if we combine the two we have a powerful mix."[41]

Again, this incarnational power is for Isherwood erotic. She asks, "Is it too outrageous to suggest that the stories of transfiguration and ascension signaled the acceptance of the departure of the man but a personal embrace of the erotic power which remains constant?"[42] In Isherwood's use the erotic, resonating with the wide sense in which Lorde used it, means more than sex; it signals empowerment and voice.

Incarnation for Isherwood necessarily implies touch. Citing Heyward, Isherwood asks, "Is this what our stories are attempting to engage us in; an intimate and transforming revolution through something as simple and powerfully frightening as touch?"[43] Elsewhere she writes, responding to September 11, that we must "commit to our flesh and the flesh of others as the sites through which redemptive praxis unfolds."[44] Yet this commitment is a challenge because of the history of Christian doctrine, which has denigrated our own bodies: "God took the risk of leaping into flesh, yet we have been encouraged to resist our enfleshment. In short, we have not dared to risk our own divine incarnation."[45]

Like Isherwood, Heyward is critical of the way in which doctrines of incarnation have pinned an exclusivity on Jesus' flesh alone. She writes that "the incarnation of God in Jesus has been interpreted historically as an essentially spiritual act, in which Jesus' bodyself ('flesh') got spiritualized. The god whom Christians believe to be the source of love and justice in the universe

---

[38] Isherwood, "Embodiment," 144 and "Times of Terror," 78.
[39] Isherwood, "Embodiment," 144. She writes here that "while incarnation remains something that happened to someone else, whose mother was genetically interfered with, and all we have to do is believe, it is my opinion that we do not do justice to the struggles in the life of Jesus and the rich narrative that we have been asked to engage with."
[40] Ibid., 145. I would not, as Isherwood does here in passing, relate disempowerment with dependency.
[41] Ibid., 153.
[42] Ibid., 146.
[43] Ibid., 147.
[44] Isherwood, "Times of Terror," 79.
[45] Isherwood, "Embodiment," 149.

did not materialize for long, if it all, in Jesus." Instead, Christ became the symbol, not of God's ongoing presence in flesh, but rather of Jesus' "accomplished" spiritualization. Because of this narrowness in doctrines of incarnation, Heyward argues that "the incarnation is not taken seriously, even in Jesus' life, much less as the character structure of all creation."[46] For Heyward, incarnation—that is, "how we ourselves 'god' in the world"[47]—happens when, even in the face of violence, persons are "struggling for justice-love, mutuality, and right relation and, as such, are acting in solidarity with their sisters and brothers."[48]

Also looking critically at the history of interpretation of incarnation, Laurel Schneider writes of a "desiccating" of the incarnation. Schneider understands incarnation as "flesh showing the divine," such that revelation starts from the flesh and in the flesh. Schneider does not draw on *eros* in the explicit way the others explored here have done, but erotic undertones are surely present. She finds that the adjective "promiscuous" is a most appropriate description for incarnation, because it implies openness and multiplicity, while also connoting the sexual and bodily.[49] The purpose of God's promiscuous incarnation is "radical, compassionate, promiscuous love of the world to such an extent that suffering in any person, any body, is a wound in God's flesh, a diminishment of God's own beloved, a gravitational pull on God to come, again. And again."[50]

Thus, all of these feminist theologies of incarnation describe an incarnation in the present tense, conveying a power that does not mask over the human body in a display of transcendent might, but instead a power that is, muscularly, ours. And they all, perhaps not surprisingly, invoke some contour of the erotic.

One thing that we feminists surely gain through the invocation of *eros* is a sense of embodied power. Put theologically, our *eros* becomes a way to express ourselves as more than passive recipients of God's power, or alternatively, victims of others' hurtful desires. We are instead, or also, agents of power, agents of desire. Our *eros* can so strongly bring us to awareness of our embodied power. So it is no surprise that feminists have often turned to the erotic when discussing that doctrine of embodied power: incarnation.

And yet, as Kathleen Sands, K. Roberts Skerrett, and Alyda Faber have emphasized, *eros* construed as a pure power for good fails to recognize the complexity and ambivalency of the power we may access in *eros*, while also failing to recognize that we may *not* access such power there. Of the feminist *eros* theologies I have reviewed earlier, Sands, Skerrett, and Faber center

---

[46] Heyward, *Touching Our Strength*, 94.
[47] Heyward, *Saving Jesus*, 120.
[48] Ibid., 121.
[49] Laurel Schneider, "Promiscuous Incarnation," in *The Embrace of Eros*, 233.
[50] Ibid., 245.

their critiques particularly on the theologies of Heyward and Brock, contesting any invocation of *eros* as a pure feminist good, and critiquing the flat association of *eros* and power.[51]

A pure feminist *eros* can again reinstate an overbearing transcendence—a sexy "power over"—that trumps particular bodies and diverse erotic strategies in the process. For example, as Skerrett writes, as "the wellspring of joy, morality, and 'our power in mutual relation,' feminist eros promises to combine the ecstasy of orgasm with the equanimity of justice." As such, Skerrett continues, "feminist eros is never confused with pain: erotic suffering is an effect of the 'sadomasochistic spirituality' generated by antisensuous Christianity."[52] Summarizing the critique of feminist *eros* begun by Sands, Skerrett writes that "by conflating erotic yearning with aspirations for 'right relation,' we deny the possibility that eros can conflict with right relation."[53]

Thus a major problem that Sands, Skerrett, and Faber see in feminist theology's championing of *eros* is its eclipsing of ethical deliberation about the complexity of sexual experience, for good or bad. As Faber summarizes, the "theoretical construction of an essentialist eros has some very serious limitations for social analysis of patriarchal sexual violence."[54] For example, Sands writes of Heyward's work that Heyward "simultaneously overburdens sex with intrinsic moral meaning and deprives it of the extrinsic moral discernment it requires."[55] Thus, as we have seen in Chapter 4, "when eros is hypostasized into an ideal, ethically wayward pleasure"—for instance, sexual masochism—"must be classified as anomalous distortions or confusions of erotic reality."[56] Because she sees in Brock's work, for example, that "the actual dynamics of sexual power as it operates in the present are treated as penultimate or only apparent,"[57] Sands describes Brock's *eros* as "an antitragic category."[58] In Heyward Sands sees that *eros*, flatly understood as part of the "natural," becomes "a sort of grace—that is, a pure but never fully manifest good that must ultimately be grasped by faith rather than through experience." Sands dubs this lofty appraisal of *eros* as part of a "justification-by-eros-through-faith."[59]

---

[51] Sands also analyzes the work of Carol Christ, and Faber reviews a joint work by Brock and Thistlethwaite, *Casting Stones*. See Kathleen Sands, "Uses of the Thea(o)logian: Sex and Theodicy in Religious Feminism." *Journal of Feminist Studies in Religion* 8.1 (1992): 7–33 and Alyda Faber, "Eros and Violence," *Feminist Theology* 12.3 (2004): 319–342.

[52] K. Roberts Skerrett, "When No Means Yes: The Passion of Carter Heyward," *Journal of Feminist Studies in Religion*, 71. For an exploration of the ways in which feminist theological celebration of *eros* also may set up a metaphysical ideal that replicates the violence it seeks to replace, see Faber, "Eros and Violence."

[53] Skerrett, 72. She refers here to Sands, "Uses."

[54] Faber, *Eros and Violence*, 320–321, cf. 327.

[55] Sands, "Uses," 21.

[56] Ibid., 21.

[57] Ibid.

[58] Ibid., 17.

[59] Ibid., 19.

Audre Lorde's classic essay "The Uses of the Erotic" argued for "the Erotic as Power," and I have argued in this book that *kenosis* is also a source of power, a kenotic power not unrelated to but also not identical with *eros*. In Chapter 3 I argued that *kenosis* is not more akin to traditional understandings of either *agape* or *eros*, but rather may carry currents of both. It is neither as self-disregarding as traditional *agape* nor as acquisitive as traditional *eros*. I make this argument despite the way in which some theologians have tended to think of *kenosis* as more closely aligned with *agape*. In contrast, when discussing power, feminist theologians have been seen to be much more likely to invoke *eros* than *agape*. As Kathleen Sands summarizes, "Countering the patriarchal preference for bloodless agape, feminists made *eros* a privileged expression of the Divine."[60] So, while Nygren's theology saw *agape* as God's privileged expression, feminists chose *eros*.

In vividly theologizing *eros*, feminist theologians have demonstrated that, similar to Valerie Saiving's claim that an exclusive emphasis on selfish pride ignores the healthfulness of self-focus for many, a narrow understanding of desire as selfish and negative translates into a sequestering of desire even in circumstances where desire's expression could release creative power for good in the world. For example, Mary Daly envisions "pure lust," through which one "casts her lot, life, with the trees and the winds, the sands and the tides, the mountains and moors. She is Outcast, casting her Self outward, inward, breaking out of the casts/castes of phallocracy's fabrications/fictions, moving out of the maze of mediated experience."[61] Daly's image bursts with eccentric motion; this lust is hardly self-centered. Similarly, we might say that a lusty *kenosis* has the power to move out of oppression, the power to resist and to remember.

In their theologies of *eros* Brock and Heyward do vigorously seek to move beyond power-over, specifically as generated by patriarchal, heterosexual sexual dynamics. They move toward a mutual power and increased emphasis on relationality. But in doing so they also set up mutuality as the pure other—the antithesis —to violence, patriarchy, and heterosexism. Doing so potentially diffuses strategies for change that might arise and function within patriarchy, under heterosexism, amidst violence. Power with, in order to function without its own overpowering omnipotence, masking difference and disparity, would need the capability to strategize under—or dare I say *with*—power over. This might mean sometimes engaging the dynamics of power over in order to sway, modify, or pervert them. For power with is finally not mutuality if the other with whom you seek to generate power must be controlled or at least legislated by your predetermined ideals of togetherness.

---

[60] Kathleen Sands, "A Response to Marcella Althaus-Reid's *Indecent Theology: Theological Perversions in Sex, Gender, and Politics*," *Feminist Theology* 11.2 (2003), 175–181, this quote page 176.
[61] Mary Daly, *Pure Lust*. Boston: Beacon, 1984, 3.

Perhaps kenotic power, as power for, might avoid duplication of these problems with erotic power—similarly to how *eros* may be tempered and textured by *kenosis*. Perhaps in our gestures and longings, actions and yieldings *for*, we might embody ways to claim the power of desire while not idealizing that desire. First, *kenosis* implies no pure *eros*, and in fact erodes such purity through its affiliation with *agape*, through its familiarity with situations of unequal power, and through its trajectory *for*. Second, *kenosis* may take on the vulnerable, ambiguous, and painful more gracefully than any ideal.

Sands finds that Heyward and Brock both look "to eros for a synthesis of love and power."[62] As I have argued, christic self-giving, as power for ourselves—for our subjectivity—carries something of the dynamics that Christian theologians have traditionally recognized in both *eros* and *agape*. It need not be flatly equated with either, or even with "love." While there is a leaning toward self-giving, in *kenosis*, the desire and generosity that may adhere in this leaning need not be contingent on the affections we often associate with love. They may redefine or widen what love can look like, but if love were constrained to romance or, even more broadly, simply to affinity, and then were *kenosis* to always flow with love, then the power of it for resistance would be undermined.

Perhaps it is not surprising that Althaus-Reid invokes *kenosis*, as a feminist theologian who does not essentialize eros, who in fact invokes what has been unessential (indecent) to eros in attempt to unessentialize God—as we saw in Chapter 3.[63] For in *kenosis* we let go of ourselves and our expectations and our regulations, so drawn are we to another body, and to a new incarnation, which will also be ours. Otherwise, we may be too busy repudiating what we are not (patriarchs, etc.) to become what we are.

Eros will not save us; pure *agape* may smother us. *Kenosis* requires a pure form of neither of these. But *kenosis* offers no guarantees of salvation either. It is its own *telos*, its own pleasure. This implies a richly tangible power, and also a momentary, fragile, and vulnerable, most surely communicable, power.

This fragility and vulnerability tether kenotic power needfully away from the ideals feminism has seen in *eros*. As Skerret writes, "A feminist whose erotic expectations are stimulated by phantasies of elemental harmony may experience unrequited love, as Heyward does, as a moral disaster, an injustice . . . Could one imagine that suffering in love does not only have to do with deprivation, prohibition, fault?"[64] Indeed, I wonder, how could Christians imagine

---

[62] Sands, "Uses," 19.

[63] For a brief appraisal of Althaus-Reid's use of *eros* in comparison to other feminist theologies, see Kathleen Sands, "Response."

Sands commends Althaus-Reid for her insistence "that S/M and fetishism do not simply repeat but mimic or parody patterns of domination" ("Response," 176). Resonating with chapter 4 in the present volume, Sands elaborates that "ironic sexuality, like humor, is a sidelong glance at the interdependence of the norm and the transgression" (176).

[64] Skerrett, 90.

otherwise? Skerrett proposes that we admit the possibility of feminist *eros* that is "sensuously rich in its deprivations"[65] rather than caught in a shameful lack in its current imperfections. She stresses that "a tragic view of eros does not imply the inevitability of antisensuous, and anti-erotic culture; it rather requires a practical wisdom that sees renunciation as a positive discipline of love."[66] *Kenosis*, self-giving, as a practice and a power and pulse *for*, yields even its visions of perfection for the sake of the other, and thus holds open the possibility of a pleasure in a tragic yet lived present.

Having let go—having emptied—our claims on the other, and having productively released our presuppositions and prerequisites for our own identity, we witness the possibility of the other's becoming. We support and serve it; we stand as martyr or witness to it. So the other survives our passion.[67] And God survives our passion, made new by it. And—through God's commitment to us, and through the other's enabled becoming—something like "we" survives our passion too, though we are changed, or wounded, or disappointed, or exalted. Most of us survive as victim-survivors, leaving any number of empty tombs behind us in the pace of kenotic trajectory.

If power with aims toward a dynamic mutuality and commonly respected interests, power for supposes only that the other need thrive, entering a realm of conflicting interests and potential violence in staking that claim, yet standing on the conviction of that *for*ness, finding one's momentary subjectivity therein: I am the "pro-you being," which is also to say, I am. I am other than you. I am in the dynamic of my relation to you: I am for you.

Power for offers no assurances of safety or purity or predictability. Mainly through feigning power over has Christian power ever offered such promises. Living power for, giving power for, stands on a covenant more fragile, often tragic, more vulnerable, more poignant. And yet it is a sustaining power.

Like Brock's "Christa/Community," kenotic power also relies on a chrism that functions in connectedness, as a gesture for. Brock writes that "christ, as the center of christianity, will share in the patriarchal broken heart as long as it supports unilateral views of power."[68] Where she turns to erotic power as the desired alternative to unilateral power, I look to the ambiguity and fluidity of kenotic power, which need not exclude *eros* but may also include forms that

---

[65] Ibid.
[66] Ibid. Skerrett writes that "acknowledging the tragic dimension of eros implies that renunciation must be part of the play of erotic praxis" (89). She elaborates: "No means No. This is not just a slogan we teach adolescent boys. Renunciation—bearing the no of the beloved—is not antisensual asceticism: it is one of the positive disciplines of love" (91).
[67] This way of being in relationship resonates with the theory of both Jessica Benjamin and Luce Irigaray. See Benjamin's *Shadow of the Other: Intersubjectivity and Gender in Psychoanalysis*. London: Routledge, 1998 and Irigaray's *I Love to You: Sketch for a Felicity Within History*, trans. Alison Martin. New York: Routledge, 1996.
[68] Brock, *Journeys by Heart*, 52.

surprise us with both the wideness and the specificity of self-giving passion. For kenotic power relies on a concept of Christ given away, a claim to Jesus given away, out of faithfulness to the Christ thus embodied.

Kenotic power, like Heyward's vision of godding, may catalyze christic presence. But without the goal of mutuality, and without a pure "erotic power," this presence may be experienced quite differently and it may function toward different ends. While self-giving could and likely often is catalyzed out of desire for mutual relation, it could also function apart from that desire. It has a wider range of pleasures, shaped by the particularities of situations and passions. Kenotic passion (which need not be the only sort of incarnating power in the world) qualifies Heyward's use of passion by giving it more specific vector and thus allowing for criticism of passions that wound, passions that, for example, assert sheer power over.[69]

Kenotic passion may thus also lead toward a different outcome than Heyward's "boundary breaking as passionate godding"[70], which Skerrett has noted as problematic.[71] Heyward finds that out of passion for justice, in "revolutionary, boundary-breaking moments, our lives give birth to God . . ."[72] Yet kenotic passion leaves open the possibility that self-giving may sometimes find its own fulfillment along the path toward the boundary of the other, able to stop before it without the passion having been in vain, without it having failed. For if mutual relation is not always the goal, then passion can still find its release in having been for, even when not received or met, and thus can honor the "no" of the other when it comes. While social norms and laws will sometimes no doubt be broken by kenotic power, this power will also sometimes be one that yields to another's boundaries, one that regards the boundary, sanctifies the boundary, through the chrism of care. In these cases it is as though the chrism on the edge of our gesture for the other stops short of touching the other, unimposing, dripping into the space between, marking the difference: not smearing christic identity where it is refused, but releasing it into the space of acknowledgment, letting Christ be embodied in just such honorable and nonpossessive acknowledgment.

Althaus-Reid describes the generative flow of kenotic power vividly when she writes in her Queer theology: "The question in theology is about how Queer lovers do theology: they wander into each other's spaces, digress at points of desire, position and reposition themselves amongst themselves and

---

[69] See the section, "What Is Passion?," in Heyward, *Saving Jesus*, 120–123 and following. Heyward does discuss the possible of "going for" another out of passion, but she seems to mean "going on behalf of," as she suggests that sometimes we must "*go for* those who are without voice, presence, or the power required in a specific context." Otherwise, we are "going with," as in "to *go with* one another in the radically mutual, interdependent world and creation that we share . . ." (*Saving Jesus*, 131).

[70] Heyward, *Saving Jesus*, 137.

[71] Skerrett, 78–81.

[72] Heyward, *Saving Jesus*, 140.

amongst others and eventually participate in some creation of new (partial) conceptualizations of love and God."[73] Althaus-Reid queers *eros*, and *kenosis* queers the strictures previously placed on our expectations of how God might come. New incarnations of God, partial and momentary, may come as a function of kenotic desire among us. We lure not only each other, but God, through the claiming of our self-emptying passion. And we need not wait for ideal conditions to claim our desires. As Althaus-Reid writes, "The nomadic Queer is the image of the unstable or irredeemable body of a theological subject who lives amidst insecurity and risk."[74] Rather than making love in a bed of mutuality and shared power, we risk ourselves in passion—agapeic, erotic, and otherwise.

We human subjects, in our kenotic passions, lure the divine toward incessant incarnation in our present day.[75] But, heeding the wisdom of Frascati-Lochhead, discussed in Chapter 2, I emphasize the continuing fluidity of such incarnation. This is no static body that we can confidently declare "the body of Christ today," for such a clearly delineated body could quickly become the cornerstone of another triumphalist Christian metaphysics.[76] If the body of Christ is kenotic, then it is fluid. To borrow Eucharistic imagery, the body is less the bread or the wine than the movement of these elements between us: body of Christ, given for you. The body of Christ is less our bodies all gathered together at Eucharist and more our bodies in motion, sent out: body of Christ, given for you. Christ is not an identity we have decided upon (this church, this person) so much as Christ is movement, erotic and agapeic. Christ is present as a kinetic power.

Christians have tended toward the appropriative: God is *this bread*, God was *that body*. God was *that male body*. When we appropriate one fixed form as the definitive location of Christ, we seek to seal up the boundaries of a body, thus disembodying our incarnation, for any living body is fluid, porous, messy. If we claim to see Christ objectively in *that* suffering person, or even in *those* particular people, over there, then we are appropriating bodies for our revelation, rather than conveying God's presence through our own bodies, drawn toward specific others: being people *for*, people who for the love of another transfer the being of God, and give Christ away.

The "Christ" is the messiah, the "anointed one." "Christ" is at its root a wet image. Present-day incarnations of Christ happen in the tumble of chrism, the spill of oil from the brow or through history, a holy designation given away,

---

[73] Althaus-Reid, *Queer God*, 50.
[74] Ibid.
[75] To her credit, Heyward insists on Christa not being defined as one particular woman, but rather being open to change, being provisional.
[76] For an exploration of kenotic Christology specifically in the context of inter-religious relationships, see David H. Jensen, *In the Company of Others: A Dialogical Christology* (Cleveland, OH: Pilgrim Press, 2001).

offered, for specific others in particular moments. Christ is a gesture given away, power *for*. We ourselves cannot fully claim the incarnation of Christ; rather, Christ becomes between us and the ones to whom we are prodigally drawn, forgetting ourselves as we pour out our anointing oil, and perhaps *also* realizing ourselves in the exchange, our own skin wet with chrism. We are the body of Christ only as we give Christ away, as we anoint, as we realize Christ in the extended chrism between us, over and over again in new moments and new Eucharist. The "anointed one" rolls down like waters through the cracks of time and place, tumbling in ever-flowing streams through the interstices of our messy and sometimes painful relating, a living chrism, which is our delight. And through our own *kenosis* we continually come into new incarnations of ourselves, tugging with us the chrism of Christ.

Passionate Christ

Heyward writes that "the whole point of the Jesus story . . . is missed if we fail to see, at its core, a passion for *life!*"[77] Yet Christians often focus on Jesus' death and the gore of his passion story, over and above the passionate vigor of Jesus' life and death.

We Christians have become accustomed to claiming that Jesus "died for us." On its own this is an almost indecipherable claim; it relies instead on various legacies of theological thought to make it interpretable. Depending on what sort of theology influences the claimant, the phrase can mean different things. It can mean "died in our place," as in the enduringly popular medieval atonement theology. It can also mean "died because of our sins." This meaning is a component of atonement theology, but it also has a place quite differently in an ancient Israelite understanding that ill circumstances come as a consequence of the corporate sins of the people. In that later sense one could hypothesize, though it sounds problematic to a modern ear, that Jesus' people may have understood Roman occupation of Palestine as part of the fallout of the people's straying from the covenant (as, for instance, the fall into Babylonian exile is interpreted in Isaiah). Jesus and other righteous Jews seeking to restore the covenant die as a consequence of the evil times that have befallen the people of God, and in so doing, leave a bright and poignant witness to the vigor of the covenant, calling people back to it even in death: dying "for us." In yet another sense "died for us" can mean "died for our cause." This interpretation holds sway in many contemporary and liberation theologies that have found inspiration in the legacy of Jesus as an oppressed person fighting for justice and being killed in the process of his resistance. For example, Heyward asserts that "the cross has nothing whatsoever to do with a deity who, in the image of a father,

---

[77] Heyward, *Saving Jesus*, 138.

would hand his son over to be crucified," but rather "the cross can be an image of JESUS' love and solidarity, of what it cost him and what it costs all of us who suffer because they love."[78]

In an assertion that, to my ear, emphasizes the commitment of God to be *for us*, Kathryn Tanner claims that "the primary meaning of 'for us' . . . is benefit rather than legal substitution; Jesus dies to benefit us so that we will no longer have to live as we do in a sin-afflicted, death-ridden world." For Tanner this newness of life is attained not solely because Jesus died, but because Jesus is the incarnate Word of God, and thus the relationship of God and God's people is itself efficacious. For "in Jesus the Word makes our cause its own . . ."[79]

Tanner reframes doctrines of atonement under doctrines of incarnation, where she argues that early Christian and patristic authors securely saw them. This reframing conveys the message that God's saving action is in communion with humanity, not in any transaction of human suffering on the cross. Thus, with a doctrine of incarnation Tanner is able to answer the concerns of many feminist and womanist theologians about the cross. It is the incarnation—the joining of God's Word with the human body, not just in Jesus' birth but in the whole of his life—that has a saving function for the plight of the human body. It is not the suffering of sacrificial acts of humans, or the human Jesus, that proves redemptive. Tanner's emphasis on the whole of incarnation answers feminist and womanist critiques of redemptive suffering.

Tanner further argues that sacrifice itself can be understood, as it has been in other times and cultures, as an enactment of community and thus, again, the work of the incarnation. Rather than as personal renunciations with no clear vector or recipient,[80] sacrifices might instead function such that they, like Tanner's description of Israelite sacrifices, "celebrate or end in joyous communion."[81] Here Tanner addresses feminist critiques by arguing that the sacrifice often *read onto* the cross (for Tanner is clear that the cross is not properly a sacrifice) must be understood as a sacrifice of God's to and for humanity.[82] Though I resonate with Tanner's relational reading of the cross, my own response to feminist concerns does not involve defining sacrifice as solely in God's domain. In some ways, despite her claim that "humans are not to offer sacrifices to God," neither does Tanner's response. For she quotes Romans and claims that humans are to offer sacrifices not "sanctified in death, but in the lives they live, for life" such that "service to the neighbor becomes the reality designated by 'sacrifices to God'."[83]

---

[78] Ibid., 122.
[79] Kathryn Tanner, "Incarnation, Cross, Sacrifice: A Feminist-Inspired Reappraisal." *ATR* 86.1: 35–56, this quotation 44.
[80] Tanner, 50.
[81] Ibid., 51
[82] Ibid., 53–55.
[83] Ibid., 55–56

The kenotic pulse of incarnation I am exploring here does, with Tanner, view the events of the cross and of Jesus' ministry in the context of incarnation. Already with the Philippians hymn, Jesus' self-emptying was integral to the process of Christ's embodiment in "the form of a human." Before the possible Pauline redaction to the hymn, which takes the vector of Jesus' life to death specifically on the cross, Jesus' *kenosis* could be read altogether as incarnation, as submission to embodied human life and its mortality. With a focus on kenotic power for incarnation, one can also see the life and power of the apostles, as in Acts or in the Pauline epistles, as part of the continuing incarnation, as in shared holy meals, in baptism, and in life together the people remember Jesus' claim to incorporate, ingest, or join "the body of Christ."

But because of the incarnation—that is, in my use of it, because of the years of the life of Jesus, but also because of the ancient, ongoing, and enduring commitment of God to be of, with, and for God's people, flesh to flesh—I cannot distinguish neatly between sacrifices from or to God and sacrifices from or to human persons. Christ is becoming incarnate still, in the flow of so much sacrifice, so much holy-making, not because God rewards our suffering with subsequent access to Christ, but because God is God among us and cannot cease to be so. Our self-emptying, when christic, is neither self-righteousness nor diffuse charity but rather always necessarily for another, for particular others to whom we are passionately drawn. That other is to some extent Christ, because we anoint Christ in our *kenosis*, and to some extent Christ is incarnate in us, but only on the outstretched figures of our gesture for, as our fingers too are wet with the chrism we have shared. Perhaps Christ is mostly glimmering between. The conveying of the chrism, the kinetics of our *kenosis* itself, brings Christ to flesh more concretely (because less concretely) than any marked or marking one himself or herself. For incarnation has always been a joining, a meeting, a communion. And as flesh, it is transient, shifting, changing—recognized as carnally alive by motion—down to our day and our bodies and—necessarily, always—beyond them.

Like Tanner, Heyward connects atonement and incarnation, though in her own manner, writing that "if we are living passionately, we are participating simultaneously in what Christian theologians have named the 'incarnation' (God's embodied place among us) and the 'atonement' (God's redemptive action among us)."[84] Though Heyward's claims are always for "right" or mutual relation, this does not mean that incarnational activity steers clear of violent settings; rather, "whenever God is incarnate (made flesh) in any context of violence . . . atonement is underway."[85]

As part of the flow of Jesus' christic self-giving, Jesus' death comes not as the exemplary instance of Jesus' *kenosis* (though Paul might have it so), but rather

---

[84] Heyward, *Saving Jesus*, 116.
[85] Ibid., 121.

as the realizing of one possible result of Jesus' passionate life. Jesus need not suffer the Roman cross for us, but Jesus could not be other than for us, and that *for*ness was in one vital instance met with the cross. Followers retelling that passionate narrative come to make this consequence stand as yet another example of Jesus' pulse of power for us, in that the cross is remembered not as, or not only as, a scene of horrible victimization, but as a mark of resistance and survival. Followers recalling and sacramentally invoking the death of their passionate Christ insist that power for be conveyed in the telling, rather than an utter victimizing and smashing of power. We insist with Gospel and sacrament that Jesus took christic subjectivity to the cross, that his suffering stands as an expression of his cry, "I am!" rather than a sign that abusers could take this from him. We remember Jesus to the last as a person for resistance to exploitation and for ongoing christic power, a power we now embody in our remembering, in our bodies and selves, in our resistance: in Christ.

A theology of the cross that emphasizes the resistance of the crucified rather than Jesus' atoning victimization may honor Christian abuse survivors by aligning them with the story and power of Christ.[86] They are bearing their cross, not in their passionless subjection to abuse, but rather in their passionate resistance to the culture of abuse.

Self-giving may convey a kenotic power to anoint Christ, to mark christic presence among us today. Yet, if these present-day incarnations of Christ were to require a ceding of one's own presence—Christ's full presence as our own full absence—then *kenosis* would function again as a tool of oppression, and thus, of pseudo-incarnation, not real presence at all. Divine *kenosis* longs for, waits for, evokes and believes in our capacity for our passionate *yes* to our kenotic power. Our yes, our kenotic desire, reveals our full presence, as we are bearing chrism and marking the full presence of Christ.

In interpreting the *kenosis* of Jesus, his "yes" is crucial, too. The fecundity of Jesus' kenotic resistance appears already in the Gospels. But in order to recognize the strength of the resistance of Jesus, it is necessary to locate power in the whole pattern of his life, and in the full-bodied current of vivacity that goes with him to the cross, and not in any bloodthirsty other who alone holds all power and who demands of Jesus an atoning sacrifice. It is necessary to recognize the agency in Jesus' kenotic risks, an agency obscured by atonement theologies in which the Father functions in his dispassionate love as an overlord orchestrating the passion of Christ. The "passion of Christ" presents us with a gory victim upon whom we may voyeuristically gaze, while the *passionate* Christ exudes kenotic power, calling us witnesses to task and luring us out from closeted corners with a passion that is *for us*, quite particularly.

---

[86] For a postcolonial feminist assertion of this sort of power in the Cross, see Wonhee Anne Joh, *Heart of the Cross: A Postcolonial Christology* (Louisville, KY: WJKP, 2006).

Drawn by Christ's passionate desire for us, we tap the kenotic power flowing from the broken side of Christ. We feast with Julian of Norwich on the fertile milk of Christ, for "our tender Mother Jesus can lead us easily into his blessed breast through his sweet open side, and show us there a part of the godhead and the joys of heaven, with inner certainty of endless bliss."[87] In bliss, we, with Augustine, "receive what we are": the body of Christ.[88] Empowered, chrism streams from our own bodies, from our own most guttural sense of self, from our own kenotic desires. Though we may also be victims, we are, with Audre Lorde, "responsible to ourselves in the deepest sense,"[89] and in the fierce pleasures of this responsibility, the passionate Christ survives.

Rather than clinging to the uniqueness of the incarnations of Christ we have known, Christ propels us forward, riding the desires for the thriving of others that we claim in ourselves, and this motion for the sake of the world generates the chrism that marks the transient musculature of Christ in our day. This chrism is given away—wet with holiness, we reach for the beloved in all her specificity—and the gesture may demonstrate the power explored in this book:

> through humility which need not seek triumph (Chapter 1);
> through gritty and tenacious solidarity (Chapter 2);
> through coming out to ourselves and enabling others to do the same (Chapter 3);
> through assertions of agency that court pain in their fervor, and might just disrupt violent dominion along the way (Chapter 4);
> through creative care that meets violence with fierce commitments otherwise (Chapter 5).

Have we not seen this power in Jesus as Christ? Have we not seen this power in Christian witnesses through the ages? Have we not seen this power in those who have claimed Christ and yet have been marginalized by the Christian tradition? And do we not feel this power now, deeply inlaid in our own muscle tissue: leaning, yielding, propelling? Holy mystery.

In this book I have explored the power *kenosis* may generate for resistance, for pleasure, and for new subjectivities, both divine and human. Because of the ways that Christianity's powerful have repeatedly distorted the rhetoric of *kenosis* to bend others under their power, any discussion of "kenotic power" will raise red flags for those committed to theological honesty about Christian power's tendency toward abuse. Theological care around questions of *kenosis* continues to be necessary because abuse continues. And meanwhile, we who feel the pull of vigorously kenotic christic currents need language to express

---

[87] Julian of Norwich, *Showings*, 60.
[88] Augustine of Hippo, *Sermon on John* 26.13.
[89] Lorde, "Uses of the Erotic," 58.

our self-giving desires, for it is precisely the expression of these desires that can contribute to the tides that will curb our abusive culture. Thus, *kenosis* merits theological reconsideration, *through and with* honesty about the hazards of kenotic doctrine.

My sense that any theological claim *for* kenotic power needs to emerge *alongside* forthrightness about the dangers of kenotic theology offers a theoretical analogy for another argument I have made in this book. While kenotic power is not a novel form of power, it does offer particular relevance to Christian life in pluralistic cultures and in a postmodern framework. This is because kenotic power need not be a pure form of energy existing as an absolute alternative to the conditions in which we already live. Emerging from our own guts, our own desires, it cannot be some "totally other power," always on top. *Kenosis* is always already on the move: down, under, with, *for*. In the context of this particular book, if I were to posit a sort of *good kenosis* in contrast to *bad*, exploitive *kenosis*, I would theoretically be setting up the same over-and-against postures that *kenosis* itself has the capability to productively confuse. Considering *kenosis* as a power *related to* and not clearly distinct from exploitive uses of it illustrates the sites where kenotic power most vividly emerges: in the thick of things.

Kenotic power does not tend toward setting itself apart in holiness; rather, it seeks to muddy our idealizations and engage us in the challenging of our repressed and oppressive social orders. Thus, it is the potential of *kenosis* to generate power even and perhaps especially in the hybridized soil of power differentials, crossed purposes, and conflictual histories that has funded my consideration of it in the chapters of this book. The currents of *kenosis* press forward, not from above and beyond, but from fissures in the thick complexity of our present circumstances. And there Christ emerges with us.

Bibliography

Adams, Carol J. "'I Just Raped My Wife! What Are You Going to Do About It, Pastor?': The Church and Sexual Violence." In *Transforming a Rape Culture*, rev. edn, edited by Emilie Buchwald, Pamela R. Fletcher, and Martha Roth, 75–104. Minneapolis, MN: Milkweed, 2005.

Adams, Carol J. and Marie M. Fortune, eds. *Violence against Woman and Children: A Christian Theological Sourcebook*. New York: Continuum, 1998.

Alsdurf, J. M. "Wife Abuse and the Church: The Response of Pastors." *Response to the Victimization of Women and Children* 8.1 (1985): 9–11.

Althaus-Reid, Marcella. *Indecent Theology: Theological Perversions in Sex, Gender, and Politics*. London: Routledge, 2000.

—. *The Queer God*. London: Routledge, 2003.

Balthasar, Hans Urs von. *The Glory of the Lord V: The Realm of Metaphysics in the Modern Age*. Edinburgh: T & T Clark, 1991. First published in German 1965.

—. *Mysterium Paschale*. Edinburgh, Scotland: T&T Clark, Ltd., 1990. First published in German as *Theologie der Drei Tage*. Einsiedeln: Benziger Verlag, 1970.

—. *Theo-drama: Theological Dramatic Theory* IV: *The Action*. San Francisco: Ignatius Press, 1994.

Bartky, Sandra Lee. "Feminine Masochism and the Politics of Personal Transformation." In *Living with Contradictions: Controversies in Feminist Social Ethics*, edited by Alison M. Jaggar, 519–529. Boulder, CO: Westview Press, 1994.

Barton, Carlin A. "Savage Miracles: The Redemption of Lost Honor in Roman Society and the Sacrament of the Gladiator and the Martyr." *Representations* 45 (1994): 41–71.

Benjamin, Jessica. *The Bonds of Love: Psychoanalysis, Feminism, and the Problem of Domination*. New York: Pantheon Books, 1988.

—. *Shadow of the Other: Intersubjectivity and Gender in Psychoanalysis*. London: Routledge, 1998.

Blodgett, Barbara J. *Constructing the Erotic: Sexual Ethics and Adolescent Girls*. Cleveland, OH: Pilgrim Press, 2002.

Bonhoeffer, Dietrich. *Christ the Center*. Translated by John Bowden. New York: Harper & Row, 1966.

—. *Letters and Papers from Prison*. New edition. New York: Collier Books, 1971.

—. *Life Together*. Dietrich Bonhoeffer's Works, vol. 5. Minneapolis, MN: Fortress Press, 1996. First published in German as *Gemeinsames Leben*. Chr. Kaiser Verlag, 1939.

—. "Lectures on Christology." *Dietrich Bonhoeffer's Works*, vol. 12. Minneapolis, MN: Fortress Press, 2009.

Boston Women's Healthbook Collective. *Our Bodies, Ourselves for the New Century*. New York: Touchstone, 1998.

Bowker, Lee H. "Women and the Clergy: An Evaluation." *The Journal of Pastoral Care* 36.4 (1982): 226–234.
Brock, Rita Nakashima. *Journeys by Heart: A Christology of Erotic Power.* New York: Crossroad, 1988.
Brock, Rita N. and Parker, Rebecca Ann. *Proverbs of Ashes: Violence, Redemptive Suffering, and the Search for What Saves Us.* Boston: Beacon Press, 2001.
—. *Saving Paradise: How Christianity Traded Love of This World for Crucifixion and Empire.* Boston: Beacon, 2008.
Brown, Joanne Carlson and Carole R. Bohn, eds. *Christianity, Patriarchy, and Abuse: A Feminist Critique.* Cleveland, OH: Pilgrim Press, 1989.
Brown, Joanne Carlson and Rebecca Parker. "For God So Loved the World?" In *Christianity, Patriarchy, and Abuse: A Feminist Critique*, edited by Joanne Carlson Brown and Carole R. Bohn, 1–30. Cleveland, OH: Pilgrim Press, 1989.
Brown, Peter. *Power and Persuasion in Late Antiquity: Towards a Christian Empire.* Madison, WI: University of Wisconsin Press, 1992.
Brumberg, Joan Jacobs. *The Body Project: An Intimate History of American Girls.* New York: Random House, 1997.
Buchwald, Emilie, Pamela R. Fletcher, and Martha Roth, eds. *Transforming a Rape Culture*, rev. edn. Minneapolis, MN: Milkweed, 2005.
Burrus, Virginia. *"Begotten, Not Made":* Conceiving Manhood in Late Antiquity. Stanford, CA: Stanford University Press, 2000.
—. *Sex Lives of Saints: An Erotics of Ancient Hagiography.* Philadelphia: University of Pennsylvania Press, 2003.
—. "Radical Orthodoxy and the Heresiological Habit: Engaging Graham Ward's Christology." In *Interpreting the Postmodern*, edited by Rosemary Radford Ruether and Marion Grau, 36–53. New York: T&T Clark, 2006.
—. "Queer Father: Gregory of Nyssa and the Subversion of Identity." In *Queer Theology: Rethinking the Western Body*, edited by Gerard Loughlin, 147–162. Malden, MA: Blackwell, 2007.
Burrus, Virginia and Catherine Keller, eds. *Toward a Theology of Eros: Transfiguring Passion at the Limits of Discipline.* New York: Fordham University Press, 2006.
Burrus, Virginia and Stephen D. Moore. "Unsafe Sex: Feminism, Pornography, and the Song of Songs." *Biblical Interpretation* 11 (2003): 24–52.
Burstow, Bonnie. *Radical Feminist Therapy: Working in the Context of Violence.* Newbury Park, CA: Sage, 1992.
Bussert, Joy. *Battered Women: From a Theology of Suffering to an Ethic of Empowerment.* New York: Lutheran Church of America, Division for Mission in North America, 1986.
Butler, Judith. *Gender Trouble: Feminism and the Subversion of Identity.* New York: Routledge Classics, 2006.
Cameron, Averil. *Christianity and the Rhetoric of Empire: The Development of Christian Discourse.* Berkeley, CA: University of California, 1991.
Campbell, Jacquelyn, Linda Rose, Joan Kub, and Daphne Nedd. "Voices of Strength and Resistance: A Contextual and Longitudinal Analysis of Women's Responses to Battering." *Journal of Interpersonal Violence* 13 (December 1998): 743–762.

Cannon, Katie G. "Erotic Justice: Authority, Resistance, and Transformation." *Journal of Feminist Studies in Religion* 23 (Spring 2007): 22–25.

Carson, Ronald A. "Motifs of Kenosis and Imitation in the work of Dietrich Bonhoeffer, with an Excursus on the Communicatio Idiomatum." *Journal of the American Academy of Religion* 43 (1975): 542–553.

Castelli, Elizabeth. *Martyrdom and Memory: Early Christian Culture Making.* New York: Columbia University Press, 2004.

Clark, Elizabeth A. *Reading Renunciation: Asceticism and Scripture in Early Christianity.* Princeton, NJ: Princeton University Press, 1999.

Coakley, Sarah. "*Kenosis*: Theological Meanings and Gender Connotations." In *The Work of Love: Creation as Kenosis*, ed. John Polkinghorne, 192–210. Grand Rapids, MI: Wlm. B. Eerdmans, 2001.

—. *Powers and Submissions: Spirituality, Philosophy, and Gender.* Oxford: Blackwell, 2002.

—. "Jail Break: Meditation as a Subversive Activity." *Christian Century* 121.13 (2004): 18–21.

—. "Is There a Future for Gender and Theology? On Gender, Contemplation, and the Systematic Task." *Svensk Teologisk Kvartalshrift* 85.2 (2009): 52–61.

—. "Pain and Its Transformations: A Discussion." *Svensk Teologisk Kvartalshrift* 85.2 (2009): 81–84.

—. "In Defense of Sacrifice: Gender, Selfhood and the Binding of Isaac." In *Feminism, Sexuality and the Return of Religion*, edited by John D. Caputo. Forthcoming.

Coates, Linda and Allen Wade. "Language and Violence: Analysis of Four Discursive Operations." *Journal of Family Violence* 22 (2007): 511–522.

Cobb, John B., Jr. *Christ in a Pluralistic Age.* Eugene, OR: Wipf and Stock, 1999.

Coleman, Monica A. *The Dinah Project: A Handbook for Congregational Response to Sexual Violence.* Cleveland, OH: Pilgrim Press, 2004.

—. *Making a Way Out of No Way: A Womanist Theology.* Minneapolis, MN: Fortress Press, 2008.

Contreras-Byrd, Melinda. "A Living Sacrifice?" *The Other Side* 38.2 (2002): 20–23.

Cook, Sarah L., Jennifer L. Woolard, and Harriet C. McCollum. "The Strengths, Competencies, and Resilience of Women Facing Domestic Violence: How Can Research and Policy Support Them?" In *Investing in Children, Youth, Families, and Communities: Strength-Based Research and Policy*, edited by Kenneth Maton, 97–115. Washington, DC: APA Books, 2004.

Cooper-White, Pamela. *The Cry of Tamar: Violence against Women and the Church's Response.* Minneapolis, MN: Fortress Press, 1995.

Costa, Mario. "For the Love of God: The Death of Desire and the Gift of Life." In *Toward a Theology of Eros*, edited by Virginia Burrus and Catherine Keller, 38–62. New York: Fordham Press, 2007.

Crysdale, Cynthia S. W. *Embracing Travail: Retrieving the Cross Today.* London: Continuum, 1999.

Dabney, D. Lyle. *Die Kenosis des Geistes: Kontinuität zwischen Schöpfung und Erlösung in Werk des Heiligen Geistes.* Neukierchen-Vluyn: Neukiechener Verlag, 1997.

Dahill, Lisa. *Reading from the Underside of Selfhood: Bonhoeffer and Spiritual Formation.* Eugene, OR: Pickwick Publications, 2009.

Daly, Mary. *Pure Lust: Elemental Feminist Philosophy.* Boston: Beacon, 1984.

Destrempes, Sylvain. *Thérèse de Lisieux et Dietrich Bonhoeffer: Kénose et altérité*. Montréal: Médiaspaul, 2002.
Elm, Susanna. *Virgins of God: The Making of Asceticism in Late Antiquity*. Oxford: Clarendon, 1994.
Evans, Stephen C., ed. *Exploring Kenotic Christology: The Self-Emptying of God*. New York: Oxford University Press, 2006.
Faber, Alyda. "Eros and Violence." *Feminist Theology* 12.3 (2004): 319–342.
Forde, Gerhard. *Justification by Faith: A Matter of Death and Life*. Mifflintown, PA: Sigler Press, 1990.
Fowl, Stephen E. *Philippians*. Grand Rapids, MI: Wm. B. Eerdmans, 2005.
Frascati-Lochhead, Marta. Kenosis *and Feminist Theology: The Challenge of Gianni Vattimo*. Albany, NY: State University of New York Press, 1998.
Friedman, Jaclyn and Jessica Valenti. *Yes Means Yes: Visions of Female Sexual Power and a World without Rape*. Berkeley, CA: Seal, 2008.
Gardner, Lucy and David Moss. "Something Like Time; Something Like the Sexes—an Essay in Reception." In *Balthasar at the End of Modernity*, by Lucy Gardner, David Moss, Ben Quash, and Graham Ward, 69–138. Edinburgh: T&T Clark, 1999.
Gebara, Ivone. *Out of the Depths: Women's Experience of Evil and Salvation*, translated by Ann Patrick Ware. Minneapolis, MN: Fortress Press, 2002.
Gilligan, Carol. *In a Different Voice: Psychological Theory and Women's Development*. Cambridge, MA: Harvard University Press, 1982.
Gillum, Tameka, Cris M. Sullivan, and Deborah I. Bybee. "The Importance of Spirituality in the Lives of Domestic Violence Survivors." *Violence Against Women* 12 (March 2006): 240–250.
Grant, Colin. "For the Love of God: Agape." *Journal of Religious Ethics* 24 (Spring 1996): 3–21.
Green, Clifford J. *Bonhoeffer: A Theology of Sociality*. Grand Rapids, MI: Wm. B. Eerdmans, 1972, 1999.
Grillmeier, Aloys. *Christ in Christian Tradition, vol.1: From the Apostolic Age to Chalcedon*, translated by J. S. Bowden. London: A. R. Mowbray and Co., 1965.
Hampson, Daphne, ed. *Swallowing a Fishbone? Feminist Theologians Debate Christianity*. London: Society for Promoting Christian Knowledge, 1996.
—. *Theology and Feminism*. Oxford: Blackwell, 1990.
Harrison, Beverly W. and Carter Heyward. "Pain and Pleasure: Avoiding the Confusions of Christian Tradition in Feminist Theory." In *Christianity, Patriarchy, and Abuse: A Feminist Critique*, edited by Joanne Carlson Brown and Carole R. Bohn, 148–173. Cleveland, OH: Pilgrim Press, 1989.
Hart, Lynda. *Between the Body and the Flesh: Performing Sadomasochism*. New York: Columbia University Press, 1998.
Heine, Susanne. "Female Masochism and the Theology of the Cross," translated by Fredrick J. Gaiser. *Word & World* 15 (1995): 299–305.
Hess, Carol Lakey. *Caretakers of Our Common House: Women's Development in Communities of Faith*. Nashville, TN: Abingdon Press, 1997.
Heyward, Isabel Carter. *The Redemption of God: A Theology of Mutual Relation*. Lanham, MD: University Press of America, 1982.
—. *Touching Our Strength: The Erotic as Power and the Love of God*. San Francisco: Harper & Row, 1989.

—. "Lamenting the Loss of Love: A Response to Colin Grant." *Journal of Religious Ethics* 24 (Spring 1996): 23–28.
Hite, Shere. *Women and Love: A Cultural Revolution in Progress.* New York: Alfred A. Knopf, 1987.
Holland, Scott. "A Poetics of Place and an Entanglement with People: A Relational Reading of Bonhoeffer's Theology." In *Theology and Conversation: Towards a Relational Theology*, edited by J. Haers and P. De Mey, 833–845. Leuven (Belgium): Leuven University Press, 2003.
Hollander, Jocelyn A. "Challenging Despair: Teaching about Women's Resistance to Violence." *Violence Against Women* 11 (June 2005): 776–791.
Hollander, Jocelyn A. and Einwohner, Rachel L. "Conceptualizing Resistance." *Sociological Forum* 19 (December 2004): 533–554.
Horsley, Richard and Neil Asher Silberman. *The Message and the Kingdom: How Jesus and Paul Ignited a Revolution and Transformed the Ancient World.* Minneapolis, MN: Fortress, 2002.
Horton, Anne and Judith Williamson, eds. *Abuse and Religion: When Praying Isn't Enough.* New York: D. C. Heath and Company, 1988.
Hunter, Nan. "Contextualizing the Sexuality Debates: A Chronology 1966–2005." In *Sex Wars: Sexual Dissent and Political Culture*, 10th anniversary edn, by Lisa Duggan and Nan D. Hunter, 15–28. New York: Routledge, 2006.
Irigaray, Luce. *I Love to You: Sketch for a Felicity Within History*, translated by Alison Martin. New York: Routledge, 1996.
Isherwood, Lisa. "The Embodiment of Feminist Liberation Theology: The Spiralling of Incarnation." *Feminist Theology* 12.2 (2004), 140–156.
—. "Incarnation in Times of Terror: Christian Theology and the Challenge of September 11th." *Feminist Theology* 14.1 (2005), 69–81.
—. *The Power of Erotic Celibacy: Queering Heteropatriarchy.* London: T & T Clark, 2006.
Jantzen, Grace. *Becoming Divine: Towards a Feminist Philosophy of Religion.* Bloomington, IN: Indiana University Press, 1999.
—. "New Creations: Eros, Beauty, and the Passion for Transformation." In *Toward a Theology of Eros*, edited by Virginia Burrus and Catherine Keller, 271–287. New York: Fordham Press, 2007.
Jasper, Alison. "Reading for Pleasure/Reading for Pain: Feminist Reflections on the Passion Narrative in John's Gospel." In *Religion and Sexuality*, edited by Michael A. Hayes, Wendy J. Porter, and David Tombs, 203–212. Sheffield, England: Sheffield Academic Press, 1998.
Jensen, David H. *In the Company of Others: A Dialogical Christology.* Cleveland, OH: Pilgrim Press, 2001.
Joh, Wonhee Anne. *Heart of the Cross: A Postcolonial Christology.* Louisville, KY: Westminster John Knox, 2006.
Jones, Serene. *Feminist Theory and Christian Theology: Cartographies of Grace.* Minneapolis, MN: Fortress, 2000.
Kellenbach, Katharina von. *Anti-Judaism in Feminist Religious Writings.* Atlanta, GA: Scholar's Press, 1994.
Keller, Catherine. *From a Broken Web: Separation, Sexism, and Self.* Boston: Beacon, 1986.

—. "Feminism and the Ethic of Inseparability." In *Weaving the Visions: New Patterns in Feminist Spirituality*, edited by Judith Plaskow and Carol P. Christ, 256–265. San Francisco: Harper San Francisco, 1989.

—. "Scoop Up the Water and the Moon Is in Your Hands: On Feminist Theology and Dynamic Self-Emptying." In *The Emptying God*, edited by John B. Cobb, Jr. and Christopher Ives, 102–115. Maryknoll, NY: Orbis Books, 1990.

—. "More on Feminism, Self-Sacrifice, and Time: Or, Too Many Words for Emptiness." *Buddhist-Christian Studies* 13 (1993): 211–217.

—. "Afterword: A Theology of Eros, After Transfiguring Passion." In *Toward a Theology of Eros: Transfiguring Passion at the Limits of Discipline*, edited by Virginia Burrus and Catherine Keller, 366–374. New York: Fordham University Press, 2006.

—. *On the Mystery: Discerning God in Process*. Minneapolis, MN: Fortress, 2008.

Kelly, Liz. *Surviving Sexual Violence*. Minneapolis, MN: University of Minnesota Press, 1988.

Kittay, Eva Feder. *Love's Labor: Essays on Women, Equality, and Dependency*. London: Routledge, 1999.

LaCugna, Catherine Mowry. *God for Us: The Trinity and Christian Life*. New York: Harper San Francisco, 1991.

Lamb, Sharon, ed. *New Versions of Victims: Feminists Struggle with the Concept*. New York: New York University Press, 1999.

Lebacqz, Karen. "Love Your Enemy: Sex, Power, and Christian Ethics." In *Feminist Theological Ethics: A Reader*, edited by Lois K. Daly, 244–261. Louisville, KY: Westminster/John Knox Press, 1994.

Linahan, Jane E. "*Kenosis*: Metaphor of Relationship." In *Theology and Conversation: Towards a Relational Theology*, eds J. Haers and P. De Mey, 299–309. Leuven: Leuven University Press, 2003.

Lorde, Audre. *Sister Outsider: Essays and Speeches*. Berkeley, CA: Crossing Press, 1984.

Luther, Martin. *A Treatise on Christian Liberty*, translated by W. A. Lambert. Philadelphia, PA: Fortress Press, 1957.

—. *Luther's Works, vol. 26: Lectures on Galatians* (1535), edited by Jaroslav Pelikan. St. Louis, MO: Concordia Publishing House, 1995.

—. "Philippians 2." In *Luther's Sammtliche Werke*, vol. 5. Weimar: Hermann Bohlaus Nachfolger, 1883.

—. "Heidelberg Disputation, 1518." In *Luther: Early Theological Works*, edited by James Atkinson. Louisville, KY: Westminster/John Knox Press, 2006.

Lyman, Rebecca. *Christology and Cosmology: Models of Divine Activity in Origen, Eusebius, and Athanasius*. New York: Oxford University Press, 1993.

MacKendrick, Karmen. *Counterpleasures*. Albany, NY: State University of New York Press, 1999.

—. "Carthage Didn't Burn Hot Enough: Saint Augustine's Divine Seduction." In *Toward a Theology of Eros: Transfiguring Passion at the Limits of Discipline*, edited by Virginia Burrus and Catherine Keller. New York: Fordham University Press, 2006.

Macquarrie, John. "Kenoticism Reconsidered." *Theology: A Monthly Review* 77.645 (1974): 115–124.

—. "The Pre-existence of Jesus Christ." *The Expository Times* 77.7 (1966): 199–202.

McAllister, Pam, ed. *Reweaving the Web of Life: Feminism and Nonviolence*. Philadelphia, PA: New Society Publishers, 1982.

Maitland, Sara. "Passionate Prayer: Masochistic Images in Women's Experience." In *Sex and God: Some Varieties of Women's Religious Experience*, 125–140. New York: Routledge and Kegan Paul, 1987.

Marchal, Joseph A. *Hierarchy, Unity, and Imitation: A Feminist Rhetorical Analysis of Power Dynamics in Paul's Letter to the Philippians*. Atlanta, GA: Society of Biblical Literature, 2006.

Martin, Ralph P. *A Hymn of Christ: Philippians 2:5–11 in Recent Interpretation and in the Setting of Early Christian Worship*. Downers Grove, IL: InterVarsity Press, 1997.

Martin, Ralph P. and Brian J. Dodd, eds. *Where Christology Began: Essays on Philippians 2*. Louisville, KY: Westminster/John Knox Press, 1998.

McGrath, Alister E. *Luther's Theology of the Cross: Martin Luther's Theological Breakthrough*. New York: Basil Blackwell, 1985.

Melanchthon, Philip. *Annotations on First Corinthians*, edited and translated by John Patrick Donnelly. Milwaukee, WI: Marquette University Press, 1995.

—. "Didymi Faventini." In *Melanchthon Werke*, vol. 1, ed. Robert Stupperich. Gütersloh: C. Bertelsmann, 1951.

—. *Loci Communes* 1521, in Melanchthon and Bucer, ed. Wilhelm Pauck. Philadelphia: Westminster Press, 1969.

Mercedes, Anna. "A Christian Politics of Vulnerability," in *The Sleeping Giant Has Awoken: The New Politics of Religion the United States*, eds Jeffrey W. Robbins and Neal Magee. New York: Continuum, 2008, 41–54.

—. "Who Are You? Christ and the Imperative of Subjectivity," in *Transformative Lutheran Theologies: Feminist, Womanist, and Mujerista Perspectives*, edited by Mary Streufert. Minneapolis, MN: Fortress Press, September 2010.

Moltmann, Jürgen. *The Crucified God: The Cross of Christ as the Foundation and Criticism of Christian Theology*. New York: Harper and Row, 1974.

—. "God Is Unselfish Love." In *The Emptying God*, edited by John B. Cobb, Jr and Christopher Ives, 116–124. Maryknoll, NY: Orbis Books, 1990.

—. "God's *Kenosis* in the Creation and Consummation of the World." In *The Work of Love: Creation as Kenosis*, edited by John Polkinghorne, 137–151. Grand Rapids, MI: Wm. B. Eerdmans, 2001.

Nason-Clark, Nancy. *The Battered Wife: How Christians Confront Family Violence*. Louisville, KY: WJKP, 1997.

—. "Shattered Silence or Holy Hush? Emerging Definitions of Violence Against Women in Sacred and Secular Contexts." *Family Ministry* 13 (Spring 1999): 39–56.

Nygren, Anders. *Agape and Eros*, revised edn, translated by Philip S. Watson. Philadelphia: Westminster Press, 1953.

Pagelow, Mildred Daley. "Secondary Battering and Alternatives of Female Victims to Spouse Abuse." In *Women and Crime in America*, edited by Lee H. Bowker, 277–300. New York: Macmillan, 1981.

—. *Woman Battering: Victims and Their Experiences*. Beverly Hills, CA: Sage Publications, 1981.

Pagels, Elaine. "Gnostic and Orthodox Views of Christ's passion: Paradigms for the Christian's Response to Persecution?" In *Rediscovery of Gnosticism*, vol. 1, edited by Bentley Layton. Ithaca, NY: Snow Lion Publications, 2002.

Pannenberg, Wolfhart. *Jesus: God and Man*, translated by Lewis L. Wilkins and Duane A. Priebe. Philadelphia, PA: Westminster Press, 1968.

Papanikolaou, Aristotle. "Person, Kenosis, and Abuse: Hans Urs von Balthasar and Feminist Theologies in Conversation." *Modern Theology* 19:1 (January 2003): 41–65.

Pelikan, Jaroslav. *The Christian Tradition, vol. 4: Reformation of Church and Dogma*. Chicago: University of Chicago Press, 1984.

Pellauer, Mary, "The Moral Significance of the Female Orgasm." In *Sexuality and the Sacred: Sources for Theological Reflection*, edited by James B. Nelson and Sandra P. Longfellow, 149–168. Louisville, KY: Westminster/John Knox Press, 1994.

Pellauer, Mary, et al., eds. *Sexual Assault and Abuse: A Handbook for Clergy and Religious Professionals*. San Francisco, CA: Harper and Row, 1987.

Pellauer, Mary D. with Susan Brooks Thistlethwaite. "Conversation on Grace and Healing: Perspectives from the Movement to End Violence against Women." In *Lift Every Voice: Constructing Christian Theologies from the Underside*, eds Susan Brooks Thistlethwaite and Mary Potter Engel, 169–185. New York: Harper Collins, 1990.

Perkins, Judith. *The Suffering Self: Pain and Narrative Representation in the Early Christian Era*. London: Routledge, 1995.

Perkins, Pheme. "Philippians." In *The Women's Bible Commentary*, edited by Carol A. Newsom and Sharon H. Ringe, 343–345. Louisville, KY: Westminster/John Knox Press, 1992.

Pitstick, Alyssa Lyra. *Light in Darkness: Hans Urs von Balthasar and the Catholic Doctrine of Christ's Descent into Hell*. Grand Rapids, MI: Wm. B. Eerdmans, 2007.

Polkinghorne, John, ed. *The Work of Love: Creation as Kenosis*. Grand Rapids, MI: Wm. B. Eerdmans, 2001.

Raphael, Melissa. *The Female Face of God in Auschwitz: A Jewish Feminist Theology of the Holocaust*. London: Routledge, 2003.

Richard, Lucien J., O.M.I. *A Kenotic Christology: In the Humanity of Jesus the Christ, the Compassion of God*. Lanham, MD: University Press of America, 1982.

Rivera, Mayra. *The Touch of Transcendence: A Postcolonial Theology of God*. Louisville, KY: Westminster/John Knox Press, 2007.

Ruether, Rosemary Radford. *Sexism and God-talk: Toward a Feminist Theology*. Boston: Beacon, 1993.

—. *Gaia and God: An Ecofeminist Theology of Earth Healing*. New York: HarperOne, 1994.

Saiving, Valerie. "The Human Situation: A Feminine View." In *Womanspirit Rising: A Feminist Reader in Religion*, edited by Carol Christ and Judith Plaskow, 25–42. San Francisco, CA: Harper San Francisco, 1979.

Sands, Kathleen. "Uses of the Thea(o)logian: Sex and Theodicy in Religious Feminism." *Journal of Feminist Studies in Religion* 8.1 (1992): 7–33.

—. "A Response to Marcella Althaus-Reid's *Indecent Theology: Theological Perversions in Sex, Gender, and Politics*." *Feminist Theology* 11.2 (2003): 175–181.

Scarry, Elaine. *The Body in Pain: The Making and Unmaking of the World*. New York: Oxford University Press, 1985.

Schmid, Heinrich. *Doctrinal Theology of the Evangelical Lutheran Church*, third revised edition, translated by Charles A. Hay and Henry E. Jacobs. Minneapolis, MN: Augsburg Publishing House, 1899.

Schneider, John R. *Philip Melanchthon's Rhetorical Construal of Biblical Authority*. Lewiston, NY: Edwin Mellen Press, 1990.

Schneider, Laurel C. "Promiscuous Incarnation." In *The Embrace of Eros: Bodies, Desires, and Sexuality in Christianity*, edited by Margaret D. Kamitsuka, 231–246. Minneapolis, MN: Fortress Press, 2010.

Skerrett, K. Roberts. "When Yes Means No: The Passion of Carter Heyward." *Journal of Feminist Studies in Religion* 12.1 (1996): 71–92.

Solberg, Mary M. *Compelling Knowledge: A Feminist Proposal for an Epistemology of the Cross*. Albany, NY: State University of New York Press, 1997.

Sykes, Stephen W. "The Strange Persistence of Kenotic Christology." In *Being and Truth: Essays in Honor of John Macquarrie*, edited by Alistair Kee and Eugene Thomas Long, 349–375. London: SCM Press, 1986.

Tanner, Kathryn. "Incarnation, Cross, Sacrifice: A Feminist-Inspired Reappraisal." *ATR* 86.1: 35–56, 2004.

Tessier, L. J. *Dancing After the Whirlwind: Feminist Reflections on Sex, Denial, and Spiritual Transformation*. Boston: Beacon, 1997.

Thielicke, Helmut. *Being Human . . . Becoming Human: An Essay in Christian Anthropology*, translated by Geoffery W. Bromiley. Garden City, NY: Doubleday & Company, 1984.

Thomasius, Gottfried. "Christ's Person and Work" (1857). In *God and Incarnation: In Mid-Nineteenth Century German Theology*, edited and translated by Claude Welsh, 23–101. New York: Oxford University Press, 1965.

Thompson, Deanna A. *Crossing the Divide: Luther, Feminism, and the Cross*. Minneapolis, MN: Fortress Press, 2004.

Townes, Emilie. *Breaking the Fine Rain of Death: African-American Health Issues and a Womanist Ethic of Care*. New York: Continuum, 1998.

Trelstad, Marit, ed. *Cross Examinations: Readings on the Meaning of the Cross Today*. Minneapolis, MN: Fortress, 2006.

Vattimo, Gianni. *Belief*, translated by Luca D'Isanto and David Webb. Stanford, CA: Stanford University Press, 1999.

Wade, Allan. "Small Acts of Living: Everyday Resistance to Violence and Other Forms of Oppression." *Contemporary Family Therapy* 19 (March 1997): 23–39.

Ward, Graham. "The Erotics of Redemption: After Karl Barth." *Theology and Sexuality* 8, 1998: 52–72.

—. "Kenosis: Death, Discourse and Resurrection." In *Balthasar at the End of Modernity*, by Lucy Gardner, David Moss, Ben Quash, and Graham Ward, 15–68. Edinburgh: T&T Clark, 1999.

—. "Suffering and Incarnation." In *Suffering Religion*, edited by Robert Gibbs and Elliot R. Wolfson, 163–180. London: Routledge, 2002.

Warner, Kate, Agnes Baro, and Helen Eigenberg. "Stories of Resistance: Exploring Women's Responses to Male Violence." *Journal of Feminist Family Therapy* 16.4 (2004): 21–-2.

Welker, Michael. *God the Spirit*, translated by John F. Hoffmeyer. Minneapolis, MN: Fortress Press, 1994.

—. "Romantic Love, Covenantal Love, Kenotic Love." In *The Work of Love: Creation as Kenosis*, edited by John Polkinghorne, 127–136. Grand Rapids, MI: Wm. B. Eerdmans, 2001.

Welsh, Sharon D. *A Feminist Ethic of Risk*, revised edn. Minneapolis, MN: Fortress Press, 2000.

Wengert, Timothy J. *Philip Melanchthon's Annotations in Johannem in Relation to Its Predessors and Contemporaries*. Geneva: Librairie Droz, 1987.

West, Traci C. *Wounds of the Spirit: Black Women, Violence, and Resistance Ethics*. New York: New York University Press, 1999.

Williams, Delores. *Sisters in the Wilderness: The Challenge of Womanist God-Talk*. Maryknoll, NY: Orbis Press, 1995.

Wood, Gale Goldberg and Susan E. Roche. "Representing Selves, Reconstructing Lives: Feminist Group Work with Women Survivors of Male Violence." *Social Work with Groups* 23.4 (2001): 5–23.

Wood, Susan. "Is Philippians 2:5–11 Incompatible with Feminist Concerns?" *Pro Ecclesia* 6.2 (1997): 172–183.

Wuest, Judith and Marilyn Merritt-Gray. "A Theoretical Understanding of Abusive Intimate Partner Relationships that Become Non-violent: Shifting the Pattern of Abusive Control." *Journal of Family Violence* 23 (May 2008): 281–293.

Index

abuse 3, 9, 10, 12, 19, 33, 40, 61, 85, 87–8, 91, 93–4, 106–7, 109–28, 132, 134, 151–3
  clergy 3, 110–13, 126
agape 8, 9, 64–5, 70, 81–3, 94, 112, 124, 130, 139, 144, 147
agency 2, 5, 6, 9, 37, 86, 88, 90, 93, 95–8, 101, 105–8, 117, 119, 130–2, 136, 141, 143, 151–2
Althaus-Reid, Marcella 63–5, 77–80, 86, 97, 131, 144, 146–7
anti-Judaism 39–41, 45, 62
asceticism 86, 89, 92–7, 99–100, 103, 106, 131
Athanasius of Alexandria 22–3
atonement 56, 59, 73, 89–90, 92, 103, 128, 148–51

Balthasar, Hans Urs von 29, 32, 65, 70–7, 82
baptism 16–17, 21, 23, 41, 61, 125, 150
Barton, Carlin 98–9
body 5, 17–18, 22, 27, 35, 54–5, 80, 88, 90–2, 94–5, 99–102, 108, 127–8, 137–42, 144, 146–52
  of Christ 9, 13, 17, 24, 34, 62, 70, 147, 150, 152
Bonhoeffer, Dietrich 8, 27, 55, 58, 65–70, 72–4, 80
Brock, Rita 103, 110, 138–9, 142–5
Brown, Joanne Carlson 110, 113
Brown, Peter 22, 104–5
Burrus, Virginia 9, 87–8, 95–8, 106–8

Cameron, Averil 98
care 3, 6–9, 110, 112–14, 117–23, 138, 146, 152

chrism 9, 59, 132–3, 137, 145–8, 150
Clark, Elizabeth A. 99
Coakley, Sarah 8, 13, 24, 27, 30–4, 80, 106
Cobb, John B., Jr. 137
Coleman, Monica 112, 137
Contreras-Byrd, Melinda 3, 10, 128
Cooper-White, Pamela 122, 133–4
covenant 38, 62, 72, 145, 148
creation 21, 29, 37, 56, 71–2, 76, 127, 136, 139, 141, 147
cross 13, 15, 17, 28, 34, 40, 47–9, 52–4, 56–8, 61, 66, 72–3, 91, 110, 112, 127–8, 130, 148–51
  see also "theology of the cross"

Dahill, Lisa 69, 126–7
Daly, Mary 82, 143
danger 3, 13, 86, 89, 118, 122, 127, 153
dependence 3, 6, 29, 30, 33–4, 36–7, 64, 75, 94, 109, 126, 138, 140n. 40
  see also need
desire 7, 9, 35, 47, 56, 59, 63–5, 70–3, 75–6, 81, 83–4, 87–90, 92–4, 96–8, 107–8, 121, 123, 130–1, 134–5, 138, 141, 144, 146, 151–3
  see also eros
domination 7, 20–1, 26, 36, 38–9, 41, 53, 55, 60, 62, 67–9, 71, 74, 82, 86, 89–90, 95, 97, 105, 107, 130–1, 133–5, 152

empowerment 7, 8, 20, 33–5, 55, 57, 61–2, 79, 89, 101, 105, 107–8, 111, 124, 129–30, 133, 135
Enlightenment 10, 20, 24, 35, 90, 97

Index

equality 15, 19, 41, 78, 116, 118, 133
  see also mutuality
eros 8–9, 63–5, 69–70, 77, 81–3, 86, 89–90, 94–7, 106–8, 130, 136–45, 147
  see also desire
Eucharist 61–2, 71–2, 74n. 61, 135, 147–8, 150–2
exploitation 6–8, 14–15, 20, 131–2, 134–5, 151, 153

Faber, Alyda 141–2
Frascati-Lochhead, Marta 39, 42–6, 78, 86, 147

gender norms 3–5, 7, 12, 19, 30–3, 35–6, 38, 40, 69, 77, 80, 83, 88, 90, 95–7, 114–15, 120, 122, 124, 126
generosity 2–3, 6, 20, 23, 39, 129–30, 144
Green, Clifford 66–8

hagiography 86, 92, 95–7, 106
Hampson, Daphne 23, 30–1
Haraway, Donna 44
Harrison, Beverly 87–90, 92–6, 99–102, 106–9, 132, 136
Hess, Carol Lakey 4–5
heterosexism 36, 43, 77–80, 89–90, 97, 122, 143
Heyward, Carter 87–96, 99–102, 106–9, 132, 136, 139–44, 146, 148, 150
hierarchy 2, 5, 7, 20–1, 35, 41, 97, 106, 134
humiliation 25, 27, 49–50, 59, 98, 107
humility 3, 13, 14, 19–20, 27–8, 35, 111–12, 126, 152

identity 5, 10, 14, 16–17, 20, 70, 78, 80, 95–7, 99, 125, 126, 135, 145, 147
  see also subjectivity
incarnation 2, 9, 12, 17, 21–2, 24–5, 27–9, 33–4, 40–2, 45, 49, 51, 54–5, 57, 59–60, 65–6, 77, 128–9, 132–3, 135, 137–41, 144, 146–52
Irenaeus 21, 100
Irigaray, Luce 82, 137, 145n. 69
Isherwood, Lisa 7, 129, 140–1

Jesus 5, 7–8, 14–17, 19, 24–8, 32, 41, 49, 56, 66–7, 73, 79, 110, 112, 126, 130, 132, 137–8, 140–1, 146, 148–52
Joh, Wonhee Anne 61, 151n. 88
joy 15, 92, 101, 107, 110, 124, 126, 142, 149, 152

Kellenbach, Katharina von 41, 62
Keller, Catherine 1, 4–5, 45, 64, 68, 80–1, 83, 126
kinetic energy 38, 70, 80, 135, 147, 152

Lebacqz, Karen 136
Logos 22–3, 27, 29, 54, 149
Lorde, Audre 63, 81, 140, 143, 152
love 6, 9–11, 18, 28–9, 32, 54, 57, 62, 68, 70–1, 75–6, 78, 82–3, 90–1, 107, 120, 132, 136–7, 139, 141, 144–5, 147, 149
Luther, Martin 40, 46–60, 64, 66–7, 72, 130
Lyman, Rebecca 23, 105

MacKendrick, Karmen 9, 11, 87, 92–4, 101, 107–9
Marchal, Joseph A. 18–19
Martin, Ralph 16
martyrdom 21–3, 85–6, 89, 95, 98, 100, 103–4, 106, 145
masochism 9, 37, 84–95, 97, 101, 106–9, 124, 131, 142
Melanchthon, Phillip 40, 46–7, 50–5, 57–8, 60, 64, 66–7, 83, 130
messiah 12, 16, 19, 59, 147
mimicry 7, 144n. 63
Moltmann, Jürgen 26–7, 32, 65, 74–6
Moore, Stephen 106–8
mutuality 7, 9, 41, 86, 89–91, 108, 130, 133–6, 139, 141–3, 145–6

Nason-Clark, Nancy 111–12
need 29, 64, 76, 110–11
  see also dependence
nihilism 42–3
Nygren, Anders 64, 143

Index

obedience 2, 17–18, 90, 126
omnipotence 14, 22–3, 28–30, 32–3, 35, 37–8, 46, 54, 60, 65–6, 72, 76, 79, 90, 107, 143
ontology 16–17, 20, 67, 72, 76, 82, 97

pain 2, 11, 37, 54, 84, 87–9, 91–3, 95–6, 99–103, 106, 108, 118–19, 124, 128, 135–6, 138, 142, 144, 152
Parker, Rebecca 103, 110, 113
passion 5, 59, 61, 66, 69, 72–5, 78, 80, 83, 94, 97, 113, 115, 117, 119–20, 137, 145–6, 148, 150–2
  of Jesus 8, 49, 130, 148, 151
passivity 5, 93, 95, 97–8, 107, 117–18, 121, 125, 131, 135, 141
patriarchy 2–7, 9, 19–20, 31–8, 40–1, 43–4, 80, 82, 84, 88–90, 93–5, 106–8, 113, 120, 122, 124, 128, 130, 136, 142–5
Paul 14–21, 23, 32, 55, 59, 150
  see also Philippians
Pellauer, Mary 121, 127
Perkins, Judith 87, 99–104
Perkins, Pheme 19
Philippians 2, 14–21, 27, 33, 40–1, 49, 55–6, 59, 66, 77, 79, 131, 150
pleasure 64, 80, 87–9, 92–3, 96, 99–102, 107–9, 123, 133, 135–7, 144, 146, 152
politics 12, 13, 21, 31, 40, 45, 53, 60–1, 81, 98, 103–4, 115, 126, 129–30, 140, 143, 153
  of empire 13–14, 19–23, 31, 77, 79, 103, 105, 113, 128
prayer 13–14, 33–5
process theology 64n. 6, 76, 137

queer theology 9, 77–80, 97, 146–7

rape 112, 122, 128
  see also abuse
Raphael, Melissa 126n. 64
relationality 10, 17, 28, 38, 41, 47, 53, 54, 56, 60–1, 64, 66–7, 70, 73, 78, 81–3, 89, 91, 94, 101, 108, 115, 121, 133, 136, 138–9, 143, 145, 149, 153
renunciation 25, 28, 41, 76, 86, 88, 90, 98–9, 103, 106, 145
resistance 2, 6–9, 20, 34, 88–9, 92, 94–5, 97–8, 103, 105–7, 109–10, 113–28, 130, 132, 144, 148, 151–2
revelation 27, 32, 34, 48, 50–4, 64–7, 69, 72, 75, 102, 114, 120, 135, 141, 147
risk 3, 33, 86, 112, 135–6, 140, 145, 147, 151
Ruether, Rosemary Radford 39–42, 44–5, 62, 79n. 100

sacrifice 2–6, 10, 29, 63, 81, 98, 101, 106, 110, 114, 124–6, 128, 135, 149–51
sadomasochism 37, 78, 85–91, 93–6, 106–8, 131, 137, 142, 144n. 63
  see also masochism
Saiving, Valerie 3, 4, 55, 64, 69, 73, 81, 88, 126, 143
Sands, Kathleen 107, 141–4
Schneider, Laurel 141
secularization 42–5
self-abnegation 3, 31, 63, 70, 89, 113, 123, 129, 135
self-centeredness 3, 14, 30–1, 68, 73–4, 143
service 5, 6, 9, 55–8, 60, 67–8, 149
sin 3, 50–2, 55, 57–8, 64, 69, 71, 73–4, 76, 88, 90–1, 95, 125–6, 134
Skerrett, K. Roberts 141–2, 144–6
slave 15, 17, 40, 56, 86, 94
solidarity 8, 111, 126, 128, 141, 149, 152
Stanton, Elizabeth Cady 1–2
Stoicism 99, 101
Stortz, Martha Ellen 134
strength 2–3, 9, 20, 22, 31–3, 69, 93–4, 106–7, 109, 119, 122, 124–5, 135, 136
subjectivity 5–6, 36, 56, 65–72, 74, 77–8, 80–4, 87, 89, 94–5, 99–105, 108, 114, 130–2, 144–5, 151
  see also identity

submission 2, 5, 20–1, 30–2, 34–7, 81, 89, 94–5, 97–8, 104, 131, 150
suffering 8, 13, 17–19, 21–2, 24, 28, 40, 47–52, 54–5, 58–9, 61, 63, 92, 97, 99, 100–2, 105, 111–12, 114, 128–9, 135, 138, 141–2, 144, 147, 149–51
   redemptive 1, 18, 46, 91, 98, 110, 128, 149
survival 6, 117, 145, 151–2
survivor 114–15, 121–4, 127–8, 145

Tanner, Kathryn 149, 150
Tessier, L. J. 123, 127
theology of the cross 8, 17, 30, 40, 46–53, 58–62, 66–7, 151
Thomasius, Gottfried 27–30, 54, 65–6
Thompson, Deanna 40n. 2, 50, 56, 61
transcendence 18, 42, 62, 68–9, 72, 80, 97, 102, 126, 135–6, 141–2, 153
transgression 11, 92–3, 97–9, 106, 108–9, 132, 144n. 63
Trinity 65, 70–7, 82

Vattimo, Gianni 39, 42–6
victim 9, 10, 13, 95, 97–9, 112, 114, 116, 121–2, 124, 127–8, 131, 141, 145, 151–2
violence 1, 8, 10, 17, 18, 36, 74, 83, 85–6, 88, 90, 97–8, 100, 110, 112, 115–16, 118–19, 121, 123–6, 130, 132, 141–3, 145–6, 150, 152
   and Christianity 1, 3, 39, 106, 113, 152
   see also abuse
vulnerability 2, 9, 13, 14, 20, 31–5, 37, 74–5, 79, 98, 125, 129–30, 144–5

Wade, Allan 116–21, 124, 127
Ward, Graham 24, 48, 56–7, 70–1, 81–2
Welker, Michael 65, 74–5
West, Traci C. 121–3, 126
womanist theology 6, 149

yield 3, 8, 34–5, 39, 134–5, 144–6, 152

www.ingramcontent.com/pod-product-compliance
Lightning Source LLC
Chambersburg PA
CBHW061838300426
44115CB00013B/2432